5008 7⁵⁵

W9-DGD-885

8

nd

*The Kefauver Committee
and the Politics of Crime
1950–1952*

THE KEFAUVER COMMITTEE AND THE POLITICS OF CRIME
1950–1952

William Howard Moore

University of Missouri Press
Columbia

ISBN 0–8262–0145–8
Copyright © 1974 by
The Curators of the University of Missouri
Library of Congress Catalog Card Number 72–93923
Printed and bound in the United States of America
University of Missouri Press, Columbia, Missouri 65201

To the Memory of My Mother and Father

Preface

Social determinists maintain that a society has the criminals it deserves. Certainly the manner in which a society perceives its criminals tells us something about its values and institutions. Medieval and early modern man, essentially religious, frequently considered criminals—as well as dissenters, the insane, and the poor—to be possessed by devils. The eighteenth and nineteenth centuries witnessed the birth of modern technology and science, including the "science" of criminology. Early criminologists were essentially of two schools—the classicists, such as Jeremy Bentham, who emphasized individual free will and institutional reform, and the Italian positivists, led by Cesare Lombroso, who explained criminality in terms of measurable physical abnormalities and atavisms.

In the twentieth century, new research and insights have blurred the sharp differences between classicists and positivists, and in the United States the debate has continued along the lines of heredity and personal factors versus environment. Despite overwhelming evidence to the contrary, in popular opinion ethnic origin continues to be considered a cause of crime. While few academicians in recent times have entertained this view, a significant number of highly trained professionals, influenced by Freud and modern psychology, have emphasized maladjustment to society and deviance from its norms as personal rather than societal failures. This "psychiatric world view," which had its major impact between 1920 and the early 1960s, is expressed in the works of David Riesman and Erich Fromm.*

The environmentalists, however, in a very general way have dominated academic criminology in the United States in the twentieth century. Progressives and reformers in the interwar generation focused on the social disorganization in the slum

*Frank Riessman and Seymour M. Miller, "Social Change Versus the 'Psychiatric World View'," *American Journal of Orthopsychiatry* (January 1964), 29–38.

areas as the major source of crime, but since the 1940s an increasing number of researchers have emphasized the influence of *anomie*—a general concept of crime causation first sketched by Emile Durkheim and developed more fully by Robert K. Merton in the 1930s. The emphasis on anomie reflects the discovery that incidence of crime, as opposed to its apprehension, occurs in all classes and includes the "white collar crime" committed by business leaders, so brilliantly analyzed by Edwin H. Sutherland in 1949.

As it has been developed, the theory of anomie emphasizes the alienation and frustrations that result from the denial of institutional means to achieve culturally encouraged aspirations, such as wealth or social position; the theory suggests that individuals faced with such frustrations may withdraw, scale down their ambitions, or look for alternative—often socially deviant—means to achieve their goals. Should they choose deviance, the specific course adopted generally depends on opportunity and environment. A youth in an urban slum may seek peer-group recognition through acts of violence or bravado; a financially pressed policeman may take "protection" payments to ignore bookie establishments on his beat; a business executive may conspire to violate the antitrust laws.

Most of the research on organized crime (gambling, prostitution, drugs, and labor and business racketeering) has been a by-product of work directed primarily toward juvenile delinquency or the study of social structures. By mid-century the "Chicago school" of sociology's studies of youth gangs and crime patterns in ethnically changing neighborhoods provided some insights into the background of organized crime, sometimes even suggestive of the concept of anomie. Such classic works as Frederic M. Thrasher's *The Gang* (1936) demonstrated how powerful an influence street gangs exerted on slum youths who were seeking recognition and how they served as schools for certain organized crime gangs with political contacts. In his *Street Corner Society* (1943) William F. Whyte concluded that the frequent connection between the rackets and politics in Italian ghettos was the result of exclusion from legitimate sources of power and influence in the broader community. Although John Landesco published his valuable *Organized Crime in Chicago* in 1929, most sociologists continued to concentrate on juvenile delinquency and related problems. Despite their limited appreciation of the modern theory of anomie, researchers had certainly demonstrated by 1950 an organic relationship between those engaged in organized criminal activities and the social conditions in urban slums.

Organized crime, however, has a dimension that can hardly be explained in sociological terms, for in a sense it is not so much a sociological problem as a legal and economic one: it is the *business* of providing certain goods and services prohibited by law. Government tries to curtail the supply of a good or service that is in reasonably high demand, but in effect it creates black markets in which normal competition is by law rendered impossible, in which the consumer has no protection, and in which strong corrupting pressures are brought to bear on the law enforcement structure. Because of physical and social dangers, an inordinately large percentage of those who are willing to operate in open defiance of the law may be concentrated in the lower economic and social classes, leading, as Daniel Bell has noted, to an ethnic succession in organized crime. If the government substitutes regulatory legislation for prohibition of gambling, the narcotics traffic, and perhaps prostitution, according to this argument, a large segment of organized crime *as crime* disappears. Although nagging social problems undoubtedly remain, they are regulatory in nature, not essentially different from those associated with legitimate business. In this scheme, the sociological theory of anomie might explain the attraction of certain ethnic groups and individuals to organized crime, but it would not answer important economic and legal questions about organized crime itself.

Unburdened by such abstractions and speculations, a large segment of the public—and a considerable number of sociologists—consider organized crime not so much an economic problem as an ethnic or subcultural conspiracy, which moves from one activity to another partially for profit, partially to satisfy its own depravity. Because they view organized crime in conspiratorial rather than socioeconomic terms, they interpret efforts at economic diversification by persons once associated with organized crime as infiltration of legitimate businesses by the underworld. This theory, which harkens back to Lombroso, ethnic depravity, and the "psychiatric world view," downgrades legal and economic considerations and underscores law enforcement and questions of morality and innate criminality. In short, it holds that the roots of orga nized crime are personal or ethnic, not societal.

In 1950, the essentials of two distinct interpretations of organized crime existed side by side in the United States. One was essentially socioeconomic, one conspiratorial. The Kefauver Crime Committee of 1950–1951 was to play a vital role in orienting both professional and popular opinion toward a conspiracy interpretation. In doing so, the Committee ignored the nascent but promising body of sociological literature, and it dismissed out of hand the economic and legal arguments for regulation. In years to come, its widely heralded reports provided the essential material for college textbooks and journalistic accounts and became a model for the McClellan investigation and other official studies.

After comparing the Committee's evidence with its conclusions, I am convinced that its emphasis was wrong. I view its work as a study in miseducation, as the strengthening of old myths that might better have been laid to rest. I have tried to explore the historical context of the conspiratorial interpretation in the hope that its essential weaknesses may become more obvious and less tolerable.

I should state, however, that this effort was intended as a study of the Committee and not of crime. My primary purpose was to examine the background pressures and considerations that shaped the Committee's conclusions rather than to criticize those conclusions as such. The real failure of the Committee, then, from my perspective, was not its conclusions as much as its hesitancy, for essentially political reasons, to consider opposing judgments or significant alternatives. For me, the study raises the fundamental question of whether the public can trust congressional committees—political creatures as they frequently are—to examine carefully and fully certain controversial issues. And can it rely on the press and the academic community to act as countervailing forces, to expose the politicians' shortcomings, when they fail? Certainly, the experience of the Kefauver Committee does not constitute strong evidence for the affirmative.

*   *   *   *

Special acknowledgments are due many persons for their assistance in the completion of this project. Mr. John Dobson and his staff at the Kefauver Collection at the University of

Tennessee and the librarians at The University of Texas, par-
ticularly those in the Newspaper and Documents Collections,
have been of inestimable help. I should also mention Mrs.
Alford B. Tunis of Baker Memorial Library at Dartmouth Col-
lege; Dr. Gene M. Gressley of the Western History Research
Center at the University of Wyoming; Miss Josephine L.
Harper of the State Historical Society Archives in Madison,
Wisconsin; Philip D. Lagerquist and his assistants at the
Harry S. Truman Library in Independence; and Mr. Harvey N.
Johnson, Jr., and his staff of the Chicago Crime Commission.
A number of individuals courteously shared their reminis-
cences with me personally. Among them were Kefauver Committee counsels Downey Rice, Rufus King, George S. Robin-
son, and Joseph Nellis; Virgil W. Peterson, formerly of the
Chicago Crime Commission; Edward Cooper, once associated
with the Senate Commerce Committee; and two of Kefauver's
colleagues, former Senators John W. Bricker and Homer
Capehart. Herbert R. O'Conor, Jr., not only talked about his
father's work with the Committee but thoughtfully provided
introductions to others who had been associated with the
investigation. Jack Gould of the New York *Times* and Walter
D. Engels of WPIX-TV of New York wrote lengthy and infor-
mative letters on the Committee's use of television. Mrs. Ruth
Hagy Brod, a Philadelphia journalist whose advice Kefauver
solicited from time to time, and Richard G. Moser, who served
as Chief Counsel for four months, shared their recollections
with me by letter. Mrs. Ray Brennan and Judge Richard B.
Austin answered my questions concerning the celebrated stolen transcript in Chicago, and Mrs. Brennan sent me some of
her late husband's papers to examine. My good friend, Frank
R. Prassel, a criminologist, and my father-in-law, Judge Carlos C. Cadena, listened carefully to my theories and voiced
both encouragement and occasional learned dissent. Another
relative, Mrs. Anna Treadway, made my research in Chicago
more pleasant by her hospitality.

Professor Robert A. Divine, a perceptive adviser and critic,
directed my research at the dissertation level. Professor Lewis
L. Gould offered a number of valuable suggestions and took an
unflagging interest in the project from its inception. Profes-
sors David D. Van Tassel of Case Western Reserve University
and Clarence G. Lasby of the University of Texas have read
the manuscript and given me the benefit of their ideas. The
University of Texas Graduate School, through a travel grant,

helped ease the financial pains of the research, while the Department of History at Ohio University afforded me the unique opportunity to teach two proseminars on the history of organized crime in America and to develop and revise my ideas for the book. Most of all, however, I should acknowledge the generosity and encouragement of my late parents and the intellectual partnership in the project of my wife Maribeth.

W. H. M.
November, 1973
Laramie, Wyoming

Contents

1

The American Approach to Organized Crime

> The extended range of our researches has developed the existence of the secret organization styled "Mafia."
> —New Orleans Grand Jury Report, May 5, 1891

A passenger on a jet airliner in the early 1960s, New York's District Attorney Frank S. Hogan glanced at a scrap of paper passed along to him by a stewardess. On the paper a fellow passenger had scribbled the question, "Dear Mr. District Attorney: Is there a Mafia?" Hogan replied without hesitation: "No, Virginia, there is not." Thus the District Attorney gave his answer to the most persistent question about organized crime in America. The Mafia, in effect he said, was a myth.

While the impulses for mythmaking about crime seemingly lie deep in the human psyche, Americans have inherited two traditions that accentuate the problem in this country. First, a Puritan conscience equating law and religion prompted the public to demand that established authority protect religious beliefs and proscriptions, a pattern that by no means died with the constitutional separation of church and state in the eighteenth century. The same mentality that divided the religious world between saints and sinners logically divided the temporal between respectable citizens and criminals. As they guarded their religious convictions by ascribing their evil impulses to the Devil, so Americans protected their socioeconomic order by defining "crime" as an attribute of an immoral, atavistic underworld. Blurring law and religion, crusaders and legislators assigned both legal and spiritual definitions to a wide assortment of traditional human vices that included gambling, prostitution, and the consumption of alcoholic beverages.

Enforcement of the laws, however, proved to be more complicated than definition of the crimes. A history of decentralized government as well as the perennial conviction that crime was a local problem best handled by local authorities dictated the concentration of law enforcement duties in the lower levels of government. With the exception of certain inherent powers involved in protecting the currency, prohibiting smuggling, collecting taxes, and regulating interstate commerce, the federal government assumed no important law enforcement functions. The ultimate responsibilities remained with the state governments which, in turn, passed along most of the duties to county and city officials. As some 40,000 squabbling, ill-defined, mostly local police units struggled to keep order under the heavy burden of federal and state statutes and local ordinances, the state authorities darted in and out of the picture attempting to improve efficiency or to end corruption in municipal police departments or in the hopelessly antiquated county sheriff's office. Not until the early twentieth century did states begin to create their own police forces and to endow them with anything approximating general law enforcement powers, but even then the efforts, primarily aimed at keeping industrial peace, were timid and temporary.[1]

This insistence on decentralization, combined with the tendency to regulate public and private morality by law, created immense problems for law enforcement agencies. Lucrative despite their illegality, gambling and other vices provided the funds for the corruption of the ramshackle law enforcement machinery, where responsibilities could easily be passed along to other levels and agencies. Segregated red-light districts usually represented the police force's compromise between the public's insistence that certain activities be banned and the public appetite for them. Noting the disparity be-

1. Richard H. Rovere, *The American Establishment and Other Reports, Opinions, and Speculations* (New York: Harcourt, Brace & World, 1962), p. 4*n;* James Harvey Grisham, "Crime Control: A Study in American Federalism" (Ph.D. diss., The University of Texas at Austin, 1953), pp. 40–41, 221–22. The office of sheriff (shirereeve) originated in thirteenth-century England, died out there, but survived in the New World. By the twentieth century it had become heavily encumbered with both civil and criminal duties, and many citizens urged its abolition. Ibid., pp. 31–38. Wallace Notestein, *The English People on the Eve of Colonization, 1603–1630* (New York: Harper & Row, 1962), pp. 202, 205.

tween definition of crime and enforcement but unprepared
either to lower the sights of the law or to make the necessary
structural changes to facilitate more effective enforcement,
distraught citizens resorted to periodic revivals of vigilante
justice, bemoaned the decline of morality or religion, or explained their plight in terms of dark criminal conspiracies.

* * * *

The implications of this moral absolutism and decentralization—a continuing problem throughout American history—
reached a near crisis point by the late nineteenth century. The
disruptive impact on society of industrialization and urbani-
zation prompted at least a limited rethinking of what constituted crime and which level of government could best deal
with it. Americans had seen nothing quite like the industrial
sabotage, collusion, stock manipulation, use of private armies,
and public corruption that accompanied the development of
Big Business in the United States. Labor often responded with
violence of its own, and agrarian protesters cried out against
interstate and international conspiracies of trusts and bankers. Increasingly, Americans came to recognize the limita-
tions of local governments in dealing with much of the antiso-
cial, if not downright criminal, activities taking place in
America's competitive, profit-driven system, and they began
to demand that the state and central governments undertake
remedies.[2]

In some cases, the states proved reasonably effective, but a
number of the new problems clearly transcended state boundaries. Hesitantly, the federal government, under its interstate
commerce and taxing powers, initiated a pattern of crime
control through regulation. An increasing number of semi-
independent agencies such as the Interstate Commerce Commission and the Federal Trade Commission were formed to

2. Morris Ploscowe, "Crime in a Competitive Society," *Annals of the
American Academy of Political and Social Science* (September 1941),
105–11. Gus Tyler, *Organized Crime in America: A Book of Readings*
(Ann Arbor: University of Michigan Press, 1967), pp. 41–49. Louis
Adamic, *Dynamite: The Story of Class Violence in America* (New
York: The Viking Press, Inc., 1931), pp. 82–98, 340, 250, 257. John McCo-
naughy, *From Cain to Capone: Racketeering Down the Ages* (New
York: Brentano's, Publishers, 1931), pp. 295–314.

supervise the offending industries and to end their more flagrant abuses.

In a few selected cases, however, Congress used its powers differently. Responding to a broad public demand in the 1890s for prohibition of abuses in interstate lotteries—particularly the huge Louisiana Lottery—the federal government attempted to limit such operations to the state and local level by first denying them the use of the mails, then of interstate commerce in general. Applying the same principle to prostitution, Congress passed the Mann Act in 1910. Partly to enforce the attack on interstate prostitution, Attorney General Charles Bonaparte, over the loud protests of certain congressmen, had already created a special Bureau of Investigation within the Justice Department.[3]

All levels of American government in general adopted an artificial, moral distinction between legitimate and illegitimate businesses. Toward morally acceptable enterprises, they applied antitrust laws and regulation to rid the industry of the offensive acts; toward morally unacceptable businesses, they applied their powers in interstate commerce in the direction of outright suppression. Regulation of acceptable enterprises tended to improve the quality of product and to remove the industry's dependence on private armies; suppression of unacceptable enterprises encouraged partnership with underworld gangs and corrupt politicians. In later days, sociology's distinction between "white collar crime" and "organized crime" mirrored the moralistic distinctions of the government between types of illegal business activities.

Probably industrialization had its most far-reaching impact in the cities. Industries attracted millions of foreign immigrants and native Americans alike to the cities, placing increasing demands on space and urban services and adding new measures of social diversity that complicated enforcement of moralistic laws. A new breed of politicians—generally called "bosses" by their middle-class opponents—mobilized the voting potential of the new arrivals by providing goods and

3. Harry and Bonaro Overstreet, *The FBI in Our Open Society* (New York: W. W. Norton & Company, Inc., 1969), pp. 12–34. Various investigations failed to establish the existence of a nationwide organization of white slaves, and the Mann Act was designed to prohibit transportation of women across state lines. Herbert Asbury, *Gem of the Prairie: An Informal History of the Chicago Underworld* (New York: Alfred A. Knopf, Inc., 1940), pp. 266–67.

services to them or to their spokesmen. Money and political organization frequently purchased tolerance for an assortment of illegal activities in the ghetto and elsewhere; the extension of new services and the construction of new buildings and transportation systems involved extensive kickbacks and bribery. Reformers frequently alienated the new urban dwellers by an unbending attitude on moral and cultural questions and by an apparent lack of sympathy for their economic plight.

By the turn of the century the slick magazines as well as the yellow press were increasingly commenting on a "system" of organized crime and politics in cities throughout the country. The vast majority of muckrakers were middle class in perspective and regrettably naive about the inner workings of the criminal justice system.[4] In 1901 Lincoln Steffens exposed the political protection of vice and the widespread business corruption in his "Shame of the Cities" series, launched with information Steffens obtained from Joseph W. Folk, an ambitious, publicity-minded St. Louis politician.[5]

An offshoot of the isolation and misunderstanding in the city was the increasing tendency to identify the immigrant with crime. Attempts to link successive waves of immigration with crime and pauperism had, of course, marked popular protest and congressional investigations throughout American history. Large-scale Irish immigration partly accounted for the founding in the 1850s of the American party, which based its appeal on the Irish stereotype as an advance agent for the Pope or as a loud, carousing, drunken criminal. By the 1890s, the Italian had displaced the Irishman as the stereotype of the immigrant criminal.[6]

To some extent this new stereotype resulted from the poverty and crowded living conditions in the Italian communities

4. Edwin H. Sutherland, "Crime and Business," *The Annals* (September 1941), 112–18. Alfred R. Lindesmith, "Organized Crime," ibid., 119–27. Mark H. Haller, "Urban Crime and Criminal Justice: The Chicago Case," *The Journal of American History,* 57 (December 1970), 635.

5. Lincoln Steffens, *The Shame of the Cities* (New York: Hill & Wang, 1969), pp. vii, 26–41. Louis G. Geiger, *Joseph W. Folk of Missouri* (Columbia: University of Missouri Press, 1953), pp. 56–57.

6. Maldwyn A. Jones, *American Immigration* (Chicago: University of Chicago Press, 1960), pp. 152–58, 257. John Higham, *Strangers in the Land: Patterns of American Nativism, 1860–1925* (New York: Atheneum Publishers, 1968), p. 160.

as well as from the failure of the cities to provide adequate police protection. Part of the stereotype evolved from the increasing numbers of immigrants from southern Italy and Sicily where the traditions of Mafia and similar organizations remained strong. During centuries of misrule by foreign invaders, Sicilians had responded to oppression by noncooperation with legally established authorities, a strong sense of family, kinship, and village loyalties, and a tradition of settling disputes by vendetta or mediation by recognized village strongmen. "Mafia" emerged as a way of life—a system of involved village and family loyalties and a code of honor—not far different from that in other sections of Europe or in the United States.

In addition to mafia as a way of life, a rather ill-defined series of organizations by the same name actually operated in western Sicily. A primitive, endemic, and decentralized organization with perhaps occasional cooperation between local leaders, the formal Mafia defended and preserved the cultural mafia while occasionally engaging in private extortion. As its excesses increased, the Mafia became respected, feared, and, not infrequently, misunderstood throughout Sicily and southern Italy. Much of the modern unpopularity of the Mafia—both as culture and society—flowed from the bad press it received as a result of Sicily's provincial hostility to Italian unification in the late nineteenth century.[7]

Unquestionably, "members" of the Mafia arrived in America among the hordes of Italian immigrants in the late nineteenth century. Certainly a number of men with criminal records—some of quite a serious nature—joined the transatlantic migration.[8] There exists, however, no evidence that the immigrants transported any extensive criminal organization to the United States. Logically, those most likely to emigrate would be those least likely to hold powerful positions in any secret or

7. Eric J. Hobsbawn, *Social Bandits and Primitive Rebels* (Glencoe, Ill.: The Free Press, 1959), pp. 30–56. Tyler, *Organized Crime in America,* pp. 326–36, 344–49. The most significant literature on the Mafia of western Sicily appeared in the last two decades of the nineteenth century. The Mafia, like the Ku Klux Klan in the United States, has actually been several organizations that capitalized upon a set of attitudes and a dread name.

8. Giovanni Schiavo, *The Truth About the Mafia and Organized Crime in America* (El Paso: Vigo Press, 1962), pp. 154–55. A catalog of crimes linked to Sicilians and Italians in New Orleans is in *Foreign Relations, 1896,* p. 706.

semisecret organization in the Old Country. Probably, most such "mafiosi" were of rather low rank, likely to have been used for "enforcement" functions and probably ignorant of the broader purposes of the organization. Such men were nevertheless in a strategic position for exploiting the Italian colonies in the new country, particularly through their special skills of extortion and intimidation, and they were not above invoking the power of the Mafia in their activities. Living in areas that were underpoliced and that held a tradition of hostility toward police authority in any event, the average Italian immigrant became easy prey for such intimidation. In addition to references to the feared Mafia, extortion letters often carried the imprint of the "Black Hand," a threatening symbol that was possibly of Spanish origin. "Black Hand" letters, because of their romantic flavor, attracted widespread newspaper coverage and speculation, which in turn only increased their effectiveness.[9]

In fact, of course, a variety of criminal activity existed in the Italian communities—crimes perpetrated by labor agents and immigrant bankers, in addition to petty theft, vendettas, and Black Hand extortion. The preponderant image of Italian crime prior to the 1920s, however, was that of the act of passion, family vendetta, or extortion. The extensive newspaper

9. An apparent exception to the generalization that most *mafiosi* were poor and themselves subject to extortion was Salvatore Bonanno, father of a major New York Italian underworld figure. Gay Talese, *Honor Thy Father* (New York: World Publishing Company, 1971), pp. 190–91; Frank Marshall White, "How the United States Fosters the Black Hand," *The Outlook,* October 30, 1909, pp. 495–500. Arthur Woods, "The Problem of the Black Hand," *McClure's Magazine* (May 1909), 40–47. Gaetano D'Amato, "The Black Hand Myth," *The North American Review* (1908), 543–49. A White Hand Society, launched in 1907 by leaders of Chicago's Italian community to combat extortion, died out after a couple of years. Humbert S. Nelli, "Italians and Crime in Chicago: The Formative Years, 1890–1920," *The American Journal of Sociology,* 74 (January 1969), 376–78. The extreme example of the local Italian gang leader, Ignazio "Lupo the Wolf" Saietta of New York, headed a counterfeiting ring and loaned his followers to other secret Sicilian societies as hired killers. By report, those who feared Saietta fled to priests to prevent his casting the evil eye on them, but to no avail. Sensational writers often trace the Mafia succession in America from Saietta. Herbert Asbury, *The Gangs of New York: An Informal History of the Underworld* (New York: Alfred A. Knopf, Inc., 1928), pp. 267–68. Ed Reid, *The Grim Reapers: The Anatomy of Organized Crime in America* (Chicago: Henry Regnery Company, 1969), p. 26.

coverage, both within the Italian settlement and in the broader community, helped fix this image, as did Social Darwinism and criminologist Cesare Lombroso, whose writings defined crime as a product of individual pathology and atavism rather than as a product of social and cultural stresses.[10]

Subtly, however, a second stream of thought emerged which suggested that Mafia or Italian crime was less a way of life than acts of an organization of mysterious and unknown scope. The perspective of a national press, focusing upon two spectacular murders, probably more than any other factor prompted the growth of this idea. In October of 1890 New Orleans Police Chief David Hennessy was assassinated at the height of an intrigue-filled trial involving control of a local pier by rival Sicilian factions. The controversial Hennessy was apparently trying to maintain the peace on the pier and at the same time award the favored position to the faction he preferred. As Hennessy lay dying he allegedly gasped, "The Dagoes did it." Swift reaction to the murder brought mass arrests of suspects, a dramatic trial, a surprise acquittal followed by the storming of the jail by outraged townspeople, and the summary hanging of eleven Italians. Reporters from around the nation descended upon New Orleans and a diplomatic crisis with Italy ensued. The silence that had been maintained by the Italians while on trial, widespread publication of the charge that the defense had been financed by contributions from Italians in all parts of the nation, and alleged subornation of the jury convinced an investigating grand jury and many others that a Mafia conspiracy of uncertain but powerful proportions did in fact exist.[11]

The murder in 1909 of a New York City police lieutenant, Joseph Petrosini, added credibility to the myth of a broad Mafia conspiracy. Petrosini had been placed in charge of a

10. Nelli, "Italians and Crime in Chicago," 373–74, 390–91. Alfred Lindesmith and Yale Levin, "The Lombrosian Myth in Criminology," *The American Journal of Sociology,* 42 (March 1937), 653–71.

11. A sampling of the literature on the "Mafia incident" is John E. Coxe, "The New Orleans Mafia Incident," *The Louisiana Historical Quarterly,* 20 (October 1937), 1067–1110; J. Alexander Karlan, "The New Orleans Lynchings of 1890 and the American Press," ibid., 24 (January 1941), 187–203; John S. Kendall, "Who Killa De Chief," ibid., 22 (April 1939), 492–530; James D. Horan, *The Pinkertons: The Detective Dynasty that Made History* (New York: Crown Publishers, Inc., 1967), pp. 419–46; Schiavo, *Truth About the Mafia,* 140–72. The *Foreign Relations* volume for 1891 contains documents on the domestic as well as diplomatic aspects of the incident.

special squad of Italian policemen to combat the growing number of Black Hand extortion cases. Both he and Police Commissioner William McAdoo were convinced that there existed no centrally directed, nationally organized secret society of extortionists but rather that many small groups of extortionists played upon isolated Italians' fears of the legendary Black Hand or Mafia. To facilitate the investigation and possible prosecution of suspected felons, Petrosini traveled to Italy and Sicily to gather background information on certain immigrants.[12] An unknown gunman killed the police lieutenant while he was on assignment in Palermo. Ironically, Petrosini's unsolved assassination, dramatically presented by the press, encouraged the belief in the very entity he had hoped to prove nonexistent—an extensive, tightly knit Black Hand organization.

After the murders of Hennessy and Petrosini, the American public increasingly thought of Italian crime less as individual acts of passion and more as an organized conspiracy. Sensationalism, more than ethnic prejudice, explains the press's slow transformation of the older, almost anarchistic, Mafia stereotype into a more modern, all-encompassing conspiratorial one. Hysteria over criminal and ethnic conspiracies joined fears of bankers' plots, trusts, and political radicalism that swept the country at the turn of the twentieth century. In the short run this speculation promoted talk of restriction of immigration;[13] in the long run it was to obscure the interpretation of organized crime for decades.

12. William McAdoo, *Guarding a Great City* (New York: Harper and Brothers, 1906), 148–54. Kendall, "Who Killa De Chief," 502–7. Gino C. Speranza, "Petrosino and the Black Hand," *The Survey* (April 1909), 11–14. Anonymous, "The Black Hand Scourge," *Cosmopolitan Magazine* (June 1909), 31–41; Michael Fiaschetti, *You Gotta Be Rough: The Adventures of Detective Fiaschetti of the Italian Squad* (Garden City, N.Y.: Doubleday, Doran and Company, 1930), pp. 82–85.

13. Jones, *American Immigration,* pp. 177–82. Hastings H. Hart, "Immigration and Crime," *The American Journal of Sociology,* 2 (November 1896), 369–77. Sydney G. Fisher, "Immigration and Crime," *Popular Science Monthly* (September 1896), 625–30. S. S. McClure, "The Increase of Lawlessness in the United States," *McClure's Magazine* (December 1904), 163–71. The report of the Immigration Commission (Dillingham Commission) in 1911 discussed the number of Italians and Sicilians with criminal records in the United States, and its confusing use of the term "Mafia" probably contributed to the new stereotype. Joseph Albini, *The American Mafia: Genesis of a Legend* (New York: Appleton-Century-Crofts, 1971), pp. 167–70.

During the interwar boom and bust, events restructured organized crime in the United States, prompted significant study of the problems of law enforcement, and brought Italian-Americans into the mainstream of American crime, feeding the idea of a nationwide crime conspiracy. The primary force in each circumstance was Prohibition. Unlike the earlier federal legislation against the interstate traffic in prostitution and lotteries, the Eighteenth Amendment provided for outright prohibition of the manufacture or transportation of alcoholic beverages. Although the federal government was undertaking much more than it had in previous legislation, no effective provisions were made for federal enforcement. While local law enforcement agencies abdicated enforcement of the Volstead Act and in many cases cooperated in its violation, a small group of inefficient agents in the Prohibition Bureau struggled against a rising tide of resentment. Walter Lippmann aptly likened the entire ill-enforced Prohibition experiment to fighting the Devil with a wooden sword.[14] Unquestionably, the most dramatic development born out of Prohibition was the rise of organized gangs to meet the public's demand for liquor. Although underworld gangs had been employed throughout the nineteenth century for political and economic purposes, none of them approached the new power and wealth of gang leaders in the 1920s. When the American liquor industry was in effect declared illegal, some brewers, such as Joseph Stenson of the Sieben Brewery in Chicago, called upon gang leaders to "front" for them and to "take falls" in case of raids.[15] Others, according to rumor, sold interests in their companies to underworld figures. Diversion of industrial and medicinal alcohol to manufacture more-or-less potable beverages, home brewing, and elaborately clandestine importation from foreign sources slaked the nation's thirst and shunted vast wealth into the coffers of those who were willing to risk apprehension. The operations of Dutch Schultz (Arthur Fleginheimer) and Big Bill Dwyer in New York and the notorious rum-running operations of the Reinfeld syndicate and of Abner "Longie" Zwillman in New Jersey caught the

14. Walter Lippmann, "The Underworld: A Stultified Conscience," *The Forum* (February 1931), 69.

15. Andrew Sinclair, *Prohibition: The Era of Excess* (Boston: Little, Brown and Company, 1962), pp. 221–22. John Landesco, *Organized Crime in Chicago* (Chicago: University of Chicago Press, 1968), pp. 89–95.

imagination of the public and made the organizers wealthy men. Older, established underworld figures, such as Arnold Rothstein in New York and the gaudy "Diamond Jim" Colosimo in Chicago provided financing, recruitment, and political contacts for younger, more vigorous underworld leaders.[16]

The new bonanza brought violence and more corruption as well as wealth. In Chicago, as the Colosimo-Torrio-Capone gang gradually prevailed over such rivals as the Genna Brothers, the Dion O'Banion and Bugs Moran gangs, and the Touhys, literally hundreds of gangland murders went unsolved and most gang leaders enjoyed immunity from arrest. Al Capone's power reached into high political and judicial circles as well as the press, and was sustained by an admiring public.[17] In the absence of reliable statistics, no one can say with certainty that a real crime wave existed in the 1920s, but surely organized crime enjoyed greater profits and power than at any time in the nation's history, larger numbers of ordinary citizens participated in the violation of the Volstead Act, and the effectiveness of federal law enforcement reached a low ebb. Even had all the prohibition agents been of impeccable honesty and vigor, they probably could not have enforced the legislation in the face of middle- and upper-class demand for

16. Rothstein, the model for Meyer Wolfsheim in F. Scott Fitzgerald's *The Great Gatsby,* made his fortune in race track gambling and has been compared to J. P. Morgan of the "upperworld." Colosimo had begun as a black hander, but acquired such wealth through prostitution, gambling, and political brokerage that he himself was subjected to threats from Black Hand groups. To protect himself, he imported Johnny Torrio from the Five Points Gang in New York. Upon Colosimo's assassination in 1920, Torrio took over the gang, expanded its operations into liquor, and after a near assassination in 1925 turned control over to Al Capone, whom he himself had imported from the Five Points Gang. Leo Katcher, *The Big Bankroll: The Life and Times of Arnold Rothstein* (New York: Harper and Brothers, 1958), pp. 236–65. Asbury, *Gem of the Prairie,* p. 317. Virgil W. Peterson, *Barbarians in Our Midst: A History of Chicago Crime and Politics* (Boston: Little, Brown and Company, 1952), pp. 121–51.

17. Peterson, *Barbarians in Our Midst,* pp. 125, 134. Ovid Demaris, *Captive City* (New York: Pocket Books, 1970), pp. 116–25. Capone sponsored huge soup kitchens in Chicago during the Depression when government agencies appeared powerless, and he once considered hiring John D. Rockefeller's public relations man. Kenneth Allsop, *The Bootleggers and Their Era* (Garden City, N.Y.: Doubleday & Company, Inc., 1961), pp. 293–324.

liquor. Actually, many of the agents were underpaid, inexperienced political hacks, and before the "Noble Experiment" died in 1933, over a fourth of them had been dismissed on various charges. Congress summarily rejected President Coolidge's suggestion that local authorities be deputized to enforce the Volstead Act, and while Herbert Hoover's success in getting jurisdiction transferred from the Treasury to the Justice Department probably brought some improvement in enforcement, this action came far too late to save the Eighteenth Amendment.[18]

President Hoover's concern over the status of law enforcement prompted his appointment in 1929 of the National Commission on the Administration of Justice, chaired by former Attorney General George Wickersham. In addition to its contradictory and confusing conclusions on the continuation of Prohibition, the Wickersham Commission surveyed and summarized a decade of study of the courts and law enforcement by a variety of private groups and interests.[19]

One of these groups, the Chicago Crime Commission, had been formed in 1919 and was financed by business interests to provide sustained public pressure on officials, maintained a staff of trained investigators who observed court proceedings. The Commission collected and explored leads and issued numerous recommendations. When its suggestions were ignored by public officials, the Commission almost invariably responded with impressive statistics to support its recommendations and sought to mobilize public opinion for its proposals.

18. President's Research Committee on Social Trends, *Recent Social Trends in the United States* (New York: McGraw-Hill, 1933), pp. 1123–35. Ralph Salerno and John S. Tompkins, *The Crime Confederation: Cosa Nostra and Allied Operations in Organized Crime* (Garden City, N.Y.: Doubleday & Company, Inc., 1969), p. 280. J. C. Burnham, "New Perspectives on the Prohibition 'Experiment' of the 1920's," *Journal of Social History* (Fall 1968), 61, 63. Harris Gaylord Warren, *Herbert Hoover and the Great Depression* (New York: Oxford University Press, 1959), p. 215. On the issue of a crime wave in the 1920s, see "The Permanent Crime Wave," *New Republic,* January 5, 1921, pp. 156–57; "Wanted: A New Crusade," *Current Opinion* (February 1921), 148–51; George W. Kirchway, "The So-Called 'Crime Wave,' " ibid., 168–72.

19. Hoover interpreted the Commission's position as being in favor of maintaining Prohibition, but Wickersham thought its thrust had been for repeal. One critic ridiculed the group as the "Liquorsham" Commission. Sinclair, *Era of Excess,* p. 364. Herbert Hoover, *The Memoirs of Herbert Hoover* (New York: The Macmillan Company, 1952), II, 278.

Basically a refined expression of the old vigilante tradition, the Chicago Crime Commission took a tough attitude toward crime, viewing it less as a cultural and social phenomenon of urban life than as an insidious enemy that could best be deterred by quick and certain punishment. Merciless publicity could best purify the criminal justice system of its long-time courtship with the underworld.[20]

Patterned on the Chicago group, similar citizen crime commissions sprang up in Kansas City, Cleveland, Los Angeles, and Baltimore, and in 1925 a National Crime Commission was organized in the New York office of Elbert H. Gary of U.S. Steel Corporation. An impressive list of public figures, including Charles Evans Hughes, Frank O. Lowden, Newton D. Baker, and Franklin D. Roosevelt served on the executive committee of the national group. Representatives of twenty-six crime commissions of varying types attended the National Crime Commission's second annual meeting in 1927 and explored the inadequacy of crime statistics, problems concerning prisons, pardon, parole, and organized crime's supposed dependence upon fences and other intermediaries. Always on the verge of insolvency, most of the local anticrime groups as well as the National Crime Commission collapsed either before or during the Depression. Those in Chicago, Cleveland, and Baltimore alone remained active through 1930.[21]

More significant during the 1920s, a series of in-depth studies of the criminal justice system was undertaken, and these often involved some of the same personnel and financing as the citizens' crime commission movement. Raymond C. Moley of Columbia University came to national attention by directing crime surveys in Cleveland in 1922, Missouri in 1924, New York in 1925, and Illinois in 1928. In general, these studies urged expanding training for law enforcement officers in modern scientific techniques and statistics, greater unification of law enforcement functions by the states, abolition of the sheriffs' responsibilities for investigation of crimes, and various improvements in regulation of parole and probation.

20. Bertram J. Cahn, "The Story of the Chicago Crime Commission" (printed speech before Chicago Literary Club, 1940). Henry Barrett Chamberlain, a former newspaperman, served as operating director of the Crime Commission for over twenty years. Asbury, *Gem of the Prairie,* pp. 369–71.

21. Virgil W. Peterson, "Citizens Crime Commissions," *Federal Probation* (March 1953), 9–10.

With the exception of John Landesco's classic analysis of organized crime in Chicago—buried in the Illinois study—the state crime surveys devoted little attention to the socioeconomic causes of crime in general or of organized crime in particular. Landesco rejected the popular notion that organized crime was fostered by traits found only in immigrant groups and stressed the environment in which underworld figures had grown up in the New World. Landesco's ecological emphasis paralleled that of Frederic Thrasher who worked with youth gangs, of Walter C. Reckless, who studied the development of prostitution in *Vice in Chicago* (1933), and of other students who were working in the Department of Sociology at the University of Chicago.[22] While the "Chicago school" of sociology at this time did not fully appreciate the extent of criminal behavior in areas of the city beyond the slums, it did suggest an alternative approach to the law enforcement orientation of the state crime surveys. The Wickersham Commission, while not oblivious to these ideas, simply took note of organized crime and racketeering as an ominous threat and in general reflected the thrust and values of the state crime studies of the 1920s.[23]

The academic emphasis on environment lost out again to procedural, law enforcement interests under the New Deal. Franklin Roosevelt and his man Friday, Louis M. Howe, had been active throughout the 1920s on the National Crime Commission, and both had become convinced of the need for the kind of structural and statistical reform the movement advocated. So discredited was federal law enforcement by the end of Prohibition, however, that both lawmakers and the FBI sought to avoid undertaking any extensive new responsibilities.

The New Deal directed its "War on Crime"—like many of its other programs—toward the dramatic rather than toward the substantive. In response to the Lindbergh, Hamm, and Urshel kidnappings and the wave of daring bank robberies by Dillinger, the Barker-Karpis gang, Pretty Boy Floyd, Bonnie and Clyde, and other free-lance products of the Depression, Howe and Attorney General Homer Cummings, with the tardy coop-

22. Mark H. Haller, "Introduction," Landesco, *Organized Crime in Chicago,* pp. vii–xviii.
23. National Commission on Law Observation and Enforcement, *Report on Criminal Procedure,* No. 8, pp. 45–58.

eration of Chairman Hatton Sumners of the House Judiciary Committee, pushed through about ten acts that armed FBI agents and expanded their authority into kidnapping, interstate transportation of stolen goods, flight from prosecution, and robbery of national banks. Other legislation prohibited the sending of extortion letters through the mails or interstate commerce; protected certain types of trade and commerce against intimidation and racketeering; provided for the registration of machine guns, sawed-off shotguns and rifles; updated federal criminal justice procedure; and provided for the granting of prior congressional consent to state law enforcement compacts.[24] Impressive on paper, the New Deal legislation covered only isolated new areas of enforcement, returned the enforcement of Prohibition rather precipitately to the states, and, over all, did little violence to the established American tradition of decentralized law enforcement.

Aside from an incidental law or two, Cummings's "War on Crime" paid little attention to organized crime. The Attorney General's Conference in December 1934 touched in passing on the problem and a "Committee on Racketeering" (a subcommittee of the Senate Commerce Committee) headed by New York Senator Royal S. Copeland held extensive though unproductive hearings in 1933–1934.[25] To some extent, the creation of such agencies as the SEC, NRA, and the NLRB retarded the

24. Fred J. Cook, *The FBI Nobody Knows* (New York: The Macmillan Company, 1964), pp. 149–55, 169–70, 178, 185, 219–26. Raymond Moley, *The First New Deal* (New York: Harcourt, Brace & World, 1966), pp. 76–77, 502–3. Franklin D. Roosevelt, *Public Papers and Addresses of Franklin D. Roosevelt,* Samuel I. Rosenman, ed., 13 vols. (New York: Random House, Inc., 1938–1950), III, 242–45. Alfred B. Rollins, Jr., *Roosevelt and Howe* (New York: Alfred A. Knopf, Inc., 1962), pp. 201–2. Cook, Moley, and Rollins contain revealing but undeveloped insights into the bureaucratic squabbling behind the New Deal's war on crime. A prosaic account of the Treasury Department's anticrime effort is in John Morton Blum, *From the Morgenthau Diaries: Years of Crisis, 1928–1938* (Boston: Houghton Mifflin Company, 1959), pp. 100–119.

25. *Proceedings of the Attorney General's Conference on Crime* (Washington: 1934), pp. 56–57, 79. Ernest S. Griffith, Director, Legislative Reference Service, to Estes Kefauver, January 20, 1950, Crime Box 37, Estes Kefauver Papers, University of Tennessee Library. *Hearings,* Subcommittee on "Rackets" of the Senate Commerce Committee, 73d Cong., 2d sess., Pts. 1–7. Copeland credited Col. Louis Howe with giving him advice and placing him in contact with many of the sociologists he heard. *Congressional Record,* January 11, 1934, p. 449.

expansion of organized crime and racketeering into certain fields, but such protection was neither purposeful nor comprehensive.

*   *   *   *

While J. Edgar Hoover, director of the Federal Bureau of Investigation, launched a dramatic, publicity-laden campaign against isolated midwestern bank robbers and kidnappers, federal officials contented themselves with leaving the more perplexing fight against organized crime and racketeering to state and local authorities. Few of the gang leaders associated with the booze bonanza of the 1920s drifted into kidnapping or bank robbery; rather, they applied their wealth, muscle, managerial experience, and political contacts to the far more lucrative fields of labor exploitation and industrial racketeering or to certain illegal business operations, such as gambling, prostitution, or narcotics.[26]

Although the word *racketeering* did not come into popular use until the late 1920s, the activities it suggests go deep into the past. Simply put, racketeering was the extortion of a private tax on the exchange of goods and services at some point in the economic process. In some cases, it was purely parasitic, differing from outright robbery only in that it left the victim some "protection" and sufficient funds to carry on his economic function. In other cases, however, it could in reality protect its patron against damage or extortion by other gangs, much as the police might, or it could suppress rivals, upstart unions or recalcitrant management, much as trade associations, arbitration councils, or regulatory agencies might do. The Capone gang, with almost seven hundred strong-arm men at its command, could easily masquerade as a labor union or a newly formed trade association and exploit both sides of a management–labor dispute. At the same time, a large enterprise such as Ford Motors might employ a Harry Bennett as head of a "Service Department" and for a modest cost be free of union difficulties. Especially susceptible to racketeer-

26. Critics pointed out that state and local officials were much more effective against bank robbers and kidnappers than the FBI suggested. On the Dillinger case, see Cook, *FBI Nobody Knows,* p. 185; John Toland, *The Dillinger Days* (New York: Avon Books, 1964); Milton S. Mayer, "Myth of the 'G-Men,' " *The Forum* (September 1935), 144–48.

ing in the 1920s and 1930s were laundries and dry-cleaning establishments, fish and artichoke marketing, garment workers' unions, restaurants, and illegal businesses such as gambling or prostitution. Interestingly, each such activity was vulnerable because of its peculiarly competitive nature or because its illegality made recourse to the police impractical.[27]

Industrial and labor racketeering, largely ignored by the federal government, provided the basis for prosecutor Thomas E. Dewey's meteoric rise to political prominence in the 1930s. Dewey, appointed in 1935 by Governor Herbert Lehman as special prosecutor for a "run away" New York grand jury, put together a highly efficient staff that within two years produced 73 indictments for racketeering and 71 convictions. Capping the young attorney's courtroom successes were the convictions of Charles "Lucky." Luciano on charges of compulsory prostitution in 1936 and later of Tammany leader Jimmy Hines for criminal conspiracy. Prosecutor Dewey, unlike Director Hoover, converted his new-found prestige into a political career that led him to the governorship of New York and would culminate in two Republican nominations to the Presidency. Crime fighting had become a quick means of political promotion.[28]

The interwar era witnessed a remarkable expansion in gambling, both legal and illegal. In the 1930s, for example, "bank night" at the movies, church-sponsored bingo games, and the ubiquitous punchboards became institutions. The numbers and policy games reached into the pockets of even the poorest slum dweller, rarely gave honest odds, and turned such profits that they soon attracted the managerial talent and

27. Murray Gurfein, "The Racket Defined," in Tyler, *Organized Crime in America,* pp. 181–89. Frederick Lewis Allen, *Only Yesterday* (Perennial Library, New York: Harper & Row, Publishers, 1964), pp. 216, 220–24. Sinclair, *Era of Excess,* pp. 224–26. Daniel Bell, *The End of Ideology: On the Exhaustion of Political Ideas in the Fifties* (New York: The Free Press, 1962), pp. 131–32. In one Chicago case, an independent cleaner and dyer took Capone into partnership rather than depend upon the police or Employers' Association. The cleaner then boasted of having "the best protection in the world." Landesco, *Organized Crime in Chicago,* pp. 158–59.

28. Stanley Walker, *Dewey: An American of This Century* (New York: McGraw-Hill Book Company, 1944), pp. 40–58. Frederick Lewis Allen, *Since Yesterday* (New York: Bantam Books, Inc., 1965), pp. 147–49.

muscle of such experienced gangsters as Dutch Schultz in New York. Machine gambling and slot machines enjoyed tremendous popularity with the continued decline of gambling houses and lotteries. The attractively boxed "one-armed bandit," designed to collect any size coin and equipped with an adjustable pay-off mechanism, spread rapidly throughout the country to all kinds of establishments. When New York's Mayor Fiorello LaGuardia in 1934 dramatically seized and destroyed large numbers of machines belonging to onetime supporter Frank Costello, Costello shifted a good portion of his operations to more hospitable Louisiana.[29]

Probably the most important form of gambling in the 1930s was that associated with the revival of horse and dog racing. The "Sport of Kings" in the late nineteenth century had increasingly fallen under the control of professional gamblers, so that state after state banned horse racing entirely. In 1906 it was legal only in Maryland, Kentucky, and New York. In the 1930s the trend reversed as, one by one, states permitted parimutuel on-track betting as a means of raising state revenues. Nevada went so far as to legalize licensed gambling in most forms, including off-track betting, in 1931.[30]

With the expansion of races and long-distance communications, off-track bookmakers, with a stake of money and means to get up-dated information, could turn a substantial profit. Taking advantage of this increased demand, newspaperman Moses Annenberg, fresh from the vicious Hearst circulation wars, in 1927 bought the General News Bureau from Chicago gambler Mont Tennes. Tennes, engaged in gambling on Chicago's North Side, had attempted in 1907 to parlay an exclusive telegraph racing-news contract out of Cincinnati into a local monopoly of bookmakers. Although he failed to monopolize race-track gambling, Tennes did emerge from a

29. Dixon Wecter, *Age of the Great Depression* (New York: The Macmillan Company, 1948), pp. 242–43. Rufus King, *Gambling and Organized Crime* (Washington: Public Affairs Press, 1969), pp. 42–43. Bell, *End of Ideology*, p. 144; Harold Lavine, "Kingpin Costello, Gamblers' Gambler," *Newsweek,* November 21, 1949, p. 31. Traditional accounts have accepted Costello's own statement that Huey Long invited Costello into Louisiana in order to finance his welfare program. Long's latest biographer doubts this story. T. Harry Williams, *Huey Long* (New York: Bantam Books, Inc., 1970), p. 866.

30. Louis A. Lawrence, "Bookmaking," *The Annals* (May 1950), 46–47. Katcher, *Big Bankroll,* pp. 49–50. King, *Gambling and Organized Crime,* p. 120.

violent struggle with rival bookmakers as the most powerful gambling figure in the Windy City. By 1927, however, Tennes was reportedly encountering difficulty with the Capone gang and was therefore happy to divest himself of General News. The purchaser, Annenberg, who had matured in the newspaper circulation wars, faced severe competition from about seventeen other racing-news services. By 1939, however, he had a powerful hold on a national gambling empire that included bookmaking, racing publications, and various "scratch" sheets. At Annenberg's trial for income tax evasion in 1940, the prosecutor showed that his racing-news wire was American Telephone and Telegraph Company's fifth largest customer.[31]

* * * *

While the full implications of Prohibition and the expansion of gambling in the interwar period are not clear, the legal and technological problems involved unquestionably called forth managerial skills and stimulated contacts and understandings between underworld groups in various cities. The automobile, telephone, and telegraph obviously made rapid transportation and communication possible. Within the Italian underworld, kinship and business ties brought together leaders from Chicago, New York, and other cities. The so-called "cannon-mob" convention in Cleveland in 1928 brought together about twenty Italians from the Northeast and Midwest, and the multi-ethnic Atlantic City meeting in 1929 was attended by Capone, Costello, and non-Italian leaders such as Enoch "Nocky" Johnson. Although there is no reliable evidence on what exactly transpired at these meetings, it is reasonable to assume that discussions centered on rationalizing the supply and delivery of liquor and reaching understandings with amenable politicians.[32] No all-encompassing orga-

31. Virgil W. Peterson, *Gambling: Should It Be Legalized* (Springfield, Ill.: Charles C. Thomas, Publisher, 1951), pp. 34–37. Landesco, *Organized Crime in Chicago,* pp. 52, 59, 77. Lawrence, "Bookmaking," 47–48.

32. A number of accounts erroneously claim that the Cleveland *Plain Dealer* referred to the 27 men meeting in that city in 1928 as a "Grand Council of the Mafia." Cleveland *Plain Dealer,* December 1–30, 1928, particularly the December 6 issue. For a variety of interpre-

nization appears either to have called such meetings or to have developed at them. Instead the prevailing pattern continued to be decentralization with city-wide or sometimes regional agreements among underworld figures themselves and with politicians, with local politicians having ultimate veto power and responding to local public opinion more than to any overwhelming outside conspiracy.

Despite the expanded role that Italians played in violations of the Prohibition and gambling laws, the press, particularly in the 1920s, made little of any supposed ethnic conspiracy. Some observers in Chicago, of course, noted Capone's strength within Italian fraternal organizations like the Unione Siciliana, but newspaper reporters, particularly those in the James M. Cox chain, probably paid more attention to Capone's frequent Florida vacations. The real basis for Capone's power was obviously public dissatisfaction with Prohibition rather than any Mafia conspiracy. His frequently issued public statements endorsing the American economic system as well as his conviction and sentencing on income tax evasion charges in 1931 made him and his associates relatively poor material for speculation on any extensive ethnic conspiracy.[33]

The Italian gangster, in fact, constituted only part of the broader image of crime in the interwar period. Old-stock Americans from the hinterland, such as Dillinger and the Barker gang, shared the public's attention with the newer polyglot products of the urban East, such as Big Bill Dwyer, Arnold Rothstein, and Italian-American underworld figures. Another factor inhibiting talk of an ethnic criminal conspiracy was the increasing willingness of gangsters to cooperate across ethnic boundaries. The Capone gang in Chicago included such Jewish figures as Jacob "Greasy Thumb" Guzik and Welsh-Americans like Murray "The Camel" Humphries, while in New York Jewish-born Arnold Rothstein promoted Irishmen like Dwyer, Italians like Costello, or other Jews like

tations on the Atlantic City meeting, see John Kobler, *Capone: The Life and World of Al Capone* (New York: G. P. Putnam's Sons, 1971), pp. 246–48; Donald R. Cressey, *Theft of the Nation: The Structure and Operations of Organized Crime in America* (New York: Harper and Row, 1969), p. 38; Hank Messick, *Lansky* (New York: G. P. Putnam's Sons, 1971), p. 59.

33. Peterson, *Barbarians in Our Midst,* p. 273; James M. Cox, *Journey Through My Years* (New York: Simon & Schuster, Inc., 1946), pp. 313–17; Allsop, *Bootleggers and Their Era,* pp. 238, 265–67, 275.

Waxey Gordon.[34] A variety of developments, then, partially explained the fact that journalists paid relatively little attention to the Mafia notion in the 1920s.

The idea of a nationwide criminal conspiracy did not, of course, disappear, and was in fact reemphasized in the 1930s by reporters and law enforcement officials. Fragments of the evidence they collected were obvious, but did not necessarily prove their claims. Important figures involved in liquor manufacture and distribution or gambling, as in other business or professional activities, might well become acquainted; similar interests, such as racing, resorts, and possibly joint investment ventures would occasion meetings for both pleasure and planning. In some cases, ethnic and family ties might strengthen these relationships. Certainly, underworld business, like upperworld business, did not proceed in a vacuum.

As befitting New Deal rhetoric, talk of national crime organizations in the mid-1930s largely took an economic rather than ethnic jargon. Journalist Martin Mooney in 1935, for example, first publicized an alleged meeting of "the executives of Crime, Incorporated" in a New York hotel. While Mooney gave no names, he did state that it included at least three important local and national politicians. Persons of prestige names in the latter half of the 1930s did not bother to refute Mooney's contention; and his book, *Crime Incorporated,* bore the endorsement of FBI Director Hoover. Prosecutor Thomas E. Dewey echoed a similar theme in addressing a citizens' anticrime group in New York in 1937.[35]

If crime fighters Hoover and Dewey occasionally gave verbal encouragement to the idea of a national crime organization in economic terms, the Federal Bureau of Narcotics revived the ethnic theme. As head of the Narcotics Bureau since its inception in 1930, Harry J. Anslinger, a veteran of the old Prohibition Bureau, dominated his agency much as Hoover did the FBI. Although he had had early encounters with Black Hand extortion, Anslinger had given little cre-

---

34. Gangs continued to operate as racially unifying forces, and underworld leaders like Capone and Costello often provided the financial wherewithal for the rise in politics of members of ethnic groups. Bell, *End of Ideology,* pp. 141–48.

35. Martin Mooney, *Crime Incorporated* (New York: Whittlesey House, 1935), p. 38. George Redston and Kendell F. Crossen, *The Conspiracy of Death* (Indianapolis: The Bobbs-Merrill Co., Inc., 1965), p. 196.

dence to talk of a pervasive Mafia organization until he examined the intelligence that had been gathered by his narcotic
agents.[36] A large portion—though not all—of the names his
investigators had collected were Italian, partly because the
bureau's European agents came into frequent contact with
Italian police officials, who remembered Mussolini's anti-
Mafia campaign of the 1920s and 1930s.[37]

As the decade came to an end, evidence for the existence of a
nationwide crime cartel seemed to mount. In the summer of
1939, J. Richard "Dixie" Davis, former "mouthpiece" for the
slain Dutch Schultz, was nearing the end of his prison term—a
light one-year sentence, which Davis had received in exchange for cooperating in Dewey's prosecution of Hines. To
finance his start in the outside world, Davis wrote a six-part
series of articles for *Collier's,* relating his life of crime and his
admittedly secondhand information on the "Americanization
of the mobs." Davis stated that a Schultz lieutenant had told
him that the highly publicized murders of Vincent "Mad Dog"
Coll and "Legs" Diamond were actually far less significant
than the bloody purges of the "Mustache Petes" by a younger
group of Italians led by "Lucky" Luciano in 1931. Supposedly,
the murders had been precipitated by the "Mustache Petes' "
unwillingness to cooperate with other ethnic groups in crime,
and Luciano had used the Unione Siciliana, which Davis described as a "mysterious, all-pervasive reality," to mobilize the
underworld on a nationwide scale. The refined Luciano organization, spawned by Italians, included important Jews such
as Meyer Lansky and Benjamin Siegel in New York and Moe
Dalitz in Cleveland. Those independents who, like Schultz,
resisted the new conglomerate, were executed. Davis's articles,

36. Harry J. Anslinger and Will Oursler, *The Murderers: The Story
of the Narcotics Gangs* (New York: Farrar, Straus & Cudahy, Inc.,
1961), pp. 20–25. Anslinger as a youth had been deeply impressed by
the horrors of opium, an ingredient of many patent medicines of the
time. In the 1930s he mobilized an impressive educational campaign
against heroin and marijuana, a campaign that contributed to the
Marijuana Act of 1937. A hard-liner on the drug problem, he has been
roundly criticized for taking a "criminal, rather than medical" approach to the problem of addiction. Ibid., pp. 38–42. Salerno, *Crime
Confederation,* p. 282.

37. During this time, a number of later important underworld
figures, including the Anastasia brothers entered the United States
illegally. Salerno, *Crime Confederation,* pp. 276–77; New York *Times,*
October 26, 1957.

admittedly sketchy, based on secondhand information, and springing from questionable motives, were nonetheless accepted at face value by those who sought evidence for a nation-wide criminal conspiracy.[38]

Less than a year after the Davis articles appeared, Brooklyn's District Attorney William O'Dwyer began an exposure of what one writer insisted was the "most startling crime story of the century." While investigating some of the hundred-odd unsolved murders still in his files, O'Dwyer's office began to look at the killings as part of a broader pattern. The investigators found a series of witnesses, notably Abe "Kid Twist" Reles, who testified that they had been part of a murder ring that was hired by groups that belonged to a nationwide crime combination. A group of men rather than a single individual directed the giant conspiracy; Henry "Dutch" Goldberg of California may have been the single most powerful figure. According to Burton Turkus of O'Dwyer's office, the term *Murder, Inc.*, as well as the nationwide implications were first suggested by a reporter, Harry Fenney of the New York *World-Telegram.* Working at peak efficiency, the O'Dwyer staff won conviction after conviction, some for murders committed as far away as the Pacific Coast. With the exception of Louis "Lepke" Buchalter, however, the prosecution never touched anyone regarded by the press as a really powerful gangster.

In late 1941, as major new cases allegedly involving national political figures were looming, the Japanese attack on Pearl Harbor brought the United States into World War II, usurping not only the headlines but also O'Dwyer, who went into Army Intelligence. The full impact of the O'Dwyer revelations were overshadowed by war and receded into the jungle of New York politics.[39]

---

38. J. Richard "Dixie" Davis, "Things I Couldn't Tell Till Now," *Collier's,* July 22, 1939, pp. 9–10, 38–41; July 29, pp. 20–21, 37–40; August 5, pp. 12–13, 43–44; August 12, pp. 16–17, 29–30; August 19, pp. 12–13, 34–38; August 26, pp. 18–19, 35–38, particularly the August 5 and August 12 articles. Daniel Bell argues that the leadership in organized crime has undergone a process of ethnic succession over the past century. First the Irish, then the Jews, and more recently the Italians have preponderantly held leadership roles. Bell, *End of Ideology,* pp. 141–45.

39. Meyer Berger, "Murder, Inc.," *Life,* September 30, 1940, pp. 86–96. Burton B. Turkus and Sid Feder, *Murder, Inc.: The Story of "The Syndicate"* (London: Victor Gollancz, Ltd., 1953), pp. 19–20. Joseph Freeman, "Murder Monopoly: The Inside Story of a Crime Trust," *The*

By the early 1940s, a number of developments indicated a growing tendency in the United States to consider organized crime as an ethnic conspiracy. The American tradition had been to overlegislate, to overburden the public law with essentially religious proscriptions. Because there existed widespread differences over the moral judgments behind the laws, many were willing to violate the law in order to obtain the goods and services supposedly suppressed. Profits from these blackmarket operations provided opportunities for otherwise disadvantaged economic groups; and once systematized, the same profits exerted corrupting pressures on the hopelessly splintered law enforcement structure. Americans were in general unwilling to reconsider the purpose of the law or to undertake a rationalization and upgrading of the law enforcement and criminal justice system. Rather they expressed their frustration in periodic reform efforts, in frantic spasms of moral self-examination, or in efforts to explain crime—particularly organized crime—as a conspiracy alien to the broader socioeconomic system. The national coverage given such crimefighters as Hoover, Dewey, and O'Dwyer encouraged Americans to look for national patterns and organizations of crime; press speculation on supposed ethnic plots, dramatized by the appearance of major Italian-American gangsters during the Prohibition period and encouraged by such men as Anslinger, stimulated a modest revival of interest in the Mafia theories. Unfortunately, academic criminologists, economists, and historians made no real effort to counter this tendency, and as a result the study of organized crime became increasingly the province of prosecutors and sensationalists.

Nation, May 25, 1940, pp. 645–49. Ironically, a case similar to "Murder, Inc.," had surfaced in August of 1921 when confessions were extracted in New York from members of an Italian murder ring said to be linked to over 125 deaths in New York, Detroit, Buffalo, Chicago, Pittsburgh, and Bridgeport. Tommaso Sassone, "Italy's Criminals in the United States," *Current History* (October 1921), 24.

2

The Postwar Crime Scare

No matter how cheap a crime story may be, it is still
better than any other type of story.
   —Gene Lowall, Denver *Post,* 1949

If the significance of one dramatic prosecution paled during
the war, crime itself remained a volatile issue, subject to
much speculation and prognostication. As financiers pre-
dicted economic setbacks and internationalists raised the
specter of isolationism in the postwar world, so law enforcement experts prophesied the advent of a new crime wave.
Virgil W. Peterson of the Chicago Crime Commission called
upon the nation to brace itself for unprecedented lawlessness
such as it had experienced after World War I, and FBI Director J. Edgar Hoover complained that permissive education
was producing more and younger criminals. He urged Americans to "build up the dikes against the coming flood."

Hoover regularly released FBI statistics on major crimes
against persons and property to document his contention. The
figures revealed a 12.4 per cent increase in crime in 1945 and
a 7.6 per cent jump in 1946—the latter supposedly representing a sixteen-year peak in criminal activity. Both the FBI Director and Attorney General Tom Clark explained the rise
primarily in terms of juvenile delinquency. Hoover noted the
large percentage of youth among those arrested, and Clark
announced a 198 per cent increase between 1939 and 1946 in
the arrest of girls under eighteen years of age. Most commentators accepted the Hoover–Clark explanations for the rising
crime rates and public opinion agreed that the cause was the
weakening of home and parental authority due to wartime
dislocations and general neglect.

Impressed by parallels he perceived in the post-World War

I period, Hoover in 1947 warned that increasing gang warfare might well be the next logical step in the evolving pattern of crime. While police authorities in several cities denied that gang activity was on the increase, a group of antigambling advocates and journalists initiated a campaign to prove them wrong.[1] This new campaign against organized crime was temporarily to overshadow and ignore juvenile delinquency and any connection it might have with the broader problem of crime.

In January 1947, as Al Capone, suffering from a stroke, pneumonia, and advanced paresis, lay dying in his Palm Beach home,[2] developments were surfacing that suggested that his crime syndicate would not only survive him but would continue to grow and prosper. In Chicago, officials released a 98-page statement by the late James M. Ragen concerning the wire-service war then disturbing Chicago and several of the nation's larger cities. In his statement, Ragen had declared that his opponents in the racing-news wire war were dominated by members of the old Capone gang, now operating as a syndicate. In 1946, when Ragen had filed the statement, he charged that his life had been threatened by Jake Guzik, Anthony Accardo, and Murray Humphries; his assassination later that year convinced the press and most officials of the truth of his charges.[3]

1. Virgil W. Peterson, "Case Dismissed: The Unreasonable Leniency of American Justice," *Atlantic Monthly* (April 1945), 69–74. J. Edgar Hoover, "The Rising Crime Wave," *The American Magazine* (March 1946), 124–28. Arnold Braithwaite, "How to Make a Crime Wave," *New Masses,* August 20, 1946, pp. 19–21. New York *Times,* March 20, May 14, 1946; March 17, August 3, 1947; October 11, 1948; March 18, 1949. Crime definition and statistics are too primitive to say with any certainty whether crime really increased in the late 1940s. Some commentators have since argued that it was really on the decline. Fred P. Graham, "A Contemporary History of American Crime," in Hugh Davis Graham and Ted Robert Gurr, *Violence in America: Historical and Comparative Perspectives* (New York: Bantam Books, Inc., 1969), pp. 490–91.

2. Ironically, the forty-eight-year-old Capone died the same week as Andrew J. Volstead, author of the act that set Prohibition into motion. The gangster's brother Ralph hospitably carried beer to reporters on a death watch outside the Capone home. Compared to the lavish gangster funerals of the 1920s, Capone's modest services in Chicago went virtually unnoticed. "The Capone Era," *Time,* February 10, 1947, pp. 24–25. "Prohibition: Seeing Ghosts," *Newsweek,* February 3, 1947, pp. 24–25; "Crime: Exit for the Big Guy," ibid., February 17, 1947, p. 31.

3. John Bartlow Martin, "Al Capone's Successors," *The American*

At the time of his murder, Ragen, a veteran of the newspaper circulation wars, had come into possession of much of the old Annenberg wire organization. In addition to his income tax difficulties in 1939, Annenberg had run afoul of the antimonopoly laws because his Nation-Wide News Service had actually owned most of the regional outlets of his racing-news wire service, and they in turn could selectively sell it to bookmakers. Faced with seemingly endless legal difficulties, Annenberg apparently simply walked out of his organization, never to return. Ragen, with Arthur B. McBride, an old associate in the rough-and-tumble circulation wars, then pieced the Annenberg organization together, renamed it Continental Press, and through subterfuge concealed his control of the distributors. Numerous title transfers occurred between the Ragen and McBride families for reasons never candidly explained. The aggressive Ragen and a local Chicago gambler linked with Guzik became embroiled in a bitter business and personal feud over ownership of a distributorship as well as rates for the wire service. Although the details still remain clouded, it appears that both parties attempted to use force. Apparently the FBI exerted pressure on Ragen to keep "gangsters" out of the wire service set-up and Ragen informed on certain of his rivals. Fearing assassination in reprisal, Ragen tried to take out "insurance" by filing the 98-page statement with the Cook County State's Attorney.[4]

The murder of Ragen lent a probably undeserved credence to his statement. Certainly, persons associated with the old Capone organization opposed Ragen, but to suggest that their opposition represented a concerted effort by a "Capone syndicate" to muscle into Continental is probably an exaggeration; surely Ragen's contention in 1946 that the frequently incoherent Capone was directing the operation amounted to simple

Mercury (June 1949), 728–34. "Heirs of Capone," *Newsweek,* January 13, 1947, pp. 24–25. Estes Kefauver, *Crime in America* (Garden City, N.Y.: Doubleday & Co., Inc., 1951), pp. 31–35.

4. Kefauver, *Crime in America,* pp. 31–35; Testimony of Thomas F. Kelly, General Manager of Continental Press, in *Hearings Before the Special Committee to Investigate Organized Crime in Interstate Commerce* (Kefauver Committee), 81st Cong., 2d sess. (1951), Pt. 5, pp. 692–701, 710–19. Cited hereafter as Crime *Hearings.* Arthur McBride testimony, ibid., Pt. 6, pp. 43–111. The Kelly testimony shows that muscle had long been used in the wire-service struggles and that cries of a "Capone takeover" dated back almost twenty years.

folly. Ragen's death was followed by several months of intense, costly, and often violent conflict between Continental and Trans-American, a rival service that was strongly supported by Guzik and others. In 1947 the two groups merged, with the more pacific McBride in ostensible control and the Guzik distributorship receiving special rates. To the bewildered public, the Ragen murder, followed by the release of his statement and the apparent "muscling" of Continental distributors in St. Louis and Kansas City by Trans-American, appeared a bold power play by a revitalized Capone combine. The dramatic slaying of Benjamin "Bugsy" Siegel in the home of his mistress in Beverly Hills later in 1947 was occasionally linked to the wire service war, although the connection was never argued with totally convincing logic.[5]

A second development in 1947 persuading police and civic officials that a strong Capone syndicate was attempting to expand occurred in Dallas, Texas. There Pat Manno of Chicago and a loquacious underling, Paul Jones, attempted to bribe Sheriff-elect Steve Guthrie and Police Lieutenant George Butler into allowing a Chicago group allegedly including Guzik and Humphries to gain control of gambling in Dallas. Manno claimed that the group he represented was already operating in St. Louis, Kansas City, New Orleans, and Little Rock. Guthrie and Butler played Manno along until they could clandestinely record his offer by a "bug." When they publicized their experiences, neither the press nor law enforcement officials discounted the Manno-Jones claim of control in other cities as possible sales overstatement.[6]

Perhaps the most convincing evidence of the existence of a Capone syndicate, as well as of its political power, came to light in 1947 with the parole of three former Capone associates from a federal penitentiary. In 1943 Paul "The Waiter" Ricca, Louis "Little New York" Campagna, and Charles "Cherry Nose" Gioe were sentenced to ten years in prison on charges of racketeering for their parts in a million-dollar shakedown of the movie industry, which they supposedly had attempted through the International Association of Theatrical Stage Employees. Through political pressure the Chicago men were first transferred from the federal penitentiary at Atlanta to the

5. Kefauver, *Crime in America,* pp. 34–36, 126–28.

6. *Newsweek,* January 13, 1947, pp. 24–25. Butler later stated that Manno said his group was "linked with the Mafia." Crime *Hearings,* Pt. 5, p. 1183.

one at Leavenworth. There they were convenient to Kansas City, and a local underworld figure, Tony Gizzo, drove Anthony Accardo, using another man's name, to the penitentiary several times for conferences. Subsequently, a favorable tax settlement was arranged, and finally, mail fraud charges against Ricca, Campagna, and Gioe were dropped, thereby setting up the possibility of parole. To cover the tax payments due the government and to speed along the parole procedures, several unidentified persons mysteriously left packages containing a total of nearly $200,000 with the men's attorney. Obviously, at least a loose, well-heeled friendship arrangement existed among certain Chicago gangsters. A House committee headed by Michigan Republican Clare E. Hoffman investigated the controversial paroles and prompted legal action to return the men to prison, but the proceedings became bogged down in the courts, and the men evaded long stays in prison.[7]

If 1947 witnessed the rediscovery of the Capone gang, it also marked the press's promotion of New York's Frank Costello to "Prime Minister of the Underworld." Herbert Asbury, who for twenty years had been writing journalistic accounts of the underworld in New Orleans, New York, Chicago, and San Francisco, now turned his attention to Costello in a two-part series for *Collier's*. Basically, Asbury argued that neither Costello's upperworld nor underworld roles were clear, but that he appeared to be the arbiter of power and political fixer for a wide assortment of illegal activities. Asbury's articles, which placed Costello in a nationwide rather than a limited New York setting, roused a flurry of interest in "America's No. 1 Mystery Man," including cover stories by *Time* and *Newsweek* and a politely refused speaking invitation from the Greater Los Angeles Press Club.[8]

7. Charles Webster, "How the Capone Mob Still Thrives!" *National Police Gazette* (August 1948), 79–80. Virgil W. Peterson, *Barbarians in Our Midst: A History of Chicago Crime and Politics* (Boston: Little, Brown and Company, 1952), pp. 230–37 *et passim*. Otto Kerner, Jr., U.S. Attorney for the Chicago area, remained skeptical as to the existence of the Capone syndicate. *The Attorney General's Conference on Organized Crime, February 15, 1950* (Washington: Department of Justice, 1950), p. 41.

8. Herbert Asbury, "America's No. 1 Mystery Man," *Collier's,* April 12, 1947, pp. 16–17, 26–33, and April 19, 1947, pp. 33–44. *Newsweek,* November 21, 1949, p. 31. *Time,* October 17, 1949, p. 27. Previous speakers at the Press Club had included President Truman, Vice President Barkley, and General Mark Clark.

Costello's links to "Big Bill" Dwyer and Arnold Rothstein during Prohibition, his role in the 1929 Atlantic City meeting with Capone and others, and his slot machine investments in New York and New Orleans had stimulated some public speculation about him and his operations throughout the 1930s. After 1943, however, he became a major political issue in New York politics. Manhattan's District Attorney Frank S. Hogan, engaged in an investigation of gangster infiltration into the night-club industry, had come to focus his attention upon the celebrated Copacabana, frequented by Costello. A legal wiretap on Costello's telephone produced little information on the night clubs but a great deal on Costello's political influence. Through his extensive contacts with Tammany Hall, including Michael Kennedy whom he helped elect leader in 1942, Costello in 1943 had arranged for the nomination of fellow Italian Thomas Aurelio to the state supreme court. Hogan's wiretap picked up Aurelio's call of appreciation. Evidence in hand, Hogan privately attempted to persuade Kennedy to press Aurelio into withdrawing his name, but both Kennedy and Costello stood firm and Hogan released the wiretap to the press. Costello's man went on to win election, but only after Costello had become a perennial political football in New York.

Mayor LaGuardia who almost a decade earlier had smashed Costello's slot machines in New York and had carried on a campaign of harassment since, rejoined the chase with vigor. The following year Costello accidentally left $27,200 in a taxi, and LaGuardia, labeling it *outlaw money,* blocked its return until the federal government could file two tax liens against it. In the legal proceedings on this action, Costello admitted to having known Rothstein and the bookie "lay-off" Frank Erickson, and he ill-advisedly referred to himself as "King of the Slots." He eventually recovered less than $130 of the outlaw money. In 1945, five Tammany district leaders, on the outs with the controlling faction, sent a wire to U.S. Attorney General Francis Biddle, in which they charged that Costello dominated Tammany and urged that the Justice Department oppose any candidate suggested by the majority. Newbold Morris, former aide to LaGuardia and Republican mayoralty candidate in 1945, agreed wholeheartedly with the Tammany malcontents. Governor Dewey and the new mayor, William

O'Dwyer of "Murder, Inc." fame, took turns denouncing the underworld "Prime Minister."[9]

The anti-Costello chant soon broadened beyond the politicians. In 1945 Garland H. Williams, local agent of the Federal Bureau of Narcotics, informed the New York newspapers that the major illicit narcotic dealers were members of the Unione Siciliana—now supposedly a branch of the Mafia—and that Costello had dominated this organization "more or less" since the purge of the "Mustache Petes" in 1931. In Williams's account, the role Luciano had played until he was sent to prison —that of Costello's chief lieutenant—had gone to gambler Joe Adonis, onetime supporter but now opponent of LaGuardia and a prominent figure in speculations about "Murder, Inc." Williams insisted that Costello was "absolute boss" of the East Harlem underworld, comprised mainly of Italians. He concluded his charges with the hedge, however, that, while no one could "prove" that Costello and Adonis had invested money in the narcotics traffic, they did allow "little men" to operate. Costello, who had risen from impoverished childhood in an immigrant family to great wealth and political influence, felt that he had been grievously maligned by this insult to his long-sought respectability. He became so indignant that he called a press conference and denied any connection with an organization known as Mafia. He charged Williams with irresponsibility, deplored the trade in narcotics, and called for a grand jury investigation before which he promised to waive immunity. District Attorney Hogan did not grant Costello the grand jury.[10]

Linked with the Williams statement was Luciano's deportation in 1946. For reasons never fully explained, but allegedly as a reward for aid given Naval Intelligence during the war, Governor Dewey commuted Luciano's 30-to-50-year prison sentence, preparatory to deportation to his native Italy. Costello attended a going-away party for Luciano and visited him when he temporarily returned to Havana the following year. When the Narcotics Bureau subsequently noticed an increase

9. *Collier's,* April 12, 1947, pp. 16–17, 26–33, and April 19, 1947, pp. 33–44; *Newsweek,* November 21, 1949; James A. Bell, "Frank Costello: Statesman of the Underworld," *The American Mercury* (August 1950), 131–37.

10. Bell, "Costello"; *Collier's,* April 12, 1947, pp. 26–33, and April 19, 1947, pp. 33–44.

in drug traffic and connected it with Luciano, Costello's visits to Cuba raised endless speculation as to who gave orders to whom.[11]

By the late 1940s, Costello had become fair game for a wide assortment of critics. Major crime stories of the past two decades were revised with an eye to the emerging Costello. Reporters speculated now that it had been Costello who loaned money to Rothstein rather than vice versa; Costello must have been a boss, rather than a rival or associate of Big Bill Dwyer in the rum-running days; Costello must have been the guiding genius behind the 1929 Atlantic City meeting; Costello had been consulted in the 1932 Lindbergh kidnapping; Costello had given the order for Louis "Lepke" Buchalter to surrender to the FBI in 1941; Costello had known members of the "Big Six," who had, it was believed, controlled the "Combination" that ran "Murder, Inc."; Costello had political pull in Kansas City, Los Angeles, and New Orleans as well as in New York; Costello must have ordered Bugsy Siegel's murder; Costello had been linked to the Capone movie extortion plot. Movie actor-producer-turned-news commentator Robert Montgomery revived an old demand that the Justice Department deport Costello, on the basis that he had lied in his naturalization papers in 1925. Later, in 1949, William O'Dwyer, New York's mayor, in his on again-off again race for reelection, split an already shaky alliance with crime fighter Hogan, and Costello appeared again as an issue. Clendenin Ryan, an eccentric millionaire and former associate of LaGuardia, not only sponsored Montgomery's campaign but also lashed out at a supposed "Costellodwyer" partnership.[12]

Costello fought these allegations. In various interviews, he blamed his early misdeeds on an underprivileged childhood, but now that was all behind him, now he was a legitimate, semiretired real estate dealer with interests in only a few scat-

11. Ralph Salerno and John S. Tompkins, *The Crime Confederation: Cosa Nostra and Allied Operations in Organized Crime* (Garden City, N.Y.: Doubleday & Company, Inc., 1969), pp. 248–49.

12. *Collier's,* April 12, 1947, pp. 16–17, 26–33, and April 19, 1947, pp. 33–44. *Newsweek,* November 21, 1949, p. 31. *American Mercury* (August 1950), 131–37. *Time,* November 28, 1948, pp. 15–18. "Montgomery vs. Costello," *Newsweek,* February 6, 1950, pp. 27–28. Joseph Lilly, Executive Director of Government Affairs Club, New York, to William H. Standley, April 19, 1949, Crime Commission Study Box, William H. Standley Papers, University of Southern California Library, Los Angeles.

tered semilegitimate gambling establishments like the swank
Beverly Club outside New Orleans. Since the Aurelio case, he
had forsaken all interest in politics. While admitting that he
had never "sold any Bibles," Costello argued that he was still
"cleaner than 99 percent of New Yorkers." In 1946 Costello
became so distraught and sleepless over the swirling rumors
and charges that he visited a Park Avenue psychiatrist, Dr.
Richard Hoffman, who suggested that he overcome his "frustrated superiority" by meeting some "nice people." In an effort
to follow this advice, Costello sponsored a $100-a-plate dinner
for the benefit of the Salvation Army in January, 1949. The
dinner caused enormous embarrassment because Hearst reporters, lurking in the background, reported that Costello, his
New Orleans associate Phil Kastel, Erickson, and Vito Genovese had hobnobbed that evening with five state supreme
court justices, including Aurelio; Congressman Arthur Klein;
and several Tammany dignitaries, among them Hugo E.
Rogers, Manhattan Borough's president. To add insult to in-
jury, the Salvation Army accepted the money but denied
knowing its benefactor had been *THE* Costello, and Dr. Hoffman revealed the analysis and advice he had earlier given
Costello.[13]

*   *   *   *

Interest in nationwide crime combinations paralleled a
growing controversy over legalizing gambling. The evidence
that is available bears out the popular impression that the
volume and intensity of public gambling in most forms increased measurably during the war. As unemployment declined, incomes rose, and rationing and war production cut
back on available consumer goods, an increasing amount of
money flowed into gambling. The "embourgeoisement" of
gambling continued, moreover, into the postwar years, despite
its illegality in many communities. Casinos and off-track betting in particular enjoyed ever widening prosperity, with
the expanding bookie operations accompanying the state-
licensed parimutuels on which they depended. Factory
managers found it necessary at times to tolerate on-job bookie
operations. In the New Orleans area, sheriffs of two rival

13. "Frank and the Nice People," *Newsweek,* February 7, 1949, p. 16.

parishes that competed for the gambling traffic cried foul
when the press ignored the wide-open conditions that prevailed in their communities.[14]

The gaping disparity between law and practice inevitably
produced suggestions for the legalization of gambling. Some
protagonists pleaded that encouraging on-track parimutuel
bets while punishing the same wager through an off-track
bookie discriminated against the workingman. Not a few
pointed to the revenues that might be gained through taxing
a larger volume of legal gambling. Still others argued that
police corruption would be reduced and public respect for law
enforcement improved by legalizing gambling. Edward Deve-
reux, Jr., a graduate student at Harvard, concluded in his sociology dissertation that gambling on a small scale probably
improved the social health of a community. Proposals for the
legalization of gambling in various forms appeared in a number of states, including Minnesota, New York, California,
Florida, Illinois, Idaho, Montana, and Arizona. New York's
Mayor William O'Dwyer clashed with a fellow crime fighter,
Governor Thomas E. Dewey, over O'Dwyer's suggestion that
off-track betting be legalized.[15]

The debate over legalization was less moral in tone than
economic; the prolegalization forces lacked the cohesion,
leadership, and favorable press of those in opposition, and the
antigambling group won out almost universally. Unquestion-

14. Paul S. Deland, "The Facilitation of Gambling," *The Annals*
(May 1950), 25. Irving Ross, "Big-Time Gamblers Invade the Facto-
ries," *Readers Digest* (August 1950), 49–52. "Plant Gambling," *Business Week,* January 21, 1950, pp. 109–10. "Louisiana: Front-Page Sin,"
Newsweek, February 17, 1947, p. 30. J. Edgar Hoover himself became
a racetrack fan and Hoover's onetime executive assistant, Spencer J.
Drayton, joined the Thoroughbred Racing Protective Bureau, formed
by the Thoroughbred Racing Association to prevent illegal bookmaking activities at the tracks. Fred J. Cook, *The FBI Nobody Knows* (New
York: The Macmillan Company, 1964), p. 239. John I. Day, "Horse
Racing and the Pari-Mutuel," *Annals* (May 1950), 60.

15. Ernest Havermann, "Gambling in the U.S.," *Life,* June 19, 1950,
pp. 96–121. "Gambling gets a Free Ride," *Business Week,* May 14, 1949,
pp. 31–34. Robert R. Brunn, "Challenge to 'Crime, Inc.,'" *The Christian Science Monitor Weekly Magazine,* November 18, 1950, p. 8.
"New York Mayor Raises Public Morality Issue," *Christian Century,*
January 25, 1950, p. 100; Howard Orr, "How to Stop Gambling," ibid.,
November 29, 1950, pp. 1424–25. Virgil W. Peterson, *Gambling: Should
It Be Legalized* (Springfield, Ill.: Charles C. Thomas, Publisher, 1951),
pp. 3–4.

ably, the most prolific and articulate of those opposed to legalization schemes was Virgil W. Peterson who had, since 1942, been operating director of the Chicago Crime Commission. A graduate of Parsons College and Northwestern University Law School, Peterson had headed FBI offices in Boston, St. Louis, and Milwaukee before returning to Chicago. As operating director, Peterson revitalized the commission, mastered its voluminous files, and channeled his various recommendations through the *Journal of Criminal Law and Criminology* as well as more popular journals and news releases. Although his FBI background had given him no special grounding in fighting organized crime or gambling, Peterson pondered the problems, observed the Chicago scene, and won growing recognition as a "walking encyclopedia" on the subjects. The more diligently Peterson studied organized crime and gambling, the more closely they seemed to merge in his mind, and he shortly became convinced that there was not only a historical but a necessary relationship between the two.

In a Crime Commission booklet, "Gambling: Should It Be Legalized?", published in 1945 and twice expanded in an article and a small book, Peterson developed his basic thesis that it was the profits, not the legality or illegality, of gambling that prompted criminals' interest in it. As a result, legalization would only lend respectability to the criminal interests involved in gambling without reducing their revenues or driving them out of the industry. Legalization for purposes of control, according to Peterson, was incompatible with legalization for purposes of raising revenue, for one or the other would necessarily be given priority and hence either create a market for illegal gambling or expand legal gambling indefinitely. Peterson saw nothing oppressive in allowing on-track wagers while prohibiting off-track betting, for society by the same technique had regulated the hours and the places for purchasing liquor, the seasons for hunting animals, and even the times that persons could walk the streets.[16] Peterson had ready-made replies for all proposals for the legal expansion of gambling, and while some of his arguments could not stand close scrutiny, others—at least within the context of the flush gambling in the late 1940s—appeared convincing. To support

16. Personal interview, Virgil W. Peterson, Riverside, Illinois, July 22, 1970; Peterson, *Gambling: Should It Be Legalized,* pp. 124, 106–10, 57 *et passim.*

those opponents of gambling who wished to refute the charge
that they were moralistic busybodies, Peterson argued that
antigambling crusades had historically been prompted by social and economic factors and not by moral ones.

Peterson had a special argument for those convention-
minded cities that hesitated to crack down on gambling and
other vice. In a speech delivered in Miami in 1948, he maintained that in fact the "myth of the wide-open town" had been
foisted upon an unthinking citizenry by corrupt political machines in league with organized crime. First, there existed no
proof that revenues declined when gambling laws were enforced. Second, because so much of the profits of illegal gambling was controlled by organized gangs centered in Chicago
and New York, little of the profits stayed in the resort town in
any event. Often these outside influences might attempt to get
gambling legalized, but they did so for selfish reasons connected with the cost of "protection" and their desire for respectability. Little, repeated Peterson, could be gained and
much could be lost by legalization.[17]

Peterson's basic arguments won acceptance and occasional
exaggeration through a revived citizens' crime commission
movement, through cooperation with the American Municipal Association, and through a concerted newspaper campaign. In each case, Peterson was personally active. The crime
commission movement of the 1920s had reflected the business
and professional classes' interest in increased police efficiency in dealing with crimes against persons and property.
Despite the leadership of well-known business and political
figures, the movement faltered during the Depression, with
only the groups in Chicago, Cleveland, and Baltimore remain-
ing active by 1930. The postwar crime wave stimulated interest in the prevention of juvenile delinquency and violent
crime and in increased effectiveness of the entire criminal

17. Virgil W. Peterson, "The Myth of the Wide-Open Town," *Journal
of Criminal Law and Criminology* (September–October 1948), 288–92.
The volume of race track betting began to decline with the recession
of 1949, and consequently may have encouraged track owners to regard off-track bookmaking with greater hostility. To a certain extent,
the legalization fight can be seen as a conflict within the gambling
industry between owners of tracks who profit from admissions and
the parimutuel operations and the illegal bookie who operates off
track. Pat Frank and Luther Voltz, "Florida's Struggle with the Hood-
lums," *Collier's,* March 25, 1950, pp. 20–21, 78–81.

justice system. As operating director of the influential Chicago
Crime Commission, Peterson personally encouraged the formation of new anticrime groups, and he took every opportunity to persuade them that most public gambling had interstate ties that made it detrimental both to local business and
to government in general.

In 1945 Governor Earl Warren of California asked the legislature for a special study group on organized crime as part of
a comprehensive review of state criminal justice. Appropriations finally became available in 1947, and Warren appointed
Adm. William H. Standley, former ambassador to Russia, as
chairman. The so-called California Crime Commission, in
reality directed by Chief Counsel Warren Olney and two former FBI agents, John Hanson and Harold G. Robinson, quickly
got in touch with Peterson, who flew to California and dazzled
the commission's members with his "knowledge of organized
crime with all its affiliations." Peterson pointed to the infiltration of gangsters from the East and called for independent
civic organizations to carry on the fight against crime. In its
reports, the commission claimed that it found indications of
a nationwide slot machine racket headed by Costello and positive evidence of an effort to gain state-wide protection for the
racket through California's Attorney General Fred Howser,
then engaged in a rancorous political feud with Governor
Warren. According to the commission, the operators of the
racket had prompted action aimed at removing Warren and
Los Angeles's Mayor Fletcher Bowron from office. Before it
expired in 1951, the commission had explored the bookie wire
service in the state, found evidence in it of a nationwide crime
syndicate, ordered all communications companies to refuse
service to bookies, and called for a broader, nationwide
study.[18]

As early as 1946, the Cox and Knight newspapers and affil-

18. Mark H. Haller, "Civic Reformers and Police Leadership:
Chicago, 1905–1935," in Harlan Hahn, ed., *Police in Urban Society*
(Beverly Hills: Sage Publications, 1971), pp. 46–48. Virgil W. Peterson,
"Citizens Crime Commissions," *Federal Probation* (March 1953), 10;
Leo Katcher, *Earl Warren: A Political Biography* (New York:
McGraw-Hill Book Company, 1967), 243–47. Hanson to Standley,
March 26, 1948; Standley to Guy E. Reed, Chairman, Board of Direc-
tors, Chicago Crime Commission, March 27, 1948; news clipping, San
Francisco *News,* April 15, 1948, Crime Study Commission Box, Stand-
ley Papers; "Swatting Costello," *Newsweek,* March 21, 1949, p. 25. Ke-
fauver, *Crime in America,* p. 129.

iated radio stations in Miami had financed an investigation by
ex-FBI agent Daniel P. Sullivan into infiltration by gangsters
on Florida's Gold Coast. A committee of the Dade County Bar
Association continued the interest and in early 1948 formed
the privately financed Crime Commission of Greater Miami
with Sullivan as operating director. Again, Peterson's advice
had been sought at various stages in the formation of the
Miami anticrime group, and he had delivered the keynote
address at a well-publicized meeting to launch the new organization. Peterson and Sullivan, both of whom had worked for
the FBI on the Dillinger case, exchanged intelligence on
the traffic between the Chicago and Miami underworlds, on
racing-news wire service activities, and on infiltration into the
hotel and horse- and dog-racing industries by underworld
figures from both Chicago and New York. Complementing one
another expertly, Sullivan and Peterson had, by 1950, built up
antigambling sentiment in Miami to a fever pitch.[19]

Citizens' crime commissions sprang up in Dallas, Kansas
City, St. Louis, and Gary as well as in other cities in 1949 and
1950. Most of them depended heavily upon the parent group
for information and advice, and most followed Peterson's lead
in attacking interstate gambling operations and their alleged
political contacts.[20]

Peterson, in addition, had contacts outside the crime commission movement. For several years, Carl H. Chatters, executive director of the American Municipal Association, had been
referring city officials to Peterson for answers to questions
concerning organized crime. Such contacts provided the basis
for Peterson's well-received speech at the group's annual
meeting in Cleveland in late 1949. After impressing the five
hundred members attending the conference with the public's
ignorance of names, places, and interstate links in the underworld, Peterson called for greater local vigilance and leadership, a systematized exchange of intelligence, and a broader
investigation. Dutifully instructed, the association, in behalf
of the ten thousand municipalities it represented, directed its
board of trustees to map a comprehensive anticrime campaign, complained of the numerous jurisdictional problems

19. Les Barnhill, "Miami Dailies Help Make Mobsters Scram," *Editor & Publisher*, December 2, 1950, p. 8. Peterson interview.
20. Peterson, "Citizens Crime Commissions," 11. "St. Louis Wants
Speedy Justice in its Courts," *The American City* (June 1949), 19.

associated with control of crime operating in interstate commerce, and asked for aid and study by the federal government.[21] By working with energetic, if somewhat egotistical, mayors such as DeLesseps S. Morrison of New Orleans, Fletcher Bowron of Los Angeles, and Dorothy McCullough Lee of Portland—all posturing as crime fighters in the LaGuardia tradition—Peterson had immensely increased the public interest in organized crime and the solutions he proposed.

The Peterson–Sullivan–Olney axis depended upon the press as well as politicians to spread its message. Indeed, the initiative in the campaign against organized crime had clearly passed from the crime commission movement to the press by 1949. In the process, the message occasionally became badly distorted, as in Peterson's dealings with gadfly Lee Mortimer. Fresh from a venture into the murky speculation surrounding the Bugsy Siegel assassination, Mortimer, a feature writer for the tabloid New York *Mirror,* tapped Peterson's command of detail and the bizarre tales of William Drury, former Chicago policeman, to produce his best-selling *Chicago Confidential.* Mortimer vastly oversimplified Peterson's concept of a loose-knit cooperation between several national crime syndicates into a seemingly all-powerful, all-encompassing Mafia dominated by Italians. Costello and Chicago's Charles Fischetti, a cousin of Al Capone, emerged as President and Vice President, respectively, of the Unione or Mafia, with a shadowy figure, Gaetano Ricca (Tony Goebels), shuttling back and forth with messages and orders. Cynically, Mortimer linked his refurbished Mafia creation to international communism, a booming narcotics traffic, and a "swishy homosexual" takeover of night spots.[22]

In California, Miami, and New York, too, crime commissions depended heavily upon enterprising, if occasionally over-dramatic journalists. Warren Olney was so impressed with a series of anti-Howser articles that appeared in the San

21. Peterson interview. Peterson, *Barbarians in Our Midst,* p. 257. "War on Syndicated Crime Urged of AMA," *The American City* (January 1950), 86–87.

22. "Gang Guns in Chicago," *Newsweek,* October 9, 1950, pp. 36–37. Jack Lait and Lee Mortimer, *Chicago Confidential* (New York: Crown Publishers, Inc., 1950). Jack Lait relied on the younger Mortimer for most of the material in the books they wrote. For Peterson's more cautious and decentralized views, see his testimony in Crime *Hearings,* Pt. 2, pp. 125–213.

Francisco *News* that, while he acknowledged that the author was so biased as to be unqualified to join the Crime Study Group's staff, he himself shared the bias. When a San Francisco *Examiner* reporter, Ed Montgomery, turned up his hearing aid to catch voices in the corner of a bar, he discovered a lead to a major scandal in the West Coast Internal Revenue Service and a Pulitzer Prize-winning story later developed by the Governor's commission.[23]

Probes by newspapermen into gambling provided vital information to crime commissions in Miami and Brooklyn. In April 1949, Don Petit, a reporter for the Miami *News*, disappeared into the underworld to emerge three weeks later with addresses and telephone numbers of bookies, numbers headquarters, and houses of prostitution as well as names of city detectives who were receiving "ice" from them. The Petit exposé was ideally timed for the convening of a new grand jury that was investigating police protection of gambling—a subject that had long interested the Crime Commission of Greater Miami.[24]

On the basis of a chance remark overheard in a tavern near his Brooklyn *Eagle* office, reporter Ed Reid began an investigation into the open secret of gambling and corruption in Brooklyn. Reid's discoveries appeared in an extensively advertised eight-article series in December 1949. Reid, who became a longshoreman in order to facilitate his thousand-odd interviews, had been convinced from the beginning of his inquiry that his story would lead to a new crime boss, since the supposed directors of "Murder, Inc." had moved out of Brooklyn in search of suburban respectability. The *Eagle* series did indeed find an unnamed "Mr. Big" (later revealed as Harry Gross) as well as ties to a nationwide crime syndicate, and it prompted an explosive grand jury investigation of police protection by Brooklyn District Attorney Miles McDonald and County Judge Samuel Leibowitz. The McDonald investigation eventually led to major shake-ups in the New York police department, tarnished the reputation of Mayor O'Dwyer, and gave birth to a new citizens' crime group in New York.[25]

23. Olney to Standley, August 3, 1949, Crime Study Box, Standley Papers. "Reporter's Crime Story Sets Off National Probe," *Editor & Publisher*, December 2, 1950, p. 31. "11 Pulitzer Prizes Won on Crime Theme," ibid., May 12, 1951, p. 7.

24. "Ice in Miami," *Time*, June 13, 1949, pp. 78–79.

25. "Reporter's Facts Put on Trail of Mob," *Editor & Publisher*,

If newsmen increasingly tended to see national patterns within the underworld, perhaps it was because they increasingly exchanged information among themselves. In early 1950 Leo Sonderegger, city editor of the Providence *Journal and Bulletin,* initiated the formation of an agreement by fourteen major newspapers to pool information on organized crime. At an organizational meeting in Chicago, the ubiquitous Peterson briefed the newsmen on the extent and influence of crime syndicates and promised the Chicago Crime Commission's aid to the newspapers' project. Stressing the fact that local crime reporting alone presented but a partial picture, the journalists planned to correct a long overdue need for a national perspective on gambling and racketeering. Shortly after the meeting in Chicago, the newspaper pool released a series of articles that centered on Costello as the "alleged overlord of an underworld federation" and on the Continental Press as the "outstanding integrating force in the farflung hoodlum world of local and regional dynasties."[26]

The newspaper pool and the crime commissions reflected in 1950 the old American proclivity to view organized crime as something set apart from the economic and social realities of American life. Talk of nationwide crime syndicates and of the rediscovered Mafia served the functions of scapegoating for the antilegalization forces and of titillating an increasing number of newspaper readers. The search for criminal conspiracies, moreover, paralleled the effort to ferret out communism and Communist sympathizers at home as the nation experienced frustration and disappointment abroad. Political forces, it became evident, would be forced to react to the vocal anticrime movement of the late 1940s.

December 31, 1949, p. 45; "Journalistic Romance is Just a Big Gamble," ibid., November 4, 1950, p. 57; "Brooklyn Lid Blows Off," ibid., May 12, 1951, p. 9. Ed Reid, "How We Tracked Down Brooklyn's 'Mr. Big,' " *Readers' Digest* (April 1951), 133–40. A similar exposé in New York by Malcolm Johnson of the *Sun,* beginning in November 1949, had focused on the waterfront but had also linked gangster influence to a "national crime syndicate." Allen Raymond, *Waterfront Priest* (New York: Henry Holt & Company, 1955), pp. 114–37.

26. Ray Erwin, "14 Papers Organize Anti-Crime Syndicate," *Editor & Publisher,* February 18, 1950, pp. 7, 40.

3

The Creation of the Committee

I had to start early because . . . , I had to allow time
for people to get use to my French Huguenot name.
—Estes Kefauver, 1950, on his 1948 senatorial campaign

The widespread publicizing of crime by citizens' commissions and newspaper reporters struck political Washington with ominous velocity. As the Truman Administration had attempted to contain and direct the "red menace" with its rhetoric and loyalty program, it also tried to ride out the hysteria over crime with modest bureaucratic directives and fumbling motions at cooperation with state and municipal officials.[1]

In 1946 Attorney General Tom Clark had called a national conference on the prevention and control of juvenile delinquency, but the renewed interest in the Capone syndicate and the press build-up of Costello one year later forced the Administration's attention to organized crime. In response to this new wave of publicity, the Justice Department in 1947 launched a special "racket squad" to visit major cities preparatory to organizing grand jury investigations. Directed by Special Assistant Attorney General Max H. Goldschein, federal grand juries soon began work in Miami, Los Angeles, Newark, Scranton, Philadelphia, and Kansas City. At the same time, by direction of Secretary of the Treasury John W. Snyder and the Justice Department, federal agents began a slow-moving audit of income tax returns of gamblers, slot

1. Athan Theoharis, "The Rhetoric of Politics: Foreign Policy, Internal Security, and Domestic Politics in the Truman Era, 1945–1950," and "The Escalation of the Loyalty Program," in Barton J. Bernstein, ed., *Politics and Policies of the Truman Administration* (Chicago: Quadrangle Books, Inc., 1970), pp. 196–268.

machine operators, and better-known racketeers.[2]

In response to pleas for federal coordination by the American Municipal Association in late 1949, Attorney General J. Howard McGrath invited representatives of the A.M.A. as well as the National Association of Attorneys General, the National Institute of Municipal Law Officers, and the United States Conference of Mayors to participate in the annual conference of United States Attorneys in Washington on February 15, 1950. To demonstrate the Administration's concern over the problem, President Truman addressed the conference, interpreted the crime wave as an inevitable result of wartime dislocations, urged cultivation of the "gentler forces" of church and home life for the young, pointed out that crime remained a local problem, and cautioned against fighting crime for personal gains and against violation of civil liberties. McGrath underlined the Administration's basic position that local officials had to carry the chief burden while the federal government worked on limited but complementary programs. The Attorney General argued that interstate gambling presented the major problem, and he attempted to focus the attention of the conference on legislative remedies. At the same time, he urged the leaders to use the press and civic organizations in their own communities "to capture the popular imagination in a stirring campaign to crush organized crime."[3]

The Administration's handling of the developing crime issue, however, began to strike sour notes. Los Angeles's Mayor Fletcher Bowron charged the Treasury Department with laxity toward racketeers; DeLesseps S. Morrison, mayor of New Orleans and past president of the American Municipal Association, charged that both he and the A.M.A. had been short-changed at the Attorney General's conference. Morrison drew heavily from his own highly publicized anticrime campaign, which in 1946 had driven Frank Costello's slot machines as well as the direct racing-news wire service out of the

2. Press release, March 29, 1951, Harry S. Truman Papers, Harry S. Truman Library, Independence, Missouri. Assistant Attorney General Peyton Ford to Kefauver, April 30, 1951, J. Howard McGrath Papers, Truman Library. New York *Times,* April 18, 1950. *Third Interim Report of Special Committee to Investigate Organized Crime in Interstate Commerce,* 82d Cong., 1st sess., p. 7. Statement of Assistant Attorney General James M. McInerney in *The Attorney General's Conference on Organized Crime,* February 15, 1950, pp. 53–54.

3. *Attorney General's Conference,* pp. v, 2–4, 5–9.

city of New Orleans proper. Through his work with the A.M.A. and its links with Virgil Peterson, Morrison found a nationwide framework for interpreting his campaign. According to Morrison, the Capone organization dominated Continental, and Costello operated a national slot-machine racket. These two groups as well as others worked together in a "loose confederation of mutual respect, cooperation, allocated territories, and huge profits." The New Orleans mayor had presented these views along with a ten-point program at the Attorney General's conference. In addition to legislation dealing with slot machines and the wire service, Morrison's programs called for easier access by municipal officials to FBI and Bureau of Internal Revenue information as well as a "coordinated masterplan of action" against nationwide rackets by the Attorney General's Office. That nothing of significance emerged from the conference irritated Morrison; that he, Mayor Bowron, and the A.M.A.'s Director Carl Chatters had been given short shrift by the conference in its appointments to important subcommittees increased his pique.[4]

The seemingly passive McGrath program failed to fill the vacuum of leadership that spirited reporters and crime fighters saw in the federal government. Hence, attention focused increasingly on the Congress, where a number of eager politicians were jockeying for the favor of the anticrime forces. New York's Representative W. Kingsland Macy, a Taftite Republican and veteran of the Seabury investigation of the early 1930s, had been following various crime commission reports, and on March 14, 1950, he called for a nationwide congressional investigation.[5]

In the upper house, Republican Joseph R. McCarthy of Wisconsin and Democrat Estes Kefauver of Tennessee, both freshmen senators with far-reaching ambitions, hoped to establish crime investigations of their own. McCarthy, looking for a dramatic issue on which to bolster his candidacy for reelection in 1952, was considering both crime and communism as subjects. His interests in the organized crime issue dated at least back to November of 1949 when Harold Lavine of *Newsweek* noted that McCarthy apparently had documen-

4. *Attorney General's Conference,* pp. 51, 26–34. DeLesseps S. Morrison to Kefauver, March 29, 1950, Crime Box 3, Kefauver Papers.
5. *Congressional Record,* March 14, 1950, p. 3348; April 26, 1950, p. 584; March 22, 1950, p. A29996–97.

tary evidence of Costello's close ties with the distributors of Whiteley's scotch whiskey.[6]

While Kefauver's interests predated those of McCarthy, they too smacked of opportunism. The only surviving son of a Madisonville, Tennessee, politician-hardware dealer, Kefauver grew up in a comfortable and respected rural middle-class atmosphere. From his mother, Kefauver seems to have taken an unruffled paternalism and an overblown and possibly inaccurate family pedigree. He developed from his small-town Progressive father a keen interest in politics, a dogged determination to achieve, and a withdrawn, contemplative disposition. Possibly he learned an appreciation for the value of publicity from a distant cousin, former Missouri Governor Joseph W. Folk, who had launched an impressive political career and presidential bid in the wake of Lincoln Steffen's exposés of corruption in St. Louis; certainly Kefauver had developed, early in his career, an uncanny nose for promotional notoriety. From the prevailing intellectual atmosphere of home, school, and political party he accepted the economic and political philosophy of Wilson's New Freedom; throughout his career, Kefauver remained basically a Brandeisian.

After attending local schools, Kefauver entered the University of Tennessee, where he played football and engaged in a variety of extracurricular activities. Despite only average academic marks and involvement in a cheating scandal, the young man's recommendations were sufficient to get him into Yale Law School, where he maintained good grades. Kefauver had once dreamed of entering Folk's Washington law firm, but Folk died prior to the young man's law school days, and Kefauver apparently anticipated no other career than practicing in Tennessee. He joined a Chattanooga firm in 1927 and quickly gained a local reputation for thorough and conscientious work while, at the same time, he entered the world of local boosterism, thereby keeping a promise to a Yale classmate to "join everything in town."[7]

6. Eric Goldman, *The Crucial Decade and After, America, 1945–1960* (New York: Vintage Books, 1960), pp. 140–41. *Newsweek,* November 21, 1949, p. 31.

7. David White, "The Early Years of Estes Kefauver" (seminar paper, Estes Kefauver Collection, University of Tennessee, May 1969), pp. 2, 4, 6, 8–13, 16. Louis G. Geiger, *Joseph W. Folk of Missouri* (Columbia: University of Missouri Press, 1953), 191 n. Joseph Bruce Gorman, "The Early Career of Estes Kefauver," East Tennessee His-

Kefauver's law practice and civil activities shortly brought him into political conflict with Judge Will Cummings, who engineered his defeat for the state senate in 1938. Nevertheless, a year later, having gained Cummings's support, Kefauver won a special election to the U.S. Congress. During his ten-year service in the House, Kefauver proved to be a loyal New Dealer and an ardent defender of the Tennessee Valley Authority. His major special interests were antimonopoly, which he channeled through his membership on the Select Committee on Small Business, and congressional reform, which he promoted through sponsorship of the Legislative Reorganization Act of 1946 as well as through a small but well-received book, *A Twentieth Century Congress.* In 1948, demonstrating his flair for publicity, Kefauver donned a coonskin cap and campaigned successfully for the Senate over the divided state machine of Boss E.H. Crump of Memphis.

The new 45-year-old senator had won his place by deliberate cultivation of the public and press and by sheer physical endurance. Kefauver constantly clipped items from newspapers and rushed congratulatory notes to hundreds of constituents and reporters; he shook thousands of hands on campaign forays into the state; and he courted the support of powerful regional newspapers such as the Nashville *Tennessean* and the Chattanooga *Times.* A poor orator but a man of incredible stamina, he had less a machine than thousands of personal contacts which necessitated periodic reactivation, a task that became more and more taxing as Kefauver aged.

An essentially aloof, keenly intelligent man who was able to tap the minds of experts and see through a maze of detail, Kefauver apparently at the same time experienced no difficulty in posing as a homespun Lincoln or Man in Coonskin Cap. Aside from his political views and his soaring ambitions, Kefauver seemed to invite hostility in Congress by his willingness to focus his press contacts on an opponent, by his persistence in buttonholing fellow legislators, and by his frequently exercised unwillingness to reciprocate favors with fellow senators. To Kefauver the immediate problem on which he worked took precedence over all other concerns, and he seemed never to appreciate why other legislators could not wholeheartedly agree.[8]

---

torical Society's *Publications* (No. 42), 1970, pp. 61, 75 *et passim.*
8. Jack Anderson and Fred Blumenthal, *The Kefauver Story* (New

Although Kefauver rarely shared his personal thoughts, his victory in 1948 almost certainly set him thinking of higher office. Scattered Tennessee newspapers mentioned the possibility of his candidacy for the Presidency the month after his election to the Senate, and Kefauver's correspondence clearly indicates that he had discussed his chances with close friends by early 1950.[9] In all probability the Democratic ticket in 1952 would not be composed of both President Truman, who would be sixty-eight years old, and Vice President Barkley, who would be seventy-five. As a young, liberal, border-state legislator with a reputation of bucking bossism, Kefauver must have concluded he had a certain availability. Politically, Kefauver needed out-of-state contacts, attention from the press, and wider public recognition; by repetition, the strange-sounding name itself might become an asset. If he could exploit the crime issue without offending the national administration, Kefauver might well open up political opportunities for himself in 1952.

To reduce charges of opportunism, Kefauver explained that his interest in organized crime had been awakened by his work as chairman of a House Judiciary subcommittee which in 1945 had probed into alleged judicial corruption in the middle district of Pennsylvania. His subcommittee's work, capping a series of investigations by the bar, grand juries, and enterprising newspaper reporters, demonstrated conflict of interest bordering on outright bribery, and it recommended the impeachment of District Judge Albert Johnson. A man with little training in criminal law, Ke-

---

York: The Dial Press, 1956), pp. 50–54, 70–72. "Kefauver, (Carey) Estes," *Current Biography* (1949), 315–17. Charles Bartlett, "The Crusading Kefauver," *The Nation*, May 3, 1952, pp. 426–29. Agnes Thornton Bird, "Resources Used in Senatorial Primary Campaigns, 1949–1964" (Ph.D. diss., University of Tennessee, 1967), pp. 19, 30, 45–55, 80. Robert L. Riggs, "The Man from Tennessee," *The Progressive* (March 1956), 7–11. Kefauver consistently scored high in the press's evaluations for effectiveness. In 1946 *Collier's* rated him among the ten best congressmen; *Time* placed him among the top ten senators in 1950; and in 1952 *New Republic* considered him second only to Paul Douglas of Illinois. *Time*, April 3, 1950, p. 20; *New Republic*, March 3, 1952, p. 11.

9. Nashville *Tennessean*, December 4, 1948. Mrs. Flora Brody to Kefauver (two undated letters but early January, 1950, and mid-February, 1950), General Correspondence, 1948–1955, A-B Box, Kefauver Papers.

fauver declared that it was the spectacle of judges extorting money from local criminals that prompted his close scrutiny of crime problems after 1945. A more accurate statement would be that the investigation placed Kefauver in contact with crime reporters such as George Martin of the Scranton *Times* and Justice Department prosecutors such as Max Goldschein, who became the subcommittee's counsel, and Boris Kostelanetz, who had successfully pushed the movie extortion case against the Capone group in 1943. The Senator cultivated the reporters, became their drinking partner, and listened to their suggestions. He read with fascinated skepticism Lait and Mortimer's theories of a Mafia overlordship in *Chicago Confidential.* In early 1949 Philip L. Graham and J. Russel Wiggins, the publisher and managing editor of the Washington *Post,* directed Kefauver's attention to the activities of the California Crime Commission and procured for him the group's progress reports. Kefauver studied these and similar documents with newsmen as well as with Goldschein and Kostelanetz.[10]

As Kefauver pondered the problem throughout the spring of 1949 he apparently intended only to introduce bills to curb the racing-news wire service and possibly to prohibit interstate transportation of slot machines. Midyear, the Senator presented a draft of a wire service bill to Attorney General Clark and Federal Communications Commission Chairman Wayne Coy; in November, he was still working on the legislation. Discussion with several experts and the calls by crime commissions and the A.M.A. for broader federal government investigations, however, shifted Kefauver's approach temporarily away from specific legislation and toward a more comprehensive congressional inquiry into gambling and racketeering. Not only would such an investigation open up important press and political contacts, but it would also allow

10. *Congressional Record,* May 2, 1950, pp. 6150–51. "Official Conduct of Albert W. Johnson and Albert L. Watson . . . ," *House Report No. 1639,* 79th Cong., 2d sess. (1946), pp. 1–50. Joseph Borkin, *The Corrupt Judge: An Inquiry into Bribery and Other High Crimes and Misdemeanors in the Federal Courts* (New York: Clarkson N. Potter, Inc., 1962), pp. 141–86. Lee Mortimer, "Will Kefauver Be President?" *The American Mercury* (May 1951), 515–24. J. R. Wiggins to Standley, May 20, 1949, Crime Commission Study Box, Standley Papers; Estes Kefauver, *Crime in America* (Garden City, N.Y.: Doubleday & Company, Inc., 1951), p. 167.

the Senator to approach more fully the alleged monopoly or cartel of organized crime by syndicated gambling figures. Both Folk and Brandeis peered out of Kefauver's rimless spectacles in late 1949.[11]

On January 5, 1950, Kefauver formally introduced Senate Resolution 202, which called for the Judiciary Committee on which he served to direct "a full and complete study and investigation of interstate gambling and racketeering activities and of the manner in which the facilities of interstate commerce are made a vehicle of organized crime." The Senator stressed that the existence of nationwide crime syndicates had been noted by crime commissions in Chicago and California, by mayors in New Orleans, Los Angeles, and Portland, and by numerous nationally known reporters and magazine writers. A federal study, such as the A.M.A. had requested, could determine whether such rumors were true and, if so, could properly gauge their use of interstate commerce. Only after this had been done could Congress legislate intelligently on the problem.[12]

As the press picked up the story, poachers appeared on the scene. McCarthy suggested that the main responsibility be transferred to the Special Investigations Committee, on which he served, while the supplementary tasks be assigned to the Judiciary and Commerce committees. The Senator from Wisconsin noted that the Special Investigations Committee, in its inquiry into the "five-percenters" the previous summer, had done some background work into the problem and had a staff "specifically trained for this sort of thing." Kefauver brushed aside McCarthy's suggestion, but he stated that he was certain the McCarthy group had information that could assist the Judiciary Committee's study. Kefauver, possibly anticipating McCarthy's interest, had filed his own resolution first, even before sounding out party leaders, and as a member of the majority party, had strong ground on which to fend off McCarthy's challenge. Recognizing Kefauver's claims as well as his coonlike tenacity in holding to them, McCarthy lumbered off in the direction of the State Department. The following month he announced the discovery of a large but imprecise number

11. Kefauver to Clark, June 3, 1949, Crime Box 2, Kefauver Papers. *Congressional Record,* May 2, 1950, pp. 6154–55.

12. *Congressional Record,* January 5, 1950, pp. 67–78. "Statement of Senator Estes Kefauver on Resolution to Investigate Gambling and Racketeering" delivered January 5, 1950, McGrath Papers.

of Communists making foreign policy for the Democrats.[13]

Congressman Emanuel Celler, chairman of the House Judiciary Committee, informally suggested to Kefauver that he alter his resolution to provide for a joint committee rather than a strictly Senate study. Wisconsin's cagey Senator Alexander Wiley, looking toward his campaign for reelection in 1950, took the opportunity in endorsing Celler's suggestion to remind Kefauver that he too had "considerable material on the subject" and that he wanted to cooperate with the Tennessee freshman. Kefauver took the hint. He explained to Celler that to change the resolution might jeopardize its approval that session but told Wiley that he would welcome his membership on the proposed Judiciary subcommittee.[14]

Kefauver easily outmaneuvered McCarthy, Celler, and Wiley, but the real test of his acumen would come in convincing senior senators and the Administration that the inquiry by the Judiciary Committee was wise or necessary at all. The first major obstacle was the bulky, cantankerous chairman of the Judiciary Committee, Nevada's Senator Pat McCarran. The bane of Senate liberals, McCarran passed on about a third of all bills before they were brought to the floor. In early 1950, McCarran had become especially obstreperous over the Administration's Displaced Persons Act and was in no mood to be crossed. Since he was seeking reelection in the wide-open state of Nevada, McCarran greeted the proposal to investigate gambling and racketeering with a grunt and almost two months of delay. He appointed a six-man subcommittee, ostensibly headed by Kefauver, to study S. Res. 202, but he himself dominated the proceedings. Kefauver tapped the staff of the Senate District Committee for digests of a recent investi-

13. Washington *Post* clipping of January, 1950, Kefauver scrapbook. Kefauver to McGrath, January 9, 1950, McGrath Papers. Goldman, *Crucial Decade,* p. 142. Much of the origin, jurisdictional squabbling, and staffing of the Kefauver Committee has striking parallels in the Truman and McClellan committees. See Matthew Yung-chun Yang, "The Truman Committee" (Ph.D. diss., Harvard, 1947), pp. 6–9. Donald H. Riddle, *The Truman Committee: A Study in Government Responsibility* (New Brunswick, N.J.: Rutgers University Press, 1964), pp. 13–14. Jonathan Daniels, *The Man of Independence* (Philadelphia: J. P. Lippincott Company, 1950), pp. 222–27. Robert F. Kennedy, *The Enemy Within* (New York: Harpers, 1960), pp. 23–24.

14. Emanuel Celler to Kefauver, February 20, 1950; Wiley to Kefauver, February 22, 1950; Kefauver to Celler, February 23, 1950; Kefauver to Wiley, February 27, 1950; Crime Box 37, Kefauver Papers.

gation of gambling in Washington, reports by the Federal Communications Commission, findings of the California and Chicago Crime Commissions, and syndicated articles by Edward Folliard in the Washington *Post,* by Bob Considine, and by Drew Pearson. He telegraphed the chairman of the Citizens' Committee of Massachusetts for its full report on state and national gambling; he discussed the problem with James M. Cox of the Miami *Daily News* and had Dan Sullivan of the Miami Crime Commission fly to Washington with information for the Judiciary Committee. Information and petitions coming his way from Virgil Peterson through the A.M.A. and from the Women's Citizens Committee of Gary, Indiana, reinforced Kefauver in his attempt to impress McCarran with the urgency of his resolution. The Senator from Nevada pleaded for more time, then raised the issue of states' rights, and finally suggested that Senator Ed Johnson of the Senate Commerce Committee ought to be consulted.[15]

As the Attorney General's Conference raised the possibility that the issue might get away from the Judiciary Committee and McCarran entirely, the leery committee chairman relented and allowed the full committee to consider Res. 202, but "assisted" it with several proposed amendments. First, McCarran and his ally, Mississippi's James Eastland, expanded the proposed investigation's scope to include all organized crime, including prostitution, narcotics, loan-sharking, organized murder, extortion, and labor racketeering as well as gambling. The subcommittee to be created was to explore with care the corrupting influence of these activities but was

15. Alfred Steinberg, *The Man from Missouri: Life and Times of Harry S. Truman* (New York: G. P. Putnam's Sons, 1962), pp. 340–41. *Congressional Record,* May 2, 1950, p. 6155. Kefauver to McCarran, January 16, 1950, Crime Box 37; Memorandum from Kefauver to Robert H. Mollohan, Clerk of the District Committee, January 17, 1950, Crime Box 1; Telegram from Kefauver to Rev. Dana McLean Greeley, January 28, 1950; Kefauver to Cox, January 26, 1950; Sullivan to Kefauver, February 28, 1950; Telegram from Steering Committee of Women's Citizens Committee of Gary to Kefauver, February 10, 1950; Chatters to Kefauver, January 10, 1950; Crime Box 2, Kefauver Papers. St. Louis *Post-Dispatch,* April 12, 1950. Nat Perlow to Peterson, March 13, 1950, File 5–10, vol. 2, Chicago Crime Commission Records. The Judiciary subcommittee assigned to study the original Kefauver resolution was composed of Kefauver, James Eastland of Mississippi, Herbert O'Conor of Maryland, Forrest C. Donnell of Missouri, and William Jenner of Indiana.

not to recommend any changes in the states' gambling laws. Having protected Nevada's gambling as far as the English language and senatorial manipulation would permit, McCarran then doubled the sum Kefauver had originally proposed (to $100,000) and allowed the Judiciary Committee to approve the Kefauver resolution unanimously on February 27. As chairman of the parent committee, McCarran could exercise substantial control over the membership and the conclusions of the proposed subcommittee.[16]

While Kefauver was bombarding McCarran with the supporting data for his proposal, he was also attempting to court the Administration. In his rush to supersede possible rival resolutions, Kefauver had been unable to reach Attorney General McGrath before introducing Res. 202. Within the week, however, he had met with McGrath and attempted to calm the Attorney General's anxiety. A free-wheeling inquiry into a number of big-city Democratic machines by a possibly vindictive McCarran, a still untested novice like Kefauver, and a few bloodthirsty Republicans on the Judiciary Committee could seriously embarrass the Administration and party in the fall elections and also ruin some promising prosecutions. On Kefauver's part, lack of cooperation by the Justice Department could destroy the effectiveness of the investigation as well as his own political advancement. McGrath attempted to regain the initiative and neutralize Kefauver's proposal by inviting the Tennessee Senator to attend the Attorney General's Conference the following month. Kefauver made the now meaningless concession of agreeing to delay actual presentation of the resolution until after the conference—a delay necessitated anyway by McCarran's rear-guard action and by the need to gather supporting materials.[17]

A cooing Kefauver attended the conference, where he flattered and reassured the mayors and prosecutors and carefully complimented the Justice Department. The A.M.A. faction, led by Mayors Bowron and Morrison, included in their ten-point program a specific endorsement of the Kefauver resolution, but the Attorney General's office convinced the resolu-

16. *Congressional Record,* May 2, 1950, p. 6155. *Senate Report 1317,* 81st Cong., 2d sess. Kefauver to Forrest C. Donnell, February 23, 1950; Telegram from Charles Neese, Administrative Assistant to Kefauver, February 27, 1950, Crime Box 37, Kefauver Papers.

17. Kefauver to McGrath, January 9, 1950, McGrath Papers. Kefauver to McGrath, January 12, 1950, Crime Box 37, Kefauver Papers.

tions committee that to support the proposal publicly would be interpreted as an attempt to dictate to the legislative branch. Both Morrison and Kefauver privately noted the undercurrent of opposition by the Administration.[18]

In an effort to channel the legislation on the wire services and slot machines away from the hostile Judiciary Committee as well as to siphon off support for a wider Kefauver inquiry, the conference's legislative committee, dominated by friends of the Administration, drafted the bills in such a way as to divert them to the Senate Commerce Committee rather than to McCarran's group. An alarmed Kefauver reached Vice President Alben Barkley in time to examine his copy of the bills before they were submitted and referred to committee. After looking over the drafts and talking with Barkley and the Senate parliamentarian, Kefauver recognized that he "could not dispute" that they should be sent to Commerce rather than to Judiciary.[19]

Meanwhile, because the proposed investigation by the Judiciary Committee asked for money from the Senate contingency fund, S. Res. 202 had moved on to a Rules and Administration subcommittee, comprised of John Stennis of Mississippi, Andrew F. Shoeppel of Kansas, and Guy Gillette of Iowa. Colorado's "Big Ed" Johnson, chairman of the Commerce Committee, then rushed to center stage, insisting that, since the Attorney General's bills would be heading his way, his committee ought to have the money for the crime study. Forlornly, Kefauver expected the Rules Committee to pass along the squabble to the floor, and he hurriedly began to try to mobilize support in the press and Congress behind an investigation by the Judiciary. On March 23, before the Attorney General's bills were filed, a group from the Judiciary Committee, consisting of Kefauver, McCarran, and would-be Republican subcommittee members Forrest C. Donnell of Missouri and Homer Ferguson of Michigan, appeared before the Rules Committee. Ed Johnson, angry and determined, came to plead his case. When Johnson first bluntly threatened to block action on any crime bills unless his group had money "forked" his

---

18. *The Attorney General's Conference on Organized Crime,* February 15, 1950, pp. 24–25, 32–34, 49–50. Chalmers M. Roberts, "Crime Probe Had Precarious Infancy," Washington *Post,* April 1, 1951. Morrison to Kefauver, March 29, 1950; Kefauver to Morrison, April 28, 1950, Crime Box 3, Kefauver Papers.

19. *Congressional Record,* May 2, 1950, pp. 6155–56.

way with which to study the problem and then stated he would study the problem regardless of appropriations, the Rules and Administration subcommittee backed off from the jurisdictional squabble.[20]

Rather than simply refusing to pass on the measure, however, the Stennis subcommittee approved S. Res. 202 while cutting its appropriations to $50,000 and requiring a report by July 31. McCarran growled that the July 31 deadline had destroyed the effectiveness of the inquiry and that under the circumstances the effort would be a waste of money. On an informal promise that neither the deadline nor the $50,000 would be considered final, however, Kefauver turned his persistence on the overworked majority leader, Senator Scott W. Lucas of Illinois. Stating that he did not think Johnson would object to his action on jurisdictional grounds, he asked if he might not take the resolution to the floor for immediate action.[21]

Lucas, engaged in a bitter campaign for reelection, frequently at odds with the Administration, and surrounded by powerful and independent-minded committee chairmen, was in no mood to appease the presumptuous Kefauver. Lucas, like many Senate elders, looked askance at the prospect of a man so new to the upper house, so insistent and so publicity-minded, being entrusted with an investigation of such political consequence. Like McCarran, Lucas tried to put Kefauver off, and Kefauver responded by attempting to mobilize the press, which was favorable to his position. His close friend, Lee Hills, managing editor of the Miami *Herald,* put him in touch with reporters who were connected with the fourteen-member newspaper syndicate that had been organized earlier in the year.[22]

At the same time, Kefauver attempted to convince the skeptical legislators that he did not plan a "sensational witch-hunt

20. *Congressional Record,* May 2, 1950, pp. 6156–57; May 3, 1950, pp. 6225–27. Kefauver to Lee Hills of Miami *Herald,* March 17, 1950, Crime Box 2, Kefauver Papers. *Congressional Record,* March 16, 1950, pp. 3434–35. Cleveland *Plain Dealer,* March 23, 1950.

21. *Congressional Record,* May 2, 1950, pp. 6156–57. Knoxville *News-Sentinel,* April 9, 1950. Telegram from Kefauver to Lucas, March 23, 1950, Crime Box 37, Kefauver Papers.

22. Miami *Daily News,* March 24, 1950. Hills to Kefauver, March 20, 1950; Hills to Kefauver, March 21, 1950; Kefauver to Hills, March 28, 1950, Crime Box 2, Kefauver Papers.

... or a lot of notoriety." Rather, he expected a low-keyed study, to be made in close cooperation with various federal agencies in an over-all effort to arrive at sound recommendations. Unpersuaded, various legislators, such as Lucas, Ernest McFarland of Arizona, and Dennis Chavez of New Mexico, blocked Kefauver's effort to get final floor approval for his resolution.[23]

Meanwhile, Johnson, undaunted by the earlier decision by the Rules Committee, pushed ahead with his own plans. On April 4 he introduced the two bills that had originated in the Attorney General's Conference, along with his own S. Res. 249, which called for an investigation by the Commerce Committee similiar to that Kefauver had advocated by Judiciary. The so-called Johnson Slot Machine Bill sailed through the Senate in two weeks and later won quick approval by the House and Administration as well. Resolution 249, however, became lodged in the hands of the bewildered Rules and Administration Committee. To complicate the jurisdictional log jam further, Johnson announced that his committee would hold hearings on the wire service or communications bill, S. Res. 3358.[24]

The communications subcommittee, headed by Ernest McFarland, soon realized that it had a thorny problem indeed. Under McGrath's benign direction, the conference had drafted the wire service bill as a regulatory, rather than criminal, measure and had thrust entire responsibility for enforcement upon a reluctant Federal Communications Commission. In effect, the telephone and telegraph industries—not the persons who used the wire services for bookmaking—would be subject to sanction if the commission found that their facilities were being used for gambling purposes. The Attorney General explained almost apologetically that he feared a return to a Prohibition-like situation if his department had to enforce criminal laws against gambling. Wayne Coy, chairman of the FCC, fiercely assailed the measure as did representatives of the communications and broadcasting media. Even Senator Kefauver, who risked much if he incurred the hostility of the Administration, voiced mild disagreement with some "details" of the bill.[25]

23. *Congressional Record,* March 28, 1950, pp. 4184–85; March 29, 1950, p. 4356; April 4, 1950, p. 4644.

24. *Congressional Record,* April 4, 1950, p. 4639; April 5, 1950, 4722. New York *Times,* April 6, 1950.

25. "Transmission of Gambling Information," *Hearings* before a Senate Commerce Subcommittee on S. 3358, 81st Cong., 2d sess. (1950),

"What For: They Ain't in the State Department"
Washington *Post,* April 11, 1950. Courtesy, The Washington Post

---

pp. 48, 53, 56, 61–66, 326–34, 525–52, 573–77, 604–5, 744–45. Kefauver to
McGrath, April 4, 1950, McGrath Papers. In the Annenberg cases, the
courts had quashed a lottery indictment, on the grounds that quotations on horse races were not lottery information. "Transmission of
Gambling Information," Senate Commerce *Hearings,* p. 48.

Republicans on the Commerce subcommittee meanwhile nudged and coaxed McFarland toward a broader investigation. Senator Homer Capehart listened in disbelief as McGrath and other officials explained that they had no information on "the national crime syndicate" so much discussed in the press. Even when Mayors Morrison, Bowron, and others expressed their conviction that such organizations existed, Capehart appeared confused. The Senator from Indiana wondered how the subcommittee could pass on this bill or why the Senate should spend money on the proposed Kefauver investigation into syndicates if no one knew whether in fact such syndicates existed.[26]

In effect, the idea of "the national crime syndicate"—particularly if the phrase used the definite article and the singular noun—conjured up the old Mafia conspiratorial tradition in American crime fighting. Less distinctly based on ethnic stereotypes and more on press sensationalism, the idea of the syndicate had been reborn in the late 1940s. Nurtured by the crime commissions' antigambling movement and propagandized by both politicians and publicists, the speculation had far outstripped law enforcement's investigative pace. This investigative lag and semantical fuzziness in part prompted Capehart's questions. He wanted to know what individual "pulled the strings" for organized crime.

McFarland, a dignified jurist with a personal revulsion for the subject he was investigating, insisted that his was a legislative, not a crime investigation; the issue of the national crime syndicate was, he asserted, irrelevant to his hearings because the bill under consideration would impair large-scale bookmaking regardless of the nature of the group sponsoring it. While in his subcommittee report McFarland attacked the "dime novel fiction writers" who published tales of nationwide crime and gambling syndicates, he finally yielded to

26. Commerce *Hearings,* pp. 65, 77, 128–29, 170, 253–62, 199–207, 279. McGrath explained that, aside from the lottery laws, his department had no responsibilities in the gambling area and that his only information was based on the Annenberg investigation and a FCC report on the use of communication facilities completed and classified in 1944. Upon returning from the McFarland testimony, however, McGrath ordered all 93 U.S. Attorneys to collect and analyze information on major racketeers and syndicates in their area. McFarland meanwhile sent similar inquiries to the states' attorneys-general and obtained a divided response. Ibid., pp. 48, 808–33. Washington *Post,* May 7, 1950. Washington *Evening Star,* July 3, 1950.

Capehart's needling and called Frank Costello, Frank Erickson, and St. Louis's "betting commissioner" J. J. Carroll—figures who might enlighten the Senator from Indiana. Carroll presented a dignified appearance and emphasized that his gambling operations had no connection with groups that engaged in violence; Costello disclaimed any bookmaking activities in the preceding fifteen years or any knowledge of crime syndicates; Erickson came ill-prepared and nervously admitted carrying on an illegal $100,000-a-year bookmaking business in New York. Without proper background briefing, Capehart and his fellow Republican, Charles W. Tobey of New Hampshire, bungled through the questioning, which uncovered little information of importance but prompted some reporters to charge that McFarland was engaged in a whitewash of the criminal establishment.[27]

While Capehart and Tobey, both seeking reelection in 1950, hurriedly snatched any political advantage they could from membership on the McFarland Subcommittee, Kefauver sat in on the hearings, asked a few questions, and reportedly sought a formal seat with the group. McFarland and Johnson countered with an offer of informal membership, which in effect would more efficiently contain the Tennessean's energies. They objected not so much to the substance of his proposed investigation as to the jurisdictional control McCarran would have over it and to the publicity it would afford the ambitious Kefauver.[28]

Kefauver refused to be deflected by what he regarded as the "superficial operations" of the McFarland Subcommittee. Rather, he intensified the same pressure on Lucas he had previously used on McCarran. He called upon the States' Attorneys General Association for resolutions and letters endorsing S. Res. 202, and for the first time made an open political argument to the majority leader. Warning that the Democratic party would probably be identified with criminal and gambling interests in the fall elections, he suggested that the

27. "Transmission of Gambling Information," Senate Commerce *Hearings*, pp. 170, 79, 381, 389, 431–49, 469–88. "Transmission of Gambling Information," *Senate Report No. 1752*, 81st Cong., 2d sess. (1950), p. 16. "Senate Soliloquy," *Newsweek*, May 8, 1950, pp. 27–28.

28. "Transmission of Gambling Information," Senate Commerce *Hearings*, pp. 76, 538, 546, 623; Personal interview, Edward Cooper, professional staff member of McFarland Subcommittee, Washington, D.C., October 30, 1969.

Democrats in Congress could undercut the charge and strengthen the party's position by supporting his resolution. Kefauver based his opinion at least partially on a growing volume of constituent mail suggesting a link between the Administration and underworld interests. *Publisher's Weekly* announced that the gossipy and inflammatory *Chicago Confidential* had already sold nearly 40,000 copies and even Mayor Morrison had been impressed.[29]

An unexpected event on April 6 blasted the jurisdictional log jam that had held back Kefauver. Charles Binaggio, gambling power and political figure in Kansas City, and his henchman, Charles Gargotta, were killed in a Democratic clubhouse beneath a large wall photograph of the President. The lurid picture, reprinted in numerous newspapers and magazines, aroused widespread speculation and charges. The Miami *Daily News* used the occasion to underline a series of exposés by former Chicago Police Captain William Drury which it had carried a month earlier; Drury had identified Binaggio as the Kansas City cog in the national Mafia dominated by Charles Fischetti. The anti-Pendergast Kansas City *Star-Times* demanded prompt federal action against the "National Crime Syndicate"; other newspapers speculated that Democratic leaders feared a complete study of big-city machines. Even the New York *Times* carried a front-page summary of the situation.

On Capitol Hill, Congressman Macy renewed his demand for a complete inquiry into politico–criminal ties in the Kansas City area. To the delight of Senator Tobey, the reluctant McFarland Subcommittee was drawn into the Binaggio controversy under the excuse of examining the wire service setup in Missouri.[30]

29. Kefauver to Morrison, April 22, 1950; Kefauver to Robert Larons, Attorney General of Iowa, April 7, 1950; Kefauver to Lucas, April 4, 1950; J. L. Bryan to Kefauver, January 7, 1950; Jack C. Halbrook to Kefauver, March 20, 1950; Malcolm Hatfield to Kefauver, April 4, 1950; Morrison to Kefauver, March 2, 1950, Crime Box 2, Kefauver Papers. Editorial, Washington *Post,* March 23, 1950.

30. "In Truman's Back Yard," *Newsweek,* April 17, 1950, pp. 25–27. "Shots End a Missouri Political Career," *Life,* April 17, 1950, pp. 41–45. Miami *Daily News,* April 7, 1950. New York *Times,* April 7, 9, 1950. Unidentified clipping from Greenville, S.C., paper, April 11, 1950, Kefauver scrapbook. Kansas City *Times,* April 8, 1950. New York *Daily Mirror,* April 7, 1950. "Transmission of Gambling Information," Senate Commerce *Hearings,* pp. 655, 789.

Under relentless pressure from all corners, Lucas finally capitulated. After lunching on April 10 with Kefauver and Leslie Biffle, the Senate's secretary and confidant of the President, Lucas announced he would back a broad investigation of organized crime by a special committee of five to seven members drawn from both Commerce and Judiciary. The matter would, he said, be discussed with Truman. The following day, the Senate Democratic Policy Committee met to discuss the Lucas compromise. Reportedly, neither McCarran, Johnson, nor Kefauver expressed enthusiasm for the new plan, but Lucas and Biffle prevailed. Informally, the group agreed that the McFarland Subcommittee was to cancel its hearings and a five-man special committee to be named by Vice President Barkley would assume the subcommittee's task. Johnson withdrew his objection to the publicity-minded freshman who was to handle the study; McCarran relinquished both the stranglehold he would have over an inquiry by the Judiciary Committee as well as his power to hurt the Administration through appointing hostile Republicans; Lucas rid himself of the annoying Kefauver; and Kefauver, at first expecting some final act of duplicity, received informal assurances that, as the member who had introduced the original resolution as well as the new substitute amendment, he would be chairman. As an extra inducement, the special committee was to enjoy greater autonomy than was provided in the original resolution, the same broad investigative field, the authority to continue to February 18, 1951, and funding at $150,000.[31]

The three months of intrigue and infighting among the Democrats over the Kefauver resolution gave way to over three weeks of bloodletting with the Republicans, who were now taking an increased interest during an election year in the crime issue. Because party leaders assumed that McCarran would appoint Homer Ferguson and Forrest C. Donnell to a Judiciary subcommittee, they had remained silent during

31. New York *Times,* April 11, 12, 1950. Philadelphia *Inquirer,* April 13, 1950. *Congressional Record,* May 2, 1950, pp. 6159, 6162. When Kefauver encountered difficulty in getting quick action on his new amendment, he agreed with McFarland that the communications subcommittee should continue its "very helpful" hearings and hence provide a great deal of information for the special committee. Due to delay in getting the final floor vote, the expiratory date for the special committee was moved up to March 31. Ibid., April 17, pp. 5285, 5287; May 2, p. 6149.

the earlier jurisdictional fight. When Binaggio's murder was followed so soon by the formation of the special committee, Republicans immediately scented an attempt by senators to whitewash crime in Kansas City by maneuvering critical minority members off the investigation. Ferguson, who had come to the Senate in 1943 in the wake of his sensational "one-man grand jury" revelations concerning crime and politics in Wayne County, Michigan, snarled that he was being "euchred" off the group; Minority Whip Kenneth Wherry inquired whether a "cover-up" could be expected; Robert A. Taft, Minority Leader, announced that Republicans would fight the measure.[32]

Taft's first weapon was Missouri's Junior Senator, James P. Kem, who developed the habit of lecturing his colleagues on the evils of Democratic politics in Kansas City. Binaggio and Pendergast had cooperated, he explained, in the President's effort in 1946 to block a local Democratic congressman from reelection. The Pendergast candidate won the nomination, but fraud was uncovered in the elections and indictments were forthcoming when, on May 27, 1947, the incriminating evidence was stolen from a courthouse safe. The Justice Department bungled the federal investigation that ensued, and even a subcommittee headed by Senator Ferguson failed to rekindle the department's interest. Since that time Binaggio had challenged Pendergast's leadership and was scheduled to appear before a federal grand jury when he was assassinated. In view of these conditions, Kem challenged, did the proposed Kefauver committee intend to go to Kansas City? Kefauver expressed uncertainty as to whether the crime was in the federal jurisdiction, but asserted that he would not "shy away" from the President's home county.[33]

Republicans and many newspapers accepted Kem's idea that the Democratic Policy Committee had engaged in chica-

32. Philadelphia *Inquirer,* April 13, 1951. Washington *Post,* April 1, 1951. *Congressional Record,* May 3, 1950, pp. 6234–37. New York *Times,* April 11, 12, 13, 1950. Senator Ferguson had briefly come to the defense of the Judiciary investigation in the feud with Johnson. Nashville *Tennessean,* March 19, 1950.

33. *Congressional Record,* April 12, 1950, pp. 5079–86; May 2, 1950, pp. 6159–61. Current rumor held that the federal grand jury directed by Max H. Goldschein in Kansas City, which had begun in August of 1949, was an effort by the Administration to embarrass the Binaggio faction. Goldschein to Kefauver, April 18, 1950, Crime Box 2, Kefauver Papers. New York *Times,* October 5, 1949.

nery to avoid a thorough investigation of conditions in Kansas
City. Columnist David Lawrence even suggested that the long
delay in acting on the original resolution indicated an effort
to delay the investigation until no significant material would
be gathered before the elections. Donnell, Taft, and Ferguson
argued that the creation of special committees, all but abol-
ished by the Reorganization Act of 1946, was an act of bad
faith and that historically the minority leadership, not the
Vice President, had had the right to name minority party committee members. The usually pro-Kefauver Washington *Post*
editorialized that creation of the special committee would set
a new and dangerous precedent, result in loss of committee
discipline, divide responsibility for bills and thereby retard
remedial legislation, exclude the investigative talent of Ferguson, and above all, launch the new committee under a
heavy cloud of suspicion.

Basically, of course, the question boiled down to personalities, and the Republicans were as guilty of playing politics as
the Democrats. Hoping to use Ferguson and Donnell as
hatchet men, they wanted to exploit the situations in Kansas
City and New York for their party in an election year. Suspi-
cions and hesitancy on the part of the Democratic leadership,
however, painted the majority party darker than it need to
have appeared.[34]

Even after obtaining agreement to his compromise plan,
Lucas ineptly delayed action on the necessary floor vote. The
Majority Leader had promised Kefauver that he could bring
the measure up after the pending Rivers and Harbors bill had
been acted upon, but he then changed his mind and began
debate on the financing for the Economic Cooperation Administration. On April 17 Kefauver asked for unanimous consent to interrupt debate in order to act on S. Res. 202 and
amendments. Peevishly, Lucas asked Kefauver if he thought
the crime study more important than the financing of the
Marshall Plan and argued that as soon as the Senate acted on
the ECA bill, the Tennessean could "have all the money" he
wanted to investigate every "crook in America." Kefauver
drawled that debate on his bill could be substituted for the ball

34. "Senate Against It, But——," *Newsweek,* April 24, 1950. *Congressional Record,* May 3, 1950, pp. 6234–42. Washington *Post,* April 13,
1950. Philadelphia *Daily News,* April 19, 1950. Knoxville *News-Sentinel,* May 6, 1950. Nashville *Tennessean,* May 12, 1950. Thomas E.
Butler to Kefauver, April 15, 1950, Crime Box 2, Kefauver Papers.

game the senators planned to attend the next day, but Lucas, Donnell, McFarland, and Styles Bridges of New Hampshire agreed that debate would be long and furious over alleged "shenanigans" by the Democratic Policy Committee and that previous commitments had been made. With an eye to Indiana politics, Homer Capehart asked Kefauver why membership on the special committee could not be enlarged to eleven, with appointments coming from Johnson and McCarran. Kefauver responded that, while he was not personally opposed, he felt honor bound to support the Lucas compromise and that a smaller group could work more closely with the staff. Capehart thereupon stumped Indiana, predicting whitewash of Democrats, smearing of Republicans, and over-all bad faith in the investigation of crime. Owen Brewster of Maine, the Republicans' campaign chairman, accused Lucas of delay and cover-up, while the Majority Leader lamely cried political red herring. Radio commentator Robert Montgomery shifted his caustic attacks from Costello to Lucas and Barkley, whom he indirectly linked with gambling interests in Illinois and Kentucky.[35]

Having suffered the bruising encounter of April 17, Lucas agreed to let the Kefauver resolution come to a vote on May 2. Republican hammering as well as encouragement from businessmen and columnists like Drew Pearson helped reshape Lucas's attitude. When Donnell, Ferguson, Kem, and Taft, repeating all the Republican arguments, cried for longer debate, Lucas snapped that he would no longer bear the "intimations and innuendoes" that charged him with delaying the adoption of the resolution, and he pushed ruthlessly on over Taft's objections, stopping only to guarantee the minority party at least two seats on the five-man special committee. The Senate defeated by a strict party vote of 39 to 31 Taft's proposal to have the minority floor leaders name the Republican members and then approved, 36 to 35, investigation by the Lucas special committee rather than the Judiciary subcommittee, still championed by the Republicans. Ironically, Vice President Barkley cast the deciding vote in setting up the special com-

35. Washington *News,* April 12, 1950. *Congressional Record,* April 17, 1950, pp. 5283–87. Undated press teletype statement by Capehart, Crime Box 1, Kefauver Papers. *Congressional Record,* April 18, 1950, pp. 5300–5303. Washington *Daily News,* April 19, 1950. Typescript of radio program of "Robert Montgomery," WJZ, Washington, April 20, 1950, Crime Box 37, Kefauver Papers.

mittee because four Southern senators had deserted the Lucas compromise. Minutes after the final vote, Kefauver strode out of the Senate chamber into an impromptu press conference. Side-stepping questions on the special committee's plans to investigate crime in Kansas City, he stressed the need for organization and promised to keep reporters fully informed. The next day, he began pestering Carl Hayden, chairman of the Committee on Rules and Administration, for office space.[36]

As Republicans continued to harass Lucas and reportedly approached Barkley to plead for the appointment of Ferguson, the Vice President pondered selection of committee members for a full week. Since the object of the special committee had been to avoid Ferguson and Donnell, and since membership was to be drawn from both Commerce and Judiciary, Barkley could easily choose the ranking Republican on each committee, in this case, Tobey and Wiley. Most speculation about the Democratic membership focused at first on Kefauver, Edwin Johnson, and McFarland, but Johnson and McFarland indicated shortly after the compromise was accepted that they were weary of the subject and did not wish to serve further. For these two Democratic seats, Barkley reportedly considered Eastland, Lyndon Johnson of Texas, Herbert O'Conor of Maryland, Lester Hunt of Wyoming, and Warren Magnuson of Washington. On May 10 he announced the selection of Kefauver, Wiley, Tobey, Hunt, and O'Conor. O'Conor, apparently reluctant to serve, finally agreed to do so. To skeptical Republicans and the press, Barkley observed that he had discussed the matter with neither Truman nor the party leadership.[37]

36. Anderson and Blumenthal, *Kefauver Story,* pp. 132–43. John Burton Tigrett, Vice President, American Buslines, Inc., to Lucas, May 3, 1950, Crime Box 2, Kefauver Papers. Undated Drew Pearson column, Box 7, Lester C. Hunt Papers, University of Wyoming, Laramie. *Congressional Record,* May 2, 1950, pp. 6145–61; May 3, 1950, pp. 6216–17, 6225–37, 6240–46. Nashville *Tennessean,* May 7, 1950. Kefauver to Hayden, May 4, 1950, Crime Box 37, Kefauver Papers. The four Southern renegades were Byrd and Robertson of Virginia, Eastland of Mississippi, and McClellan of Arkansas. Washington *Post,* May 4, 1950.

37. *Congressional Record,* May 9, 1950, pp. 6701–14; May 10, 1950, p. 6773. Washington *Star,* May 10, 1950. Washington *Evening Star,* May 3, 1950. Philadelphia *Inquirer,* April 17, 1950. Memphis *Press-Scimitar,* May 9, 1950. *Congressional Record,* May 10, 1950, p. 6776. Wilmington *Morning News,* May 13, 1950. Scuttlebutt in Washington had it that O'Conor would have been replaced by Magnuson had he refused to serve. O'Conor's son suggests that his father was feigning disinterest in the Kefauver Committee. New York *Times,* May 8, 1950.

"But We Wanted to Be Policemen, Too"
Washington *Evening Star,* May 5, 1950. Courtesy, The Washington
(D.C.) Star-News

Washington *Post,* May 10, 1950. Personal interview, Herbert R.
O'Conor, Jr., Baltimore, Maryland, October 27, 1969.

Kefauver, who earlier criticized Ferguson's inquisitorial methods and who probably would have had difficulty with the Michigan Republican had he been chosen, privately expressed satisfaction with Barkley's appointments. The group first met on May 11 and quickly chose the Tennessee freshman their chairman. Kefauver stressed to the newly formed committee the need to avoid publicity and sensationalism and urged unanimity in reports even if this meant muting some conclusions. With one or two exceptions, Kefauver obtained the essential unanimity he sought.[38]

* * * *

A conservative, cautious, and ambitious Catholic youth who grew to be a conservative, cautious, and successful Catholic politician, Herbert R. O'Conor maintained a polished calm while holding his political cards close to his chest. Successively a newspaper reporter, state attorney general, and wartime governor, he had moved on to the Senate in 1947, where he was appointed to the doddering successor to the Truman Committee as well as McCarran's Internal Security Subcommittee. Passed over for the Vice Presidential nomination in 1948, O'Conor felt increasingly out of sympathy with New Deal–Fair Deal liberalism and was privately contemplating retirement in 1952. Whether McCarran recommended O'Conor to Barkley is not known, but O'Conor and McCarran were friendly, and the Maryland senator, coming from a state where gambling interests were entrenched, might be expected to be reasonably sympathetic to legalized gambling elsewhere.[39]

If O'Conor could be considered McCarran's man, Lester C. Hunt could be thought of as "Big Ed" Johnson's. Hunt worked his way through Saint Louis University's College of Dentistry and immediately moved to Lander, Wyoming, which he had earlier visited as a semiprofessional baseball player. Through

38. Estes Kefauver, "Let's Cut Out the Congressional High Jinks," *American Magazine* (April 1948), 25, 143. Personal interview, Joseph L. Nellis, former Kefauver Committee counsel, Washington, D.C., August 11, 1969. New York *Times,* May 12, 1950. Undated typewritten statement, Crime Box 37, Kefauver Papers.

39. Harry W. Kirwan, *The Inevitable Success: Herbert R. O'Conor* (Westminster, Md.: Newman Press, 1962), pp. 447 *et passim.*

his activities in the state dental society, he became interested in politics and moved from the state assembly to secretary of state to six years' service as governor. Something of a states' righter as governor, Hunt campaigned on a Fair Deal platform in 1948 to win a seat in the Senate. His major committee assignments included Armed Services and, through the influence of Johnson, a fellow mountain-state politician, the Commerce Committee. Although inactive on the McFarland Subcommittee, Hunt became increasingly interested in the Kefauver investigation, particularly assailing lawyers defending committee witnesses and the telephone and telegraph companies.[40]

Charles W. Tobey, a seventy-year-old, elfish Yankee gadfly, won unquestioned acclaim as the Kefauver Committee's most colorful and eccentric character. While attending the Roxbury Latin School outside of Boston, Tobey had added a taste for literary and classical allusions to the biblical quotations learned at the knee of his strict Baptist mother. Sprinkled liberally throughout his running, occasionally tearful, commentary on the hearings, these quotations added to Tobey's stature and convinced a few he was a learned man. Actually, his family had been too poor to finance a college education, and Tobey had successively been clerk, chicken farmer, insurance salesman, banker, and shoe manufacturer. The possibility of a political career had beckoned when Tobey thrilled to Charles Evans Hughes orating on the evils of gambling in 1902. A Bull Moose Republican, Tobey was first elected to the school board in Temple, New Hampshire, in 1908, and he rose slowly through the party ranks, serving as governor, congressman, and finally, in 1939, as U.S. Senator. Tobey attracted attention in the prewar period by his rabid opposition to Roosevelt's foreign policy, but he had soon mellowed and accepted the broad outlines of internationalism. As the leader among a small group of Republican liberals, Tobey was anathema to conservative forces in New Hampshire, led by Senator Styles Bridges and editor William Loeb, and was as usual engaged in a heated reelection campaign in 1950. Tobey used

40. New York *Times,* June 20, 1954; Hunt to Douglas J. Murphey, March 24, 1951, Box 7, Hunt Papers. Ralph Jerome Woody, "The United States Senate Career of Lester C. Hunt" (M.A. thesis, University of Wyoming, 1964), pp. 10, 34. Miami *Herald,* July 30, 1950. Kefauver to Woody, July 24, 1963, Judiciary Committee Correspondence —88th Congress Box, Kefauver Papers. New York *Times,* June 9, 1954.

his appointment to the Kefauver Committee to his political advantage in New Hampshire and made it into a forum for his intense showmanship, but he also genuinely enjoyed the sleuthing, energetically pursuing leads from taxicab drivers and porters, and continually referring rumormongers to an indulgent Committee staff. Titillated by his spadework on the McFarland Subcommittee, Tobey urged the Kefauver group onward to "drive the rats out of the meal of democracy."[41]

A busy Babbitt from Chippewa Falls, Wisconsin, sixty-six-year-old Alexander Wiley kept a careful eye on the political opportunities opened up by the Committee. Until his election to the Senate in 1938, Wiley had held only one elective office; from 1909–1915 he had served as district attorney of Chippewa County. In the meantime, however, he had been school board member, banker, dairy farmer, local booster, and a member of the Kiwanis Club, the Masons, the Elks, the Knights of Pythias, and the Sons of Norway. In the Senate the hefty 220-pound Wiley continued his propagandizing for the Wisconsin dairy industry, once giving a party around a centerpiece bust of Vice President John Nance Garner carved from cheddar cheese. A gregarious, baby-kissing, polka-dancing politician, Wiley enjoyed collecting jokes for his small book and charming luncheon guests with his conversational banter. An isolationist before World War II, the Senator from Wisconsin had followed Arthur Vandenberg into mild internationalism and after Vandenberg's death in 1950 became ranking Republican on the Foreign Relations Committee. After dropping strong hints to Kefauver that he wanted a seat on the Crime Committee, Wiley, as senior Republican on the Judiciary Committee, became the obvious choice to Democrats who hoped to exclude Ferguson. The Wisconsin senator, engaged in a strenuous campaign for reelection, occasionally attacked Kefauver and Democratic influence and urged the Committee to em-

41. St. Louis *Star-Times,* June 13, 1950. "Autobiography," typescript of notes dictated by Tobey in November, 1948, Box 62; Arthur J. Freund to Tobey, June 7, 1950, Box 102; Tobey to John E. Joseph, March 5, 1951, Box 101, Charles W. Tobey Papers, Dartmouth College, Hanover, N.H. Nellis interview. Knoxville *News-Sentinel,* May 11, 1950. Washington *Post,* May 5, 1950. Tobey had amused the reporters when he announced during the McFarland hearings that he had been "credibly informed" that a bookie had been operating in the Senate Office Building, but that "no senator would patronize" him. Ibid., May 2, 1950.

phasize the Chicago investigations, from which he might benefit most.[42]

If election-year politics had shaped thought on the make-up of the Committee, it continued to a lesser extent to influence the selection of the Committee's staff. As early as January Kefauver had begun sounding out crime commission officials and other personal contacts for recommendations, and by April had mulled over the suggestions of Dan Sullivan, Virgil Peterson, and *Police Gazette* reporter Nat Perlow. Sensing final approval on his resolution by late April, the Senator from Tennessee kept in close contact with a number of New York law firms, particularly those of former Secretary of War Robert Patterson and Gen. William O. Donovan, with whom Kefauver's brother-in-law, Malcolm Fooshee, was associated. For chief counsel, Kefauver had in mind General Donovan himself; Boris Kostelanetz, who had prosecuted the 1943 movie extortion case and who had worked with Kefauver in the 1945 House investigation; Max H. Goldschein, counsel for the investigation in 1945 and more recently director of the special federal grand juries that were inquiring into organized crime; Thomas Murphy, the celebrated prosecutor of Alger Hiss; and young Rudolph Halley, who had served with the Truman Committee. Donovan expected to travel abroad, but he suggested an associate, Col. Francis Brick, whom Kefauver personally liked but did not consider because of his lack of experience with congressional committees. Kostelanetz also had planned a European trip, but he agreed to investigate international ties of American criminal figures. The Department of Justice wanted Goldschein to stay on with the Kansas City grand jury then in progress. Kefauver later claimed that the Justice Department and National Democratic Committee Chairman William Boyle recommended Murphy "very highly," but that he had vetoed the selection of Murphy, like that of Brick, because of his inexperience with

42. New York *Times,* October 27, 1967. "Wiley, Alexander," *Current Biography* (1947), 679–81. *Congressional Record,* June 15, 1951, pp. A3576–77. Judge Irving Kaufman to Wiley, May 4, 1951, Series 1, Box 3, Folder 5, Alexander Wiley Papers, State Historical Society, Madison, Wisconsin. Wiley to Kefauver, January 12, 1950; Wiley to Kefauver, February 22, 1950; Kefauver to Wiley, February 27, 1950; Kefauver to Wiley, March 3, 1950, Crime Box 37, Kefauver Papers. New York *Times,* May 28, 1950. Washington *Star,* May 28, 1950. Julius Cahn to Wiley, June 9, 1950, Series 7, Box 58, Folder 4, Wiley Papers.

congressional committees. After conferring with Ferdinand Pecora, celebrated counsel for the Banking Committee hearings of 1932, Kefauver decided on the "boy genius," Rudolph Halley.[43]

A shy, precocious youngster with a recurrent lisp, Halley zipped through Townsend Harris High School in New York and sought admission to Columbia Law School at the age of fourteen. After graduating fourth in his class in 1934, he joined the office of a U.S. District Court judge, studied the court technique for three years, and then joined the U.S. District Attorney's office in 1937. There he assisted Hugh Fulton in the dramatic prosecution of utility magnate Howard Hopson, followed Fulton to the Truman Committee, and after the war joined Fulton's law firm in Manhattan. Nephew of Broadway playwright Sam Shipman and protégé of Pecora, Halley quickly conceived of the Committee's field hearings as early acts of a play that would culminate in the exposure of a "Mr. Big"—the much-pilloried Costello—in a grand finale in New York. Halley gloried in the orchestration of witnesses and occasionally played upon friction within the Committee's staff to prompt extra effort—a habit that grievously pained Kefauver. Endorsed by the Chairman as an experienced congressional committee counsel, Halley won quick approval by the Committee as well as by party leaders.[44]

Senator Wiley, who had suggested the name of a Chicago Republican as the chief counsel, resolved to have as associate or minority counsel a man of his choosing—in this case, a second Chicago Republican, Nathaniel S. Ruvell. Jack Anderson, Drew Pearson's associate, and Senator Margaret Chase Smith of Maine, however, suggested George S. Robinson, an Air Force investigator and former Justice Department official

43. Sullivan to Kefauver, January 25, 1950; Nat Perlow to Kefauver, March 4, 10, 1950; Peterson to A. F. Lorenzen, April 3, 1950; Kefauver to Fooshee, May 8, 1950, all in Crime Box 2; Kefauver to John S. Knight, October 3, 1950; Fooshee to Kefauver, April 29, 1950; Kefauver to Donovan, May 15, 1950; Kefauver to Peyton Ford, May 13, 1950; telegram from Turney Gratz to Kefauver, May 12, 1950; Kefauver to Pecora, May 20, 1950, Crime Box 37, Kefauver Papers.

44. Lester Velie, "Rudolph Halley—How He Nailed America's Racketeers," *Collier's,* May 19, 1951, pp. 24–25, 78–79, 80, 82. Nellis interview. Kefauver to William Boyle, May 13, 1950, Crime Box 37, Kefauver Papers. Kefauver obtained special permission to pay his chief counsel up to $17,500 per year. *Congressional Record,* May 3, 1950, pp. 6262–63.

who had taken part in the inquiry into the Annenberg racing-news wire service. Tobey, impressed by Senator Smith's recommendation, strongly opposed Ruvell and insisted on Robinson. Kefauver personally liked Robinson but expressed his willingness to go along with the choice of the two Republican senators. Halley meantime had obtained inconclusive evidence from Virgil Peterson that linked Ruvell to a real estate transaction involving Ralph Capone. Robinson refused to accept a joint appointment with Ruvell and in effect began functioning as associate counsel without formal appointment. Wiley, back from a campaign swing, upbraided Robinson in a personal encounter, attacked Kefauver for his apparent indecision, and threatened drastic action, including resignation, should his candidate not receive proper consideration. Eventually, Wiley accepted Robinson's appointment although he occasionally sniped at the minority counsel, particularly over his role in the investigation in Chicago.[45]

Aside from the Halley and Robinson appointments, the filling of staff jobs created no special problems, and apparently little patronage pressure came from the Hill. As chief investigator, the Committee hired Harold G. Robinson, who had worked with Halley on the Truman Committee and more recently had directed investigations for the California Crime Commission. Through J. Russell Wiggins of the Washington *Post,* Kefauver met and hired as counsel Downey Rice, a former FBI agent whose training with the "pin register" technique of tracing telephone calls had been invaluable in a local Washington inquiry. Kefauver took on William Garrett, C.P.A. and attorney from General Donovan's New York law firm, to analyze subpoenaed records and accounts. Veteran committee investigators Henry Patrick Kiley and Jack Elich, along with public relations director Al Klein, a reporter from the Philadelphia *Record,* rounded out the original staff. In time this staff expanded to include race track investigator John M.

45. Personal interview, George S. Robinson, Vienna, Va., October 28, 1969. Tobey to Kefauver, May 19, 1950, Box 102, Tobey Papers. File memorandum from Peterson, June 22, June 29, 1950, File No. 65–50A, vol. 27, Chicago Crime Commission Records. Telegrams from Tobey to Wiley, Wiley to Julius Cahn, June 7, 1950; letter from Cahn to Wiley, June 9, 1950, Series 7, Box 58, Folder 4, Wiley Papers. Wiley to Kefauver, June 19, 1950; Wiley to Kefauver, June 23, 1950, Crime Box 37, Kefauver Papers. Unidentified news clipping, September 1, 1950, Wiley Scrapbook ?6, Wiley Papers.

McCormick, FBI agent Ralph Mills, reporter George Martin, and Washington attorney Joseph Nellis. In the field, crime commission officials, newspaper reporters, local policemen, as well as personnel of the Narcotics Bureau and Justice Department might assist the Committee's investigators either on a per-diem or loan basis. Kefauver and Halley's assignment of core staff members to pioneer city investigations led to considerable jostling among counsel, especially as television and radio began to pick up the stories and thrust Kefauver into the national limelight. Investigators not infrequently took their complaints directly to the Chairman rather than going through Halley, who increasingly concentrated his own energies on operations in New York. Infighting probably reached its peak in March of 1951 during the hearings in New York and pitted Halley, Klein, and Nellis against Rice, Martin, and others.[46]

The political atmosphere that engulfed the resolution for the creation of the committee did not lift with final approval by the Senate in May of 1950. Conceived in Kefauver's political ambitions and nourished in the shrill speculation of postwar crime reporters, the original proposal had been greeted by a sluggish and embarrassed Administration and an inept and peevish Senate leadership. Delay, attempted diversion, and the vicious maneuvering for control of the Committee by both parties had led to general skepticism of its intentions. Friends as well as the press warned Kefauver of public cynicism while at the same time they speculated on whether the chairmanship would make him a vice presidential or presidential candidate in 1952. Sensing the dangers from the outset but confident as perhaps only a novice could be, the Senator from Tennessee attempted to regain the initiative. Explaining that he intended to cooperate with existing agencies and to "avoid sensationalism at all times," he warned that, with Congress still in session and necessary background work to be done, some observers might be disappointed at his speed or even at the direction in which he moved. In short, he proposed to limit and direct the Committee and the press on an investigation of

46. Gladys M. Kammerer, *Congressional Committee Staffing Since 1946* (Lexington: University of Kentucky Press, 1951), pp. 51–52. Olney to Standley, May 16, 1950, Crime Commission Study Box, Standley Papers. Personal interview, Downey Rice, Washington, D.C., August 8, 1969. Staff summary sheet, Crime Box 37, Kefauver Papers. Nellis interview.

the newly discovered underworld; he would have publicity for himself and for his study and he would also have what the glib Wiley called "silent sleuthing." The determined young Senator would soon learn that the politics of crime were more easily analyzed than practiced.[47]

47. C. J. Gaskell to Kefauver, May 10, 1950; Manley W. Immell to Kefauver, May 11, 1950, Crime Box 2, Kefauver Papers. *Christian Science Monitor,* May 10, 1950. Washington *Daily News,* June 7, 1950. Chattanooga *Times,* May 8, 1950. Nashville *Tennessean,* May 19, 1950. Memphis *Commercial Appeal,* May 3, 1950. Typescript of Kefauver radio interview, Congressional Series no. 73, Labor's League for Political Education, May 26, 1950, Box 7, Hunt Papers. Washington *Post,* May 14, 1950.

4

The Wire Service Story

Continental Press Service is a giant monopoly whose slimy
tentacles reach into every metropolitan area in the country.
—J. E. Taylor, Attorney General of Missouri, 1951

The power of Congress to investigate, derived from English
parliamentary tradition and supposedly implied in the legislative function, has encountered intermittent but generally
fruitless challenge throughout American history. In the twentieth century, as the policy-making initiative gradually passed
from the Congress to the executive branch, congressional
investigations "in the grand manner," such as the Pujo Committee of 1911–1912, the Walsh Committee of the 1920s, the
Pecora investigation of 1932, the Nye Committee of 1934–1936,
and the Truman Committee of World War II days served as
dramatic reminders of the legislative branch's onetime dominant position in the federal structure. Generally, the tone of
congressional investigations reflected the degree of cooperation or hostility between the Administration and Congress;
hence, the New Deal benefited from the activities of the
Pecora and Black committees from 1932–1934 but experienced
increasing difficulty after 1938 with the Dies Committee and
to a lesser extent with Senator Truman's Committee. In the
80th, 81st, and 82d Congresses, an expanding number of committees and critics found fault with the Truman Administration. Among these were J. William Fulbright in his scrutiny of
the Reconstruction Finance Corporation, Senator Clyde Hoey
and his exposure of the "five-percenters," Joseph R. McCarthy
and the Republican attack on Communists in the State Department, and to a lesser extent, the Kefauver investigation of
organized crime. Headline-catching committee work helped
young and ambitious senators to circumvent the seniority sys-

tem and get their names before the public; not a few found ready-made targets in the Administration.[1]

Aside from their political and legislative utility, congressional committees increasingly assumed a broader informing or educational function for the public, a development that attracted Woodrow Wilson's attention in 1885. What has rarely been appreciated is that congressional committees were better dramatists than investigators, that the limited staff and training available, the political atmosphere in which committees worked, and the necessity of arriving at solutions rather than in-depth understanding of problems severely curtailed the amount of serious research a committee could pursue. For information and guidance, committees or independent senators depended upon lobbyists or other pressure groups. The Nye Committee relied upon pacifists like Dorothy Detzer; Walsh depended heavily upon reporters to expose the Harding scandals; the La Follette Committee looked to the National Labor Relations Board; and the maverick McCarthy depended upon an ill-chosen assortment of Hearst and McCormick reporters and the so-called "China Lobby." Investigating committees do little real investigating, but rather, they dramatize a particular perspective on a problem and place the prestige of a Senate body behind the chosen point of view.[2]

1. William E. Leuchtenburg, *Franklin D. Roosevelt and the New Deal, 1932–1940* (New York: Harper & Row, Publishers, 1963), pp. 59, 156, 280–81. Harry S. Truman, "Can We Lose the War in Washington," *American Magazine* (November 1942), 22–23, 104–6. Jules Abels, *The Truman Scandals* (Chicago: Henry Regnery Company, 1956), pp. 3–5, 43. The best analysis of the function of the congressional committee from a pro-Congress point of view is James Burnham, *Congress and the American Tradition* (Chicago: Henry Regnery Company, 1959), pp. 221–52. Also Telford Taylor, *Grand Inquest: The Story of Congressional Investigations* (New York: Simon & Schuster, Inc., 1955), and the more strident Alan Barth, *Government by Investigation* (New York: The Viking Press, Inc., 1955).

2. Woodrow Wilson, *Congressional Government: A Study in Politics* (Boston: Houghton Mifflin Company, 1885), p. 303. John E. Wiltz, *In Search of Peace: The Senate Munitions Inquiry, 1934–1936* (Baton Rouge: Louisiana State University Press, 1963), pp. 24, 47. "Letter from the Publisher," *Time*, April 9, 1951, p. 14. Jerold S. Auerbach, *Labor and Liberty: The La Follette Committee and the New Deal* (Indianapolis: The Bobbs-Merrill Co., Inc., 1966), pp. 81–84. Robert Griffith, *The Politics of Fear: Joseph R. McCarthy and the Senate* (Lexington: University of Kentucky Press, 1970), pp. 60–65. Taylor, *Grand Inquest*, p. 279.

The Kefauver Committee illustrated both the strengths and weaknesses of traditional committee investigations; the novelty of the subject and its explosive political possibilities, not its personnel or the quality of their performance, transformed its actions into a significant event in postwar American history. By accumulating evidence on an important but neglected aspect of American life it awakened the interest of both the public and law enforcement agencies to the problem of organized crime, but its antilegalization bias and its dependence on slanted sources resulted in misinformation and frustration.

*   *   *   *

Kefauver interpreted his sweeping mandate as a directive to survey the total structure of organized crime operating in interstate commerce and the corrupting influences that such activities had created in American politics. Basically, he was attempting to sketch a picture of the American underworld. Perhaps because this assignment was much broader than his original proposal, which was simply to study gambling and racketeering, perhaps because his committee had been born under a dark cloud and needed to prove itself quickly, and perhaps because the new chairman was relatively inexperienced at organizing an investigation of such scope, the Committee's first steps were hesitant. Although he almost certainly was convinced that national crime syndicates existed, Kefauver felt compelled to defend the statement by Attorney General McGrath and other officials that they had no evidence of such syndicates. By this action, he both improved his position with the Justice Department and staved off popular acceptance of any conclusion on national crime syndicates until his committee could complete its reports.[3]

3. Kefauver at first explained that unless federal statutes were violated the Justice Department would have no occasion to look into "national crime syndicates." Later he stressed that McGrath had actually said he knew of no "nationwide crime syndicate presided over by one czar." Kefauver observed that preliminary investigation from accounts in the press and reports of crime commissions led him to believe that there were several crime rings, some intertwined and some essentially separate. He denied being "too much concerned about finding some super-chief of rackets in the country." New York *Times,* April 18, 19, 1950. Kefauver radio interview, Labor's League for Political Education, May 26, 1950, Box 7, Hunt Papers.

Kefauver appeared especially indecisive over which problem to investigate first. Prior to creation of the special committee, the Senator from Tennessee had received nineteen requests for specific investigations. Lawyers of Oak Ridge, Tennessee, urged Kefauver to look into gangster-controlled gambling in the atomic plants, and the local Washington press suggested that the Committee scrutinize gambling and corruption in Baltimore and the District of Columbia; without much hesitation, Kefauver passed these requests on to local authorities in Tennessee and the House District Committee. The pro-Kefauver Nashville *Tennessean* recommended a look into a "Memphis baby racket," but the chief investigator backed off from what he feared would lead to an avalanche of "domestic relations complaints." Some suggested that the Committee look at the impact of "horror comics" on rising crime rates. Kefauver inquired into racketeering in the stock market in an executive session, but dropped the matter when little of substance developed. Before Kefauver left the chairmanship, he had placed on the agenda an investigation into collegiate and professional sports, but the press of time forced the Committee to leave this area relatively unexplored.

In February of 1950, syndicated columnist Victor Riesel began urging Kefauver to look into the "infiltration" of the "mobs" into labor unions and into "inter-plant gambling." One member of Kefauver's office staff, noting the "terrific labor following" the Senator might acquire from Riesel's twenty million readers, encouraged consideration of the columnist's suggestion. The Memphis *Commercial Appeal* also endorsed the idea of a labor investigation, and Kefauver himself, despairing of action by the Justice Department and the FBI, mentioned to Halley the possibility of looking into the attempted assassinations of labor leaders Victor and Walter Reuther. Aside from two days of hearings in Detroit in February of 1951 and an incidental recommendation to the Interstate Commerce Commission, however, the Committee stayed out of the labor–management field.[4]

4. *Congressional Record,* May 2, 1950, pp. 6158–59. Washington *Post,* May 28, June 9, 1950. Kefauver to Mrs. Dolly Keleher, June 9, 1950; Kefauver to Downey Rice, December 14, 1950; Kefauver to Coleman Harwell, October 3, 1950, Crime Box 2; memorandum from H. G. Robinson to Kefauver, October 3, 1950, Crime Box 37; Ellen Walpole to Kefauver, May 25, 1950; memorandum from Halley to Kefauver; telegram from H. L. Wallace to Kefauver, March 10, 1950, Crime Box 1;

On May 2, while Kefauver mulled over the various suggestions and sweated through final approval of his resolutions by the Senate, District Attorney Frank Hogan seized upon Frank Erickson's admissions of bookmaking before the McFarland Subcommittee and raided the gambler's offices in New York. Although he feared that Hogan might steal his thunder, Kefauver complimented the District Attorney on the success of his raid. At the same time, however, he restated that his own study would necessarily be delayed until he assembled an expert staff, collected reliable data, and explored early leads in executive session. The Committee briefly considered abandoning the investigation of gambling to McFarland and Hogan and focusing its attention on the narcotics traffic and its corrupting influences.[5]

Kefauver returned to his original interest in gambling just as the McFarland Subcommittee hearings ended. Essentially, the Chairman decided to explore the existence of national crime syndicates by further study of the racing-news wire services and by examination of the increase of wealth in the hands of known criminals. The groundwork for the wire service investigation had been laid by the Federal Communications Commission Report of 1944, by the Peterson–Sullivan crime commission axis, by the California Crime Commission reports, and by the McFarland Subcommittee. Kefauver explained that he singled out gambling because the activity sup-

Carlile Bolton-Smith to Kefauver, April 30, 1951; Kefauver to Bolton-Smith, May 15, 1951; Paul R. Rowan to Kefauver, June 22, 1950, Crime Box 2; typed Kefauver statement, December 20, 1954, Crime and Corruption Box 1; Victor Riesel to Kefauver, February 1, 1950; Kefauver to Riesel, February 7, Crime Box 2; office memorandum from Henry P. Kiley [?] to Kefauver, March 3, 1950, Crime Box 37; Riesel to Kefauver, April 4; Kefauver to Riesel, April 14, 1950, Crime Box 1; memorandum from Kefauver to Halley, August 11, 1950, Crime Box 2, Kefauver Papers. Memphis *Commercial Appeal,* May 19, 1950. Crime *Hearings,* Pt. 9. *Third Interim Report,* p. 19. The "baby racket" and "horror comics" suggestions were later treated by Kefauver as chairman of the Senate Judiciary Subcommittee on Juvenile Delinquency in 1955–1956, and the McClellan Committee began a study of labor and management racketeering in 1957. Jack Anderson and Fred Blumenthal, *The Kefauver Story* (New York: The Dial Press, 1956), pp. 158–63. John L. McClellan, *Crime Without Punishment* (New York: Popular Library, 1963), p. 25.

5. New York *Times,* May 3, 12, 1950. Kefauver radio statement, Labor's League for Political Education, May 26, 1950, Box 7, Hunt Papers. Crime *Hearings,* Pt. 14, p. 146.

plied substantial money for corruption and that the absence of federal laws in the gambling field, unlike that of narcotics, counterfeiting, or white slavery, made it the most urgent task. More readily available data existed on gambling (the estimated "take" being between $15 billion and $28 billion), and greater public interest and lobbying pressure could be mobilized for its study. The Senator logically concluded that such an investigation had the most promise, both substantively and politically.[6]

While Kefauver and his staff pored over seemingly endless testimony and records on the underworld structure as reflected in the racing-news wire services, the Committee neither inquired into the social and economic causes of crime nor considered the advisability of legalizing gambling. Although the senators heard the testimony of Virgil Peterson, James V. Bennett, Director of the Bureau of Prisons, and a number of medical doctors at the Public Health Hospital in Lexington, not one academic expert, sociologist, or criminologist appeared among the thousand-odd witnesses called in hearings covering fifteen months of testimony. Instead, the Committee relied for its information on law enforcement officers, crime commission officials, local politicians, and alleged criminals. Interpreting crime simply as a violation of a law, the Committee saw the underworld as an alien, corrupting, atavistic, conspiratorial group, a view that strongly suggested that individuals became part of it, not through environmental circumstances, but through personal choice. Senator Hunt concluded that crime was rampant "because the human heart is despicable and wicked in all things in its normal state"; Senator Tobey increasingly shouted for "righteous indignation" as the only cure of the nation's crime.[7]

Possibly inspired by Bennett's suggestion for a series of specialized studies, Kefauver early in July requested the Ameri-

6. Washington *Post,* May 7, 1950. Chicago *Daily Tribune,* May 23, 1950. Kefauver speech before the American Bar Association, September 19, 1950, *Congressional Record,* September 19, 1950, pp. A6686–88. New York *Times,* July 30, 1950. Memphis *Commercial Appeal,* June 11, 1950.

7. H. H. Wilson, "Pressure to Buy and Corrupt," *The Nation,* July 21, 1951, pp. 45–48. By contrast, the Wickersham Commission as well as the Copeland "Rackets" Committee relied heavily on expert or academic opinion. National Commission on Law Observation and Enforcement, *Reports,* pp. 1–14; "Rackets" *Hearings,* Pts. 1–7.

can Bar Association to sponsor research projects. The research would explore ways to update and modernize criminal law procedures and curtail the growing movement of attorneys away from practice in criminal law. The outgoing president of the association, Harold J. Gallagher, prevailed upon former Secretary of War Robert Patterson to head up a commission on organized crime to cooperate with Kefauver. Although the Patterson group drafted a few model statutes and although its executive director, New York Judge Morris Ploscowe, a reputable scholar who had worked with the Wickersham Commission, actually helped write the Kefauver Committee's reports, no significant social study came from the A.B.A. Commission. Instead, the Patterson Commission served primarily as a pro-Kefauver lobby that approved Kefauver's recommendations and conclusions and occasionally requested Congress to renew funds or extend the life of the Special Committee.[8]

More damning than the absence of academic testimony were the assumptions the Committee brought to the gambling problem. With the exception of William O'Dwyer, the senators called no prolegalization spokesman, but they listened respectfully to Peterson and depended upon his group and other citizens' crime commissions for data and advice. Kefauver attempted to argue that material produced in a one-day hearing at Las Vegas and in other scattered sessions documented Peterson's contention that legalization only gave respectability to hoodlum elements and neither drove them out of business nor yielded substantial revenues. Nevada had had difficulty, of course, with its gambling establishment in the flush days of the late 1940s, but so had states where gambling was illegal; in any event, Nevada was such an atypical state that conclusions based on its experience one way or another were far from convincing. While Senator Hunt argued that gamblers were essentially gangsters, that "large gamblers frequently are the scum of the earth," Kefauver noted that he opposed gambling not for moral but for economic reasons.

8. Kefauver to Harold J. Gallagher, July 10; Gallagher to Patterson, August 10; telegram from Kefauver to Patterson, September 22; Patterson to Kefauver, October 20; Howard L. Barkdull to Patterson, November 3, 1950, Box 28, Robert P. Patterson Papers, Library of Congress. Kefauver thought the creation of the A.B.A. Commission "the most important backing the Committee" had received up to November of 1950. Washington *Post,* October 28, 1950.

"Syndicate" control, he explained, meant that one party to the bet was not really gambling and that criminal groups were draining away immense profits, which then financed corruption or infiltration of legitimate business. The Committee's chairman readily admitted his reliance upon Peterson for answers to all prolegalization arguments. In fact, he had devoured Peterson's pamphlet on legalized gambling and was urgently requesting the galleys on the book edition in late 1950. The Peterson thesis was on its way to Senate approval.[9]

*   *   *   *

To document their conclusions, the Committee called upon a variety of government agencies, both federal and local. In addition to materials from the Narcotics Bureau, the Committee sought information from the Department of Justice and the Internal Revenue Bureau—the latter in order to trace the accumulation of wealth and financial transactions among underworld figures. In late May Kefauver first suggested obtaining access to IRB reports, investigative data, and returns—all generally considered confidential. Although the Justice Department seemed reluctant for the President to issue executive orders opening the material to the Kefauver Committee, White House Counsel Charles S. Murphy reminded the Chief Executive that Roosevelt had opened such files to the Truman Committee, that no obvious harm would result from the Committee's inspection, and that "for psychological reasons" the Administration should cooperate with Kefauver. Justice sought a written agreement between itself, Treasury, and the

9. *Third Interim Report,* pp. 192–95. Estes Kefauver, *Crime in America* (Garden City, N.Y.: Doubleday & Company, Inc., 1951), pp. 124–29. Hunt to D. G. Robeson, March 23, 1951, Box 7, Hunt Papers. Kefauver to David B. Parke, May 1, 1951, Crime Box 2; Kefauver to Robert E. Merriam, October 31, 1951, Crime Box 3; Kefauver to Peterson, October 9, 1950; Peterson to Kefauver, October 12, 1950; Kefauver to Peterson, October 16, 1950; Kefauver to Irwin R. Tucker, October 16, 1950, Crime Box 5, Kefauver Papers. The Committee explained that the recent conclusions of the British Royal Commission on Betting, Lotteries, and Gaming, which had found no great problem with off-track betting in England, were not appropriate to the problem in the United States due to the difference in size of the gambling turnover in the two countries and to the historic influence of gangsters in American gambling. *Third Interim Report,* pp. 192–95.

Kefauver Committee that access should not impair investigations or prosecutions in process and succeeded in persuading
Truman to delete a clause that would open extensive personnel files to the Committee. Information that emanated from
the Internal Revenue Bureau was generally to be held confidential, but portions that were deemed appropriate could be
submitted to the Senate. On June 1, Halley, Kefauver, and
other members of the Committee called upon the President
and obtained promise that tax data, immigration and naturalization records, and summaries of FBI reports would be made
available to them. Truman, in addition, promised the general
cooperation of all executive departments. Kefauver boasted
that he had received everything the Committee asked for, and
Republican Tobey agreed that the President had given the
Committee 100-per-cent support.[10]

   The IRB materials in particular were essential to the investigation, although bureaucratic difficulty in locating requested files occasionally frustrated the staff. Early speculation that the Committee would use Immigration and
Naturalization records to explore operations by the Black
Hand and Mafia or possibly to enter the controversy over Costello's deportation was not valid. On the wire service, the Committee received galleys of the McFarland hearings as well as
an extensive list of wire "drops"—mostly bookie joints—that
the Commerce subcommittee had compiled. Upon Kefauver's
request the Federal Communications Commission ordered
telephone companies and Western Union to hold, rather than
destroy, records of toll charges. These records, which stated
the time, number called, and names of persons in person-to-
person calls, might reveal underworld patterns. Chief Investigator Harold G. Robinson, formerly with the California
Crime Commission, had used these data to harass bookie operations when the state ordered suspension of service to Conti-

   10. Memorandum from Charles S. Murphy to Truman, May 29, 1950;
Acting Attorney General Peyton Ford to Truman, June 16; Truman to
"Heads of All Executive Departments and Agencies," June 17, 1950,
OF, Truman Papers. Washington *Post,* June 2, 1950. The appropriate
executive orders were issued on June 17 and are reprinted in Crime
Hearings, Pt. 2, pp. 2–5. The fear of having prosecutions interrupted
had possibly been prompted by a teapot-size tempest between Mayor
Bowron and the Treasury Department, which accused the Mayor of
damaging a California prosecution. The order on secrecy about tax
information was so loosely drawn as to be essentially useless. See
Attorney General's Conference on Organized Crime, p. 54.

nental Press. Attorney General McGrath's compilation of material from the ninety-three U.S. Attorneys on national crime syndicates and the one hundred fifty so-called "king-pins of crime" had attracted Kefauver's attention in early May. He had obtained a promise of access to the material then, but delays by the Justice Department in collecting and interpreting the information postponed actual examination of the data by the Kefauver Committee until late September. Meanwhile, in July, McGrath had ordered the U.S. Attorneys to cooperate with Kefauver.[11]

At the same time Kefauver solicited leads from state attorneys general, sheriffs, prosecuting attorneys, and mayors. Both Halley and Kefauver gained access to Hogan's voluminous files as well as to those of Brooklyn's District Attorney Miles McDonald and other prosecutors and grand juries around the country. Upon arriving in an area, investigators as a practice approached local newspaper editors and crime reporters, solicited intelligence, and in exchange for temporary secrecy promised complete details when the results of the Committee's investigation became public. Kefauver meanwhile cultivated such widely read columnists and investigative reporters as Drew Pearson and Lester Velie, tried to coordinate his investigation with the sixteen-member newspaper syndicate that was organized in early 1950, and sought out and attempted to pick the brains of recognized crime reporters such as Mac Lowery of the Miami *Daily News,* Ray Brennan

11. Kefauver to Commissioner George J. Schoeneman, June 5, 1950, Crime Box 2, Kefauver Papers. Rice interview. Washington *Post,* June 13, 1950. Kefauver to Edwin Johnson, June 7, 1950, Crime Box 2, Kefauver Papers. "Transmission of Gambling Information," Senate Commerce *Hearings,* pp. 835–69. Kefauver to Wayne Coy, May 15, June 1, 1950, Crime Box 37, Kefauver Papers. Washington *Post,* May 24, 9, 1950. McGrath to Kefauver, June 20, 1950, McGrath Papers. James M. McInerney to Kefauver, September 21, 1950, Crime Box 2; Kefauver Press Release, September 27, 1950, Crime Box 37, Kefauver Papers. McGrath speech before American Bar Association, September 19, 1950, in *Congressional Record,* September 19, 1950, pp. A6679–80. The Federal Communications Commission's study of Continental Press, made in 1943–1944, which had been available to the McFarland Subcommittee, was also at the Kefauver Committee's disposal. Kefauver experienced difficulty in obtaining access to a 1948 study of Continental and allied organizations completed by the security-conscious, self-contained FBI. Kefauver to J. Edgar Hoover, July 11, 1950, Crime Box 37; Kefauver to Peyton Ford, August 14, 1950, Crime Box 2, Kefauver Papers.

of the Chicago *Sun-Times,* Ted Link of the St. Louis *Post-Dispatch,* and Gene Lowall of the Denver *Post.*[12]

Kefauver's courtships of Nat Perlow of the *Police Gazette* and the erratic Lee Mortimer were less rewarding. Perlow, in communication with Kefauver since early February of 1950, had encouraged the Senator during the struggle to win final approval of his resolution, had advised him on the hiring of staff, and had put him in contact with gambling expert John Scarne. In the midst of the Republicans' charges that the Committee would whitewash crime in Kansas City, Perlow supplied Kefauver with the welcome news that the Pendergast machine at the moment opposed the gambling interests, and Kefauver came increasingly to rely on Perlow for insights into the Kansas City story. The Senator at times telegraphed for Perlow's advice and information and came to consider the reporter a personal friend. At the same time, however, Perlow's presence in Kansas City and his attempts to speak publicly for the Committee brought no little embarrassment to the Chairman.[13]

The Senator's friendship with Mortimer proved to be disastrous. Although Mortimer claimed that Kefauver sought him out after reading *Chicago Confidential,* the evidence suggests that the attraction from the beginning was mutual; certainly the author was not offended by Kefauver's lavish compliments. Mortimer declined to put into writing the documentation for his sensational charges, but he expanded the Senator's requests for information into personal meetings and after-dinner conversations. Kefauver the rustic found Mortimer a

12. St. Louis *Globe-Democrat,* October 1, 1950. Washington *Post,* May 1, 9, 23, 25, 1950. Rice interview. Kefauver to Drew Pearson, June 14, 1950; telegram from Kefauver to Henrietta O'Donaghue, June 19, 1950, Crime Box 2; undated clipping from New York *Mirror* [?] in Kefauver Scrapbook IV; Kefauver to Dan Mahoney, Publisher, Miami *Daily News,* April 22, 1950, Crime Box 1; Kefauver to Marshall Field, June 8, 1950, Crime Box 2, Kefauver Papers; "Link Discloses Perils Faced in Crime Reporting," *Editor & Publisher,* April 28, 1951, p. 136. Kefauver to Benjamin H. Reese, May 22, 1950; Gene Lowall to Kefauver, April 3, 1950; telegram from Kefauver to Palmer Hoyt, May 20, 1950; Kefauver to Lowall, May 31, 1950, Crime Box 2; Kefauver to Hoyt, May 15, 1950, Crime Box 37, Kefauver Papers.

13. Telegram from Perlow to Kefauver, February 18, 1950; Kefauver to Perlow, February 25, 1950; Perlow to Kefauver, February 27, 28, March 10, April 12, 13, 14, 1950; Kefauver to H. H. Roswell, May 20, June 30, July 12, 1950, Crime Box 2; Kefauver to Constantine Soloyanis, December 4, 1950, Crime Box 1, Kefauver Papers.

fascinating source of gossip, and he flattered him on the floor of the Senate, in book ads, and in a testimonial to publisher William Randolph Hearst. Mortimer at first recommended former Chicago policemen William Drury and Thomas Connelly as investigators for the Committee, then sought a place for himself on the staff. When Halley expressed vehement opposition to Mortimer, Kefauver was forced to explain to the journalist that his appointment might lead other newspapermen to insist on Committee assignments. Although Kefauver offered to acknowledge Mortimer's aid in the hearings, the relationship soon cooled as Mortimer asserted that he had discovered in Halley's background a link with—in his terms—a gangster-dominated railroad. Eventually, Mortimer became one of the bitterest critics of the Committee, writing acid judgments of Kefauver, Tobey, and O'Conor as well as of Halley, and, of course, selling more books. Kefauver, although stung by these attacks, passed them off as the opinions of a man who was still a "nice guy at heart."[14]

With the possible exception of the press, the citizens' crime commissions continued to be Kefauver's greatest outside help, and, quite understandably, the Senator recommended creation of similar groups throughout the country. Sullivan and his powerful press and radio allies in Miami had been in contact with Kefauver for months prior to the Committee's creation, and they maintained a spirited correspondence, supplying the senators specific data, suggesting lines of inquiries, and in some instances helping directly in pursuing leads, correlating and summarizing information, and planning the

14. Jack Lait and Lee Mortimer, *U.S.A. Confidential* (New York: Crown Publishers, Inc., 1952), p. 253. Mortimer to Kefauver, March 7; Kefauver to Mortimer, March 7; telegram from Kefauver to Lait and Mortimer, March 17; Mortimer to Kefauver, March 29; Kefauver to William R. Hearst, May 23; Mortimer to Kefauver, March 9, 1950, Crime Box 2; memorandums from Kefauver to Halley, July 12, 22; telegram from Kefauver to Mortimer, July 29, 1950; telephone interview, Julius N. Cahn, Washington, D.C., October 26, 1969; Mortimer to Kefauver, July 12, August 11, 1950, Crime Box 37, Kefauver Papers. Lait and Mortimer, *U.S.A. Confidential,* pp. 298, 253–63, 100–106, 360–365. Ellen Walpole to Kefauver, February 11, 1951, "Crime in America" Box, Kefauver Papers. Mortimer's sales were not hurt by a $500,000 libel suit filed against him in early 1950 by Frank Costello or by a beating administered him by unidentified assailants in the washroom of a Trenton, New Jersey, night club. New York *Daily Mirror,* May 18, 25, 1950.

hearings. When Sullivan opened his files to Kefauver, the
Senator's staff virtually denuded the Director's scrapbooks. As
a private group, the Crime Commission had no subpoena
power, but Sullivan and his men helped serve the Committee's
subpoenas and examine materials located by the subpoenas.
In one case when the Committee subpoenaed the records of
Continental Press, Sullivan flew to Chicago for the hearings
and prepared for Halley and Kefauver a complete summary of
the documents. The Crime Commission of Greater Miami considered itself the champion of a besieged antigambling public
in southern Florida, and not surprisingly the Kefauver Committee took on this coloration as well.[15]

Virgil Peterson and his staff provided similar material and
leg work in Chicago as well as the overview of the American
underworld that the Committee adopted. As soon as Chief
Counsel Halley took on his assignment, he approached Peterson with a request for access to the Chicago Crime Commission's records and confirmed plans already in progress for the
operating director to testify before the Kefauver Committee.
Carl Chatters of the American Municipal Association reassured Peterson that he could look forward to "complete cooperation from the Committee," and Halley expressed a desire
to work "even closer ... in the future" with the Chicago Crime
Commission. Peterson spent almost two days dazzling the
senators with his command of the subject, and at the request
of the Committee's staff, he suggested names of people to be
subpoenaed for the Chicago hearings and assigned some of his
men to serving a large number of them for the Committee.
Associate Counsel George Robinson, who headed the investigation in Chicago, temporarily set up his office in the Chicago
Crime Commission's headquarters, examined the Commis-

15. Washington *Post,* May 30, 1950. Sullivan to Kefauver, February
28, 1950; Sullivan to Halley, September 8, 1950, Crime Box 2; Sullivan
to Kefauver, May 3, 1950, Crime Box 3; Sullivan to H. G. Robinson,
September 13, 15, 1950; Sullivan to Halley, September 14, 23, 1950;
Downey Rice to Henry P. Kiley, August 7, 1957, Crime Box 5, Kefauver
Papers. Miami *Herald,* December 1, 1950. Sullivan to author, November 25, 1969. Sullivan to Halley, December 16, 1950; Sullivan to Kefauver, December 16, 1950, Crime Box 5, Kefauver Papers. Kefauver
respected Sullivan very highly and apparently considered him for the
position of chief investigator for the Committee. H. G. Robinson of the
California Crime Commission was selected for the position. Sullivan
to Kefauver, May 1, 1950; Kefauver to Sullivan, May 29, 1950, Crime
Box 37, Kefauver Papers.

sion's materials at Peterson's elbow, and before leaving allowed Peterson's staff to duplicate any material they desired
in the Committee's files. Peterson, who carefully guarded his
group's independence by refusing remuneration for any services rendered the Committee, forwarded leads and reminders to the Committee's staff and enjoyed immense respect
within Committee circles both for his personal modesty and
unquestioned competence. In a certain sense, the investigation was more the work of Peterson and Sullivan than of Kefauver.[16]

* * * *

Although Kefauver had initially intended to question New
York witnesses first, Hogan's raid on Erickson's Park Avenue
office at once lessened the dramatic effect of a debut in New
York and opened up new avenues of investigation to the south.
Halley caught the significance of Hogan's seizure of Erickson's documents and hurried to the District Attorney's office,
where he was shown evidence linking the New York lay-off
man to gambling establishments in Florida. After quietly de-
ploying Counsel Downey Rice to prepare for hearings in
Florida, Halley, Kefauver, and Hunt suddenly descended on
Miami as soon as Hogan had presented his case to a New York
grand jury. Although most of the gambling figures temporarily escaped service of the Committee's subpoenas, sizable
quantities of gambling records were seized and gambling

16. Washington *Star,* May 16, 1950. New York *Times,* July 3, 1950.
Memorandum from Dan Hanks to Peterson, May 11; Carl Chatters to
Halley, June 9; Halley to Peterson, June 17; Peterson to H. G. Robinson,
July 28; Halley to Peterson, July 29, August 11; Peterson to Halley,
August 4; Peterson to George S. Robinson, October 18, 25, 1950, File No.
65–50A; George S. Robinson to Peterson, April 11; Peterson to George
S. Robinson, April 17, 1951, File No. 17252, Chicago Crime Commis-
sion Records. Crime *Hearings,* Pt. 2, pp. 125–213. New York *Times,*
July 13, 1950. George S. Robinson and Peterson interviews. Peterson to
George S. Robinson, November 1, 1950, Crime Box 5, Kefauver Papers.
In the midst of the Chicago investigation, a reporter for the *Daily
Tribune* slanted a Kefauver statement in such a way that Peterson
might have taken offense, but a quick explanation by Kefauver
smoothed over any possible hostility. Chicago *Daily Tribune,* Septem-
ber 8, 1950. Peterson to Kefauver, September 14, 1950, Crime Box 5,
Kefauver Papers.

bookkeepers and accountants were subpoenaed. Rather melo-
dramatically, the Committee held two days of executive hearings in the Federal Building after investigators had checked
the entire floor for possible eavesdroppers. Most noteworthy of
the Committee's finds was a batch of canceled checks from
John O'Rourke, alleged Erickson partner in the Boca Raton
Club, to Los Angeles gambler Mickey Cohen. Although the
O'Rourke–Cohen dealings had been revealed a year previously by the Miami *Daily News,* the uncovering of checks
totaling $75,000 reportedly stunned O'Rourke. Elsewhere, the
Committee uncovered evidence of police protection of gambling in South Florida—a discovery they could hardly have
avoided. Having dramatically opened its inquiry while maintaining its image of working quietly, the senators and Halley
departed as quickly as they came, leaving Rice and four other
former FBI agents to conduct a follow-up study. Newspaperman Lee Hills congratulated Kefauver on the "shock treatment" administered "every top hoodlum in the U.S. through
the technique of secret hearings in a public place."[17]

While Rice continued the inquiry in Miami and additional
Kefauver investigators began to explore crime conditions in
other cities, the Committee members were tied down in Washington as election-year work and the outbreak of the Korean
conflict delayed the congressional recess. Kefauver bore the
brunt of preelection out-of-town hearings, including closed
sessions in St. Louis on July 18, Kansas City on July 19–20,
Chicago on October 5–7 and 17–19, New York on October 11–
12, and Philadelphia on October 13–14 and open hearings in
Kansas City on September 28–30. Meanwhile, a number of the
hearings were scheduled in Washington and heard representatives of federal agencies such as Anslinger of the Narcotics Bureau, Bennett of the Bureau of Prisons, and Wayne Coy
of the Federal Communications Commission. On July 6–7 Virgil Peterson impressed the Committee with his overview of a
"loose arrangement" among the nation's major crime syndicates.[18]

17. Washington *Star,* May 21, 1950. Lester Velie, "Rudolph Halley—
How He Nailed America's Racketeers," *Collier's,* May 19, 1951, pp.
79–80. Washington *Star,* May 27, 28, 1950. Washington *Post,* June 1, 5,
1950. Hills to Kefauver, n.d., Crime Box 2, Kefauver Papers.
18. Crime *Hearings,* Pt. 4-A, pp. 67–522; Pt. 5, pp. 111–848; Pt. 7, pp.
35–242; Pt. 11, pp. 1–224; Pt. 4, pp. 35–409; Pt. 2, pp. 88–96, 104–5, 49–64,
4–31, 125–213. New York *Times,* July 13, 1950.

Peterson first carefully catalogued the members of the two "major criminal gangs"—labeling the gangs as those of Capone and Costello while pointing out that such a categorization was an "oversimplification of the problem." Second, he demonstrated beyond question that most of the men in his "Crooks' Peerage" had intertwined legitimate and/or illegitimate links, many of them in gambling enterprises in Florida. For example, seized books belonging to West Coast gangsters contained names, addresses, and telephone numbers of important underworld figures in Chicago and Miami or on the East Coast. Peterson emphasized evidence of an occasional business transaction between Joe Adonis or Meyer Lansky, in the Costello group, with a Capone gangster in Chicago. From this web of associations, the witness claimed, he had proved the existence and operation of a nationwide pattern of racketeering and gambling. Far more questionable than Peterson's conclusions that organized crime was an interstate problem were his assumptions about the underworld structure itself. First, his testimony underscored the old American belief that crime was something set apart, that there was no honor among thieves, that there indeed existed a distinct group of men so totally depraved and so completely hostile to societal values that one could label them an *underworld.* From these assumptions Peterson concluded that the gangsters' involvements in such marginal enterprises as gambling or such totally legitimate enterprises as resort hotels represented the "infiltration" of the upperworld by the lower. That investment in legitimate businesses might represent a normal drive for profit and respectability, a motive many gambling figures shared with the solid middle class, did not influence his thinking. Perhaps Peterson's assumption also contributed to his view of a national criminal network composed of conspiratorial "syndicates" or "mobs" (such as the Capone syndicate among Chicago figures, the Costello group in the New York–New Jersey area, the Cleveland syndicate, the Detroit group headed by Mert Wertheimer, or the Minneapolis gang of Isadore "Kid Cann" Blumenfield) rather than individual entrepreneurs or partnerships that frequently maintained contact with others engaged in similar businesses in different areas of the country. While the Cleveland group, composed of about six Jewish figures with long-standing associations, might properly be called a syndicate, it would be more difficult to establish that the forty-odd men in the Chicago area constituted a single syndicate, with all the internal discipline such a term suggested. Certainly Peterson's description of a Costello syndicate—except in the very loosest sense of the word—was an oversimplification. In all probability, the structure of Peterson's underworld was less regimented and less conspiratorial than his testimony would suggest.[19]

If Peterson reflected the older law enforcement definition of crime, he also reflected an older attitude toward the solution. Not extensive experimentation with change in the legal structure and certainly not thoroughgoing review of what activities should be legalized or illegalized, but rather the insistent pressure of public opinion, aware of the economic consequences of wide-open gambling, represented the only effective control. Civic groups, such as his own Chicago Crime Commission, could enlighten the public as to the existence of the problem and could stimulate citizen participation in good government. "If the people actually want it [good law enforcement], want it sincerely instead of lip service, they will get it on the local level." Lincoln Steffens, in describing politicians as "political merchants," would hardly have put it differently.[20]

Whatever the shortcomings of Peterson's analysis, it was the result of long and sincere study. Press accounts to the contrary notwithstanding, Peterson had steered clear of the quagmire debate about a Mafia and had not capped his regional syndicates with a Mafia overlordship. He did make occasional references to the "alleged Mafia" connections of sundry gamblers, but these did not figure prominently in his final analysis. The major tragedy concerning Peterson's testimony was the fact that it underwent extensive exaggeration and distortion by the press before it reached the public—a process that Peterson did not effectively oppose.[21]

Peterson's testimony became the centerpiece for the entire investigation of the wire service. In successive visits to Miami,

19. Peterson testimony, Crime *Hearings,* Pt. 2, pp. 127, 159, 160, 162, 170–72, 175–78, 133–55.

20. Crime *Hearings,* Pt. 2, pp. 202–3. Lincoln Steffens, *The Shame of the Cities* (New York: Hill & Wang, 1969), p. 5.

21. Crime *Hearings,* Pt. 2, pp. 132, 162, 174, 188. Even the New York *Times* wildly exaggerated Peterson's actual statements on the Mafia. See Harold Hinton's special article, New York *Times,* July 30, 1950. Peterson later recalled that his designation of Costello as "the most influential underworld leader in America" led to unsubstantiated and unintended conclusions. Peterson interview.

Kansas City, St. Louis, New Orleans, Las Vegas, California, Chicago, and Cleveland, the senators used local stories about the wire service to demonstrate the close affiliation of the underworld figures Peterson had mentioned and to show how immense gambling profits made possible by the wire service led to struggles for national monopolies and to extensive corruption of local officials.

Nowhere was the Peterson thesis better illustrated than in South Florida, where Dan Sullivan and his Miami Crime Commission helped Kefauver's counsel to organize the open hearings of July 13–15.[22] Pointing to a series of charts and diagrams, the operating director explained the gambling, racing, night-club, and hotel and real estate investments of Erickson, Meyer and Jake Lansky, Adonis, Vincent Alo, Mert Wertheimer, as well as various members of the Cleveland and Chicago syndicates.

With increasing frequency since the 1930s, underworld figures from throughout the nation met in Florida hotels and night clubs, relaxed in the balmy tropical sun, occasionally entered into joint investments, and made of the Miami area what Sullivan feared was the headquarters of an interlocking gangster directorship. Sullivan stated, moreover, that the same figures reaped immense profits from a wide variety of local gambling establishments, including casino and table games in Broward County to the north of Miami and bookie operations on horse and dog racing throughout the area. The legal parimutuel betting system, engorged by the ready cash of free-spending postwar vacationers, had stimulated an unprecedented boom in illegal off-track bookmaking that apparently reached its peak by 1946–1948 and then began leveling off. According to testimony developed at the Miami hearings, outside figures such as Erickson conducted extensive bookmaking activities out of the Wofford Hotel and the Boulevard Hotel but experienced difficulty cutting themselves in to competing local bookie operations, which were protected by local political and police contacts. Among the larger independent operations were those of Raymond Craig in Miami and the S. & G. Syndicate in Miami Beach.[23]

22. Sullivan testimony, Crime *Hearings,* Pt. 1, pp. 152–74.

23. Crime *Hearings,* Pt. 1, p. 511. "Interim Report on Investigations in Florida and Preliminary General Conclusions," *Senate Report No. 2370,* 81st Cong., 2d sess. (1950), pp. 2–3. Cited hereafter as *Florida Interim Report.*

"I'll BET We Find Something Here"
Washington *Evening Star,* May 27, 1950. Courtesy, The Washington
(D.C.) Star-News

The S. & G. Syndicate had been formed in 1944 by five local, previously independent, bookmakers who agreed to finance several hundred other local bookies, supply them with wire service and "hot" information from tracks around the country, and, of course, systematize the purchase of protection. Close business contacts between one of the S. & G. members and Miami Beach's City Councilman William Burbridge helped to cement the syndicate's hold on the local police. In 1947 Erickson, backing O'Rourke, obtained the gambling concessions at the Boca Raton Club and the Roney Plaza Hotel, both of which had previously been held by the S. & G. Meyer Schine, owner of the Roney Plaza, had been warned by Pat Perdue, the Miami Beach police "one-man vice squad," that the concession should go to an S. & G. affiliate rather than to Erickson. After operations had started under the Erickson franchise, Perdue dramatically raided the Roney Plaza operation and closed it for the remainder of the season. An S. & G. bookie, however, operated out of the hotel the following season.[24]

The Committee held that the Capone syndicate had stronger weapons against S. & G. than did Erickson. In what may have been its most important case, the Kefauver group argued that Capone gangsters in early 1949 had "muscled" into the lush $26,500,000 operations of S. & G. through Harry V. Russell, purportedly a front for the Capone syndicate. Supposedly, political contacts with Governor Fuller Warren had been the first weapon employed. On the basis of a 300-page document compiled by Virgil Peterson and former FBI agent Jim Birthright, Rice, Halley, and Dan Sullivan became convinced that William H. Johnson, part owner of five horse and dog tracks in Chicago and Florida, was himself a front for the Capone syndicate. The Committee found particularly damning the fact that Johnson was associated in some of these enterprises with John Patton, former "boy mayor" of the Capone-dominated Chicago suburb of Burnham. Johnson vehemently denied the charge that he fronted for the Chicago underworld; he attempted to explain that his original track investment had been his own; he argued that, even if Patton and certain track employees had had a "few skeletons in their closets" twenty-

24. *Third Interim Report,* pp. 31–33. Crime *Hearings,* Pt. 1, p. 561. Harold Salvay, the S. & G. member linked with Burbridge, explained that he had known the city commissioner for many years and had admired him for his fight against the Ku Klux Klan in Jacksonville. The S. & G. group, as well as Harry Russell, were Jewish. Ibid., p. 581.

five or thirty years earlier, he had always known them as
respected or reformed citizens; and he observed that, since he
had met thousands of people in his work, a casual meeting
with alleged Capone figures had no significance. Johnson admitted to an almost limitless confidence in Governor Warren,
whose 1948 campaign he had largely financed with C. V.
Griffith, a citrus grower, and a youthful Jacksonville businessman, Louis Wolfson. Newspaper and political gossip in the
state capital described Johnson as "Mr. Big" in Florida, and
numerous lobbyists and special-interest groups attempted to
gain the governor's ear through him. Indeed, the Kefauver
Committee tried to link Johnson to an effort to legalize off-
track bookmaking, but Johnson retorted that off-track betting
ran counter to his vested interests, that he recalled no such
effort for legalization on his part, and that in any event, Warren had favored a law enforcement over a legalization approach to the gambling problem by endorsing the state an-
tiwire service bill in 1949.[25]

Unconvinced by Johnson's denials, the Committee theorized
that Warren's appointment of a special gambling investigator,
W. O. "Bing" Crosby, and Crosby's exclusive raids in the Miami
area on S. & G. bookies were prompted by Johnson as a spokesman for the Capone interests. Crosby, who had known the
governor for twenty years, denied that Johnson had influenced
him although he admitted knowing and talking with the race
track owner and acknowledged getting some suggestions for
raids from Russell. By tapping the governor's law enforcement
power through Johnson's influence, Kefauver argued, the
Chicago-based group had effectively countered S. & G.'s local
police contacts and disrupted their operations.[26]

The Capone syndicate also used their supposed Continental
wire service monopoly to cripple S. & G. By cutting off service
to S. & G., Continental's local distributor impeded the rapid
turnover of bets and thereby drastically reduced S. & G.'s
profits. When efforts to get its own wire service restored
proved futile, S. & G. tried to get the service through local
bookmakers, but this allegedly led to temporary termination

25. *Third Interim Report,* pp. 33–34. Rice to Kiley, August 7, 1957,
Crime Box 5, Kefauver Papers. Johnson testimony, Crime *Hearings,*
Pt. 1, pp. 600–609, 616–55. Lester Velie, "Secret Mr. Big of Florida,"
Collier's, May 5, 1951, pp. 13, 68–71.

26. *Third Interim Report,* p. 33. Crosby testimony, Crime *Hearings,*
Pt. 1, pp. 370–86.

of service to the entire state. For two weeks, S. & G. suspended operations entirely, and when it reopened, it was with Russell as a sixth partner, with wire service renewed, and with Crosby's raids suspended. Supposedly, Russell was allowed to buy into the syndicate's $26,500,000 operations for $20,000, the same sum the S. & G. paid to Russell's former associate Anthony Accardo for a yacht. Moreover, as additional evidence for their contention that Russell was merely a front for the Chicago group, the Committee discovered that the partnership of Guzik and Accardo showed a loss of $7,240 for the operation of S. & G. on its 1949 income tax return.[27]

S. & G. denied any connection between either the raids or the suspension of the wire service and Russell's entry into the local syndicate. The loss of profits by S. & G. in 1949, argued Ben Cohen, attorney for the local group, was due to general economic conditions that year and not to the problem over the wire service. S. & G. took Russell in as a partner because it feared his aggressive campaign for concessions on the beach and because it wanted to tap his experience in baseball pools, not because it had been muscled. Cohen, testifying in August of 1950, complained that local newspapers and Sullivan's crime commission had maligned the members of S. & G. by trying to link them to prostitution, narcotics, and interstate crime syndicates. The pressure and embarrassment to the men's families had become so intense, Cohen explained, that S. & G. had decided to dissolve.[28]

The Committee's work in Miami, climaxed by the "Russell muscle" story, received widespread acclaim and acceptance around the country. Again, however, it had been based almost wholly upon material provided by Peterson, Sullivan, and their allies and not through any independent investigation by the Committee. This evidence, while in general impressive, was weak at points. The Committee, for example, never proved its case against W. H. Johnson—something that Sullivan must have recognized, for he subsequently forwarded additional ideas and suggestions for strengthening the Committee's effort to portray Johnson as a front for the Capone mob.[29] The conclusions, moreover, reflected two assumptions

27. *Third Interim Report,* pp. 33–34.
28. Cohen testimony, Crime *Hearings,* Pt. 1, pp. 492–531.
29. Crime *Hearings,* Pt. 1, pp. 522–23. Sullivan to Halley, September 7, 8, 1950, Crime Box 2; Sullivan to H. G. Robinson, September 13, 1950; Sullivan to Halley, September 14, 23, 1950, Crime Box 5, Kefauver

that—at least to that point—the Committee had not demonstrated. First, the Russell muscle had assumed a control of the wire service by the Chicago mob or Capone syndicate when only Guzik and Accardo could be linked with the Russell case. A loan from a Johnson subordinate to Paul "The Waiter" Ricca possibly involved one more former Capone associate. The Committee, moreover, following the crime commission's lead, assumed from the beginning a hostile attitude toward gambling interests and the effort to legalize gambling. When the Chief Counsel confused a Miami Beach progambling newspaper with a similar one in Miami, Kefauver explained that "it does about the same thing. It condemns the committee and takes up for gambling operations." In a bumbling and inconclusive effort, Halley opened a drive, continued under O'Conor's leadership, to show that gangster money from Chicago had sponsored a local newspaper that advocated legalized gambling.[30]

The Kefauver hearings demonstrated beyond question that large sums of money, moving in illegal channels, had extensive power to corrupt and that conflicting and overlapping law enforcement jurisdictions encouraged the diffusing of responsibility. James Sullivan and Walter Clark, sheriffs of Dade and Broward counties, respectively, enjoyed income they could never satisfactorily explain to the Committee, and Clark was openly a part owner of a gambling enterprise in Broward County. Sheriff Sullivan argued that enforcement of gambling laws was not the county sheriff's responsibility, and former Miami Beach Police Chief Phil Short, in assigning Perdue to a one-man vice squad, explained that he did not want to know about the gambling problem. Governor Warren, at the same time, adopted a passive attitude toward his responsibilities. Not clearly shown by the Committee was whether the gambling interests were controlling the law enforcement structure or whether local officials were levying a private tax on gambling.[31]

Papers. Peterson hedged about a Johnson–Capone syndicate relationship, claiming that his testimony linked Johnson to Patton, not to the Capone men. Crime *Hearings,* Pt. 2, p. 168.

30. *Third Interim Report,* p. 52. Crime *Hearings,* Pt. 1, p. 554, Pt. 16, pp. 198–205, 21–52.

31. *Third Interim Report,* pp. 34–36. James Sullivan to Kefauver, n.d., Crime *Hearings,* Pt. 1, pp. 242–43. Fuller Warren to Halley, August 8, 1950, ibid., pp. 798–800. Warren publicly urged local officials to

The Russell muscle had set the pattern for developing investigations in St. Louis, Kansas City, Chicago, New Orleans, and Cleveland and on the West Coast. In the St. Louis area, the Committee discovered that certain politicians, such as East St. Louis's Police Commissioner John T. English, reported inexplicably large incomes and that the enduring jurisdictional disputes obscured the responsibilities of law enforcement officials. The senators also exposed another instance of the effect of outside muscle in the wire service. The Pioneer News Service, which dated back to the early 1920s, had become a local outlet for Continental and was caught up in the racing-news wire fight between Ragen and Trans-American in 1946–1947. William Molasky, the largest stockholder, and a local partner Gully Owen found themselves competing with Reliable News Service, a rival Trans-American outlet located across the river in East St. Louis. Led by Bev Brown, who also maintained an interest in Pioneer, Reliable maintained close contact with Frank "Buster" Wortman, a local gangster who was reportedly working with the Capone syndicate. When Continental absorbed Trans-American, Reliable disappeared and Brown and his family moved back into Pioneer, a series of developments that led the Committee to conclude that Pioneer had fallen under the Capone group's control. The availability of the wire service in the St. Louis area stimulated a rapid turnover of cash that resulted in immense profits—which in turn could be drained off by those who controlled the wire service.[32]

The inquiry into the ties between political and criminal figures in Kansas City had become so significant a test of the Committee's sincerity that Kefauver felt compelled to hold both executive and public hearings in the city prior to the elections. The basic pattern for gambling operations in Miami held true in the President's home county. On the basis of evi-

enforce the gambling laws and temporarily suspended both Sullivan and Clark from office. Warren statements, February 18, 1949, August 7, 1950, ibid., pp. 801–2. *Florida Interim Report,* p. 5; *Third Interim Report,* p. 36.

32. *Third Interim Report,* pp. 43–46. Crime *Hearings,* Pt. 4-A, pp. 68–79, 553–57. The Committee never showed, however, that in fact the new Pioneer News Service abused the Carroll–Mooney $20 million-a-year "lay-off" operation or the C. J. Rich concern, possibly the two largest bookmaking enterprises in the area. While not a totally unbiased source, J. J. Carroll insisted that "no one has ever exacted any tribute from us." *Third Interim Report,* pp. 44–45. Crime *Hearings,* Pt. 12, p. 339.

dence assembled by Kefauver's old friend Max Goldschein
during his federal grand jury investigation in Kansas City, the
Committee explored the political circumstances surrounding
Binaggio's murder as well as another wire service muscle.
Rather convincingly, Kefauver showed that Binaggio had,
after 1946, begun to contest the remnants of the Pendergast
machine and had allegedly contributed $150,000 to the anti-
Pendergast gubernatorial race of Forrest Smith, with obvious
expectation of some *quid pro quo* when Smith became governor in 1949. The key to Binaggio's hope seemed to be the governor's power to appoint the police commissioners of the city,
who could pretty well determine the degree of law enforcement directed against Binaggio's extensive gambling investments. Before the election, Binaggio had explained to former
Missouri Attorney General Roy McKittrick that he "had to
have a governor," but Smith, clearly ungrateful, had failed to
name commissioners who were sufficiently progambling to
suit Binaggio. Former Police Commissioner R. Robert Cohn
testified that a distraught Binaggio had pleaded for the commissioners' endorsement of his choice for police superintendent, had explained that "the boys" were making it "hot" on
him because of his failure to "open up" the town as they expected, and once had actually thrown money at Cohn in a
desperate attempt at bribery. Kefauver theorized that, when
Cohn and another holdover commissioner remained adamant
and when Smith continued to be unresponsive, gambling interests who had followed and possibly helped finance Binaggio's political brokerage engineered his assassination in the
Democratic Club's headquarters. The Committee concluded
that, while it had "no substantial evidence" that Governor
Smith had made any commitments to Binaggio in exchange
for his support, Smith's contention that he did not know of the
gambler's background and had not discussed in some form a
quid pro quo was "simply not credible."[33]

33. Robert L. Riggs, "The Man from Tennessee," *The Progressive*
(March 1956), 7–11; *Third Interim Report,* pp. 37–43. McKittrick testimony, Pt. 4, pp. 62–81; Pt. 4-A, pp. 35–66; Cohn testimony, Pt. 4, pp.
193–203; Pt. 4-A. pp. 203–15, Crime *Hearings.* See also Smith's testimony, labeling much of what Kefauver heard as "idle gossip," as well
as the statements of two other police commissioners, ibid., Pt. 4, pp.
204–26, 39–62; Pt. 4-A, pp. 231–52. Although the Kefauver report contended that Binaggio made "vigorous efforts" to influence the St. Louis
Police Commissioners, no such evidence was produced in the hearings. Molasky, however, admitted contributing to Smith's campaign,

The Committee showed that Binaggio, Gargotta, Gizzo, Thomas Lococo, Morris "Snag" Klein, and Phillip E. Osadchey (Eddie Spitz) had dominated an estimated $34 million-a-year gambling industry in Kansas City and that Osadchey and Klein had muscled into gambling operations as distant as Council Bluffs, Iowa. Kefauver contended that the gambling boom in Kansas City, as elsewhere, had been stimulated in part by the convenience of the local wire service, which he argued had fallen to the Capones through a deal between the nominal head of Trans-American and Osadchey. According to the Committee, Osadchey, representing Trans-American, had approached Simon Partnoy, operator of Harmony Publishing Company, a Continental distributor, and had convinced Partnoy, a twenty-five-year veteran of wire service intrigue and threat, to turn over his facilities to Trans-American. Actually, the Committee never clearly showed that Osadchey was in the back pocket of the so-called Capone syndicate nor that he had muscled Partnoy who, because of a long-standing financial grievance against the tight-fisted Ragen, was receptive to any new offer that might be made to him.[34]

As it had in Florida, the Committee demonstrated that a profitable illegal but socially approved operation leads to widespread attempts at corruption and at least occasional violence. Unquestionably, the study of the wire service implied interstate links, although the exact nature and significance of the ties were not as obvious as the Committee suggested. While the Kefauver group stressed the gamblers' political power, the evidence suggests that the politicians used the gamblers, their funds, and their organization more frequently than the gamblers used the politicians. As Jim Pendergast, heir to the now decrepit Kansas City political machine observed, Binaggio's troubles lay, not with his ability, but in his inability, to control the city's police force.[35]

---

and the Committee produced some testimony that Molasky attempted to get his controversial attorney, Morris Shenker, appointed to the St. Louis Board of Police Commissioners. Ibid., 105–9.

34. *Third Interim Report,* pp. 39–40. Missouri Attorney General J. E. Taylor statement and Partnoy testimony, Crime *Hearings,* Pt. 4-A, pp. 560, 337–51.

35. Kefauver statement, Crime *Hearings,* Pt. 4, p. 405. Pendergast testimony, ibid., Pt. 4-A, pp. 477–85. In general, Kefauver thought the Kansas City picture materially improved since Goldschein's grand jury inquiry, the formation of the Kansas City Crime Commission, and his own investigation. He pointed out, however, that conditions in

The hearings in New Orleans on January 25–26, 1951, followed the pattern of the sessions in Miami and Missouri. Based on investigations directed by Henry Patrick Kiley and Downey Rice and on material provided by Mayor DeLesseps Morrison, the Louisiana hearings dramatized most effectively the pervasive corruption among local law enforcement officers that had long characterized the New Orleans area. Jefferson Parish's Sheriff Frank J. "King" Clancy, while denying that he had accepted outright bribery, admitted he had purposefully failed to enforce gambling laws in order to ensure the employment of over two thousand persons in the numerous gambling establishments in his parish. When slot machines had been forced out of New Orleans following the election of Morrison in 1946, Costello and his associates had unsuccessfully attempted legal action to halt the destruction of their machines while at the same time they opened the swank Beverly Club in Clancy's Jefferson Parish, suburban to New Orleans. Costello's local representative, "Dandy Phil" Kastel, a former associate of Arnold Rothstein, had approached Clancy for permission to open the Beverly, and the Sheriff granted the concession on the condition that local people were employed. Clancy, who held a law degree, at first tried to fence with the Committee but came off so poorly that he later traveled to Washington at his own expense to purge himself of charges of contempt. His story was simply the most striking of tales by several local sheriffs and marshals that demonstrated the corrupting influence of widespread illegal gambling.[36]

In Carlos Marcello, Kefauver argued, he had found the local

surrounding Jackson County as well as in the counties adjacent to St. Louis, demanded more spirited enforcement of the laws. *Third Interim Report,* pp. 42–43. Crime *Hearings,* Pt. 4-A, pp. 575–82, 726–33, 164–65.

36. Crime *Hearings,* Pt. 8, pp. 1–3, 5–31, 369–423. *Third Interim Report,* pp. 84–90. Orleans Parish (coterminous with New Orleans) Criminal Sheriff John J. Grosch, whom the Committee "most clearly established" had accepted outright protection payments, argued that, as chief of detectives from 1930–1945 and sheriff since 1946, he had more important crimes to solve than violations of gambling laws. Both Grosch and Sheriff C. F. "Dutch" Rowley of St. Bernard Parish pointed to the long history of wide-open conditions in Greater New Orleans; Rowley reminded the Committee that New Orleans constables and justices of the peace in the 1870s received their pay from gambling funds. Ibid., pp. 87, 85. Crime *Hearings,* Pt. 8, pp. 182–85.

cog in interstate crime. An original partner in Costello's Beverly Club, Marcello owned shares in another plush gambling establishment, in slot machine operations outside the city limits, and, apparently through his interest in the local racing-news wire distributorship, in various horse parlors and bookie operations. On the basis of an earlier narcotics conviction, the Committee speculated that Marcello might also currently be involved in the drug traffic.[37]

Although persons associated with the local racing-news wire service had fled the scene by the time of the New Orleans hearings, the Committee noted a "typical, successful, and mysterious attempt at muscling in." John J. Fogarty, head of the *Daily Sports News,* had been in the business of publishing and disseminating racing news for thirty years prior to the eruption of the Continental-Trans-American fight in Chicago. Suddenly a rival Trans-American outlet opened under the ostensible direction of a local underworld figure whom the Committee linked with the Capone gang. From Western Union records the Senate Committee concluded that the two groups eventually merged, with Marcello as an important figure in the new operation.[38]

While the Committee demonstrated the existence of interstate contacts and investments, it failed to show extensive interstate control of the gambling operations; by painting Marcello as a central figure, it suggested that local decision-making was far from being a mere "front." One might well contend—and indeed the Committee did suggest—that local law enforcement officials, as the brokers between the law and the reality, were more important in setting policy than the gamblers.[39] The more strongly the Committee stressed the independent judgment of local politicians, the weaker became its argument that local officials were overwhelmed by wealth and force from outside the state.

En route to California for its hearings there, the Committee held a one-day session in Las Vegas on November 15. Although technically the Committee was prohibited from recommending changes in any state's gambling laws, the group's hostile attitudes quickly emerged and found their way into a report recommending that other states not follow Neva-

37. *Third Interim Report,* pp. 82–83.
38. *Third Interim Report,* pp. 80–81.
39. *Third Interim Report,* p. 89.

da's example. The basic Nevada gambling laws, enacted in 1931, had authorized gambling operations upon payment of a license fee and receipt of that license from county officials. Various changes had been instituted since 1931, including an amendment in 1949 that required a state as well as county license; the state license was to be issued or revoked by the State Tax Commission, which had the power to hold hearings. Kefauver personally expressed disappointment that the state commission had taken no effective action to examine the backgrounds of the figures who dominated the Nevada gambling industry. Many of them, the Senator noted, either had been or were supposedly involved in illegal gambling or vice in other states. Moe Sedway, long-time friend of the late "Bugsy" Siegel, Mert Wertheimer of Detroit, Benny Binion of Dallas, the Cleveland syndicate, and other important gambling figures operated in the state, many blanketed in by a "grandfather clause" that was upheld by the Tax Commission. In addition to personalities and investments, gambling in Nevada touched interstate commerce through the receipt of out-of-state bets and through the use of the telephone, telegraph, and the mails to carry on bookie operations. The postwar gambling boom, the Committee argued, had thrown gamblers of questionable background and ͵ oliticians too closely together, and in wide-open Nevada, where gambling had been legalized, there was no countervailing power, such as the press in other states, to expose corruption and to protect the public interest.[40]

To document its contention that gamblers employed monopolistic techniques and occasional violence, the Committee took a quick look into the involvement of the wire services in the assassination of Siegel in 1947. In addition to pioneering the development of the "Strip" with the construction of the Flamingo Hotel, Siegel, the smooth, handsome transplanted New York playboy-gangster, allegedly controlled the wire service in Nevada through Sedway. A ruthless overlord, Siegel supposedly refused service unless the local bookies cut him in on their profits. Siegel became embroiled in the Continental-Trans-American fight, supposedly on the side of Trans-

40. *Third Interim Report*, pp. 90–94. Both Lt. Gov. Clifford Jones and William J. Moore of the State Tax Commission received substantial returns from their gambling investments, and Moore received a special rate on the wire service that he supposedly was to regulate. Ibid., pp. 93–94.

American, and was murdered in the Beverly Hills home of his mistress shortly after Trans-American suspended operations. When Sedway and his associates first quarreled among themselves and then attempted to continue Siegel's wire service monopoly, alarmed Nevada prosecutors and politicians, fearing an outbreak of open gang warfare, prompted hearings before the State Tax Commission. These hearings led to enactment of the 1949 law as well as a ruling that empowered the commission to set rates for the wire services and required, in general, impartial distribution of the service to all licensed bookmakers. The Committee noted, however, that the commission, as of late 1950, had taken no action to fix rates or to prohibit the wire service from charging a fixed percentage of the bookmakers' take. Kefauver believed that the levying of a fixed percentage in effect made those who controlled the service partners in local bookmaking, that it created tremendous wealth for them, and that it consequently invited conflict for nationwide control of the wire services.[41]

While gambling in Nevada had thrust politicians into questionable relationships with interstate gambling figures and had occasioned vicious business practices—at their extreme, suspected murder—the situation was not peculiar to legalized gambling.[42] In a sense, while Nevada attempted regulation of private gambling within the framework of law, other areas had regulated the activity illegally through the selling of protection by law enforcement officials. The Committee, reflecting its antigambling bias, had seized upon the undesirable situation in Nevada and attempted to make of it far more than the facts justified.

41. *Third Interim Report,* pp. 91–94. Some writers have linked Siegel's death more closely to the building of the costly Flamingo, which supposedly outraged his coinvestors, than with the wire-service controversy. Dean Jennings, *We Only Kill Each Other: The Life and Bad Times of Bugsy Siegel* (Greenwich, Conn.: Fawcett Publications, Inc., 1968).

42. Popular writers since Kefauver have pointed to the large amounts of cash involved in gambling operations and the ease of "skimming" before reporting taxable income. Professor Thomas C. Schelling of Harvard University argues, however, that legalized gambling is no more subject to extortion than any other business. Schelling testimony, "The Improvement and Reform of Law Enforcement and Criminal Justice in the United States," *Hearings* before the Select House Committee on Crime, 91st Cong., 1st sess. (1969), pp. 70–91, particularly pp. 84–85.

In two swings through Los Angeles and San Francisco, the
Committee in effect performed an encore for the California
Crime Commission. With H. G. Robinson, former chief investigator for the Commission, and Robinson's close friend, Downey Rice, laying the groundwork for the Committee in California, there was little danger of the Senate's investigation
differing markedly from the Governor's Study Commission.
As usual, the most convincing evidence of interstate links in
the underworld involved the wire service. Former chief counsel for the California Crime Commission Warren Olney, under
Robinson's coaching had related the story of how his group
had prompted the Public Service Commission to order Western Union and other utilities to refuse service to Continental,
how this measure had severely curtailed the larger operations
where rapid turnover of information and money was so vital,
and how telephones had then been used to bootleg the information into the state or to take Californians' bets from centers
outside the state. The struggle for control of the wire service
in Chicago had precipitated violence in California, for example, when Joe Sica, reputed associate and heir-apparent to
aging gangster Jack Dragna, and the former pugilist Mickey
Cohen had severely beaten Russell Brophy, son-in-law to Ragen and a local Continental distributor. Through examination
of myriad records of income tax deductions and payments, the
Committee concluded that local outlets were, in effect, dummies for Continental in Chicago.[43]

The Governor's commission pointed the Senate investigators to another predictable point of interest—the corrupting
powers of gambling in an area of conflicting law enforcement
jurisdiction. Supposedly Los Angeles's Mayor Fletcher Bowron and Police Chief William H. Parker had made gambling
operations so hazardous that gamblers had initiated an unsuccessful recall petition against Bowron and had made an attempt on Parker's life. Their operations meanwhile had centered in the Guarantee Finance Company, a large lay-off
operation in the Sunset Strip section, an isolated pocket of
county territory surrounded by city boundaries. Guarantee's
books strongly suggested a pay-off of $216,000 for "juice," the
California equivalent of "protection" or "ice"; a captain in the
county sheriff's office, who made over $11,000 in a quick liquor
franchise transaction, had apparently hamstrung an over-

43. *Third Interim Report,* pp. 98–99. Olney testimony, Crime *Hearings,* Pt. 2, pp. 215–41. ·

zealous city policeman who had raided Guarantee's offices in January of 1948; the office of Sheriff Eugene Warren Biscailuz, according to Robinson, had been less than cooperative with the California Crime Commission. The Committee found that the Sheriff's use of the "vice squad" pattern, similar to that of Pat Perdue in Miami Beach, simply gave control of vice payments to a few officials and demoralized law enforcement in general. Biscailuz pointed out that Los Angeles County consisted of forty-five different municipalities and that his was the largest sheriff's office in the world; something had simply gone wrong in his vast bureaucracy—something that resulted in the failure to cooperate with Robinson. He was, he stated, personally unfamiliar with such figures as Mickey Cohen. Regardless of any conflicts between Robinson and Biscailuz's office that may have led to the Committee's bringing the spotlight to bear on the Los Angeles County Sheriff's office, the general corrupting powers of gambling and the failure of decentralized law enforcement never appeared more obvious.[44]

The Kefauver Committee briefly peered at two other situations in California that revealed organized crime in a different perspective. Rumblings of scandal in the West Coast Internal Revenue Office had been noted by the Governor's Study Group and passed along, in turn, to the Senate Committee. Essentially the story showed that agents in the IRB field offices in Nevada and California had extorted payments from prominent California gambler Elmer "Bones" Remmer, convicted abortionist Gertrude Jenkins, and brothel keeper Anna "Tugboat Annie" Schultz. To Remmer and Miss Jenkins, the aged Patrick Mooney of the Reno office had suggested that purchase of worthless stock in an unproductive Nevada copper mine, of which he was an officer, would reduce their tax penalties and end the possibilities of criminal prosecution. The Internal Revenue office hearings showed—as had the Louisiana study of Sheriff Clancy—that established law enforcement and investigative officers were in many cases the exploiters rather than the exploited in their relationships with the underworld. The IRB findings, having briefly served the Committee's function, were passed along to a House subcommittee headed by Congressman Cecil King of California.[45]

44. *Third Interim Report,* pp. 95–99. Biscailuz testimony, Crime *Hearings,* Pt. 10, pp. 279–304.
45. *Third Interim Report,* pp. 99–100. Kefauver, *Crime in America,* 131–34. Crime *Hearings,* Pt. 10, p. 1224.

Unquestionably the most discussed issue in California by
1950 was the influence of Arthur H. Samish, a superlobbyist
for various concerns and a man the Committee decided was
indeed "Mr. Big" in California. Samish's immense funds and
widespread activities had first drawn the fire of Governor
Frank Merriam in 1938, who commissioned an investigator,
Howard Philbrick, to compile information on Samish's lobbying activities with the legislature. Philbrick's report, presented to the legislature, printed and then expunged from the
record, constituted a slashing indictment of Samish, Merriam's onetime supporter. The events of World War II diverted
attention from the Samish case, and the portly lobbyist continued his activities with only brief interruption. The issue
reemerged in the late 1940s, and in 1949, *Collier's* published
a two-part series that underscored Samish's control of the
legislature through campaign financing.[46]

One of Samish's major clients was the California State
Brewers Institute, a trade association whose members brewed
86 per cent of the beer produced in California. The brewers
institute, over a period of six years, had contributed approximately $2 million to two separate funds that Samish used at
his discretion. Although no reliable books were kept, Samish
unquestionably used these funds to promote any number of
causes and candidates, and Governor Warren maintained
that, on the subjects that concerned the lobbyist, he com-
manded more influence in the legislature than the state's
chief executive. Kefauver interested himself particularly in
the possibility that Samish had been violating the Federal
Corrupt Practices Act through expenditures for campaigns
and lobbying, and he suggested not only that some of the funds
should have been reported by Samish as personal income but
also that the brewers should not be allowed to deduct their
contributions as business expenses. Rather lamely, the Committee tried to link Samish with gambling figures in other
parts of the country by showing that while in the resort town
of Hot Springs, Arkansas, he had talked with Joe Adonis, that
he had once called the Costello–Kastel Beverly Club in New
Orleans, and that he frequently called a bookie establishment

46. *Third Interim Report*, p. 100. Samish testimony, Crime *Hearings*, Pt. 10, pp. 1177–80. Lester Velie, "The Secret Mr. Big of California," *Collier's*, August 13, 1949, pp. 12–13, 71–73; August 20, 1949, pp.
12–13, 60–63.

in Chicago. Aside from a possible meeting with Adonis in New York, the Senate investigators found no other evidence to associate the California lobbyist with interstate gambling figures.[47] Given the fact that the Committee considered Hot Springs, along with Miami, as a breeding place for gambling–gangster activities, the surprising part of the Samish story was the absence of contact with underworld figures, not their presence. Apparently the IRB's cases as well as the Samish exposé were mere publicity-laden sideshows that the Committee picked up briefly, possibly with the encouragement of H. G. Robinson and the California Crime Commission.

The investigations of gambling conditions and conflicts over the wire service in Florida, Missouri, Louisiana, and California had laid the groundwork for the hearings in Chicago and Cleveland. In both Illinois and Ohio the Committee deferentially listened to the stories of Governors Adlai E. Stevenson and Frank Lausche, who complained that corruption of local law enforcement officials by gambling interests had forced them reluctantly to step in with state troopers to restore order. The Committee also found the city administrations of both Cleveland and Chicago making sincere efforts to fight the gambling interests. What disturbed the Senate group most was again the inefficiency and buck-passing facilitated by jurisdictional and boundary lines. Hence, Kefauver deplored the conflict between Cook County's Republican Sheriff Elmer Walsh and the county's Democratic State's Attorney John S. Boyle over responsibilities against slot machines and hand-books. In Ohio the vigor of Cleveland officials and Governor Lausche had driven the Cleveland syndicate, composed of Moe Dalitz, Morris Kleinman, Samuel "Gameboy" Miller, Louis Rothkopf, Samuel Tucker, and Thomas J. McGinty, out of Ohio. The main foci of their activities had become Las Vegas and the northern Kentucky counties of Campbell and Kenton, a historic gambling area across the river from Cincinnati.[48]

More important, the Committee attempted to come to grips with the meaning of the complex issue of the wire service. Despite the denials by such witnesses as J. J. Carroll and

47. Kefauver, *Crime in America,* 136–41. *Third Interim Report,* p. 104.

48. Crime *Hearings,* Pt. 5, pp. 209–19; Pt. 6, pp. 3–13. *Third Interim Report,* pp. 68–69, 60.

Frank Erickson, the Kefauver Committee had accepted the
contention of the California Crime Commission and the
McFarland Subcommittee that up-to-the-minute reports on
track conditions, shifts of jockeys, and changes in odds promoted more fervent play and a more rapid turnover of money
by the bigger bookmakers, which in turn ensured larger
profits. Despite the broadcast of such information by radio
and the possibility of direct contact with race tracks by telephone, the Senate Committee concluded that in terms of volume Continental Press enjoyed a virtual monopoly through its
leased telegraph wires, telephone lines, ticker set-up, and assorted intelligence system for purchasing or purloining vital
racing information. Discriminatory prices by Continental and
its distributors and subdistributors—the vast majority of
which the Committee considered legal dummies erected to
insulate the parent concern from gambling prosecution
—established to the Senate group's satisfaction that a
monopoly did in fact exist and that the information supplied
was indeed vital to larger bookmakers and horse parlors. The
fact that distributors, subdistributors, or even larger sub-
scribers frequently demanded a set percentage of profits from
the bookmakers made them, in effect, partners in the operations and in turn set the stage for the movement of local profits
up the wire service structure to the coffers of Continental in
Chicago.[49]

Two of the objectives of the wire service investigation were
to demonstrate that the Capone syndicate existed and that it
controlled Continental. In both matters, the Committee
achieved only partial success, although the public believed
that the Senate group had accomplished much more. Kefau-

49. "Transmission of Gambling Information," Senate Commerce
Hearings, pp. 381, 472–73. Olney testimony, Crime *Hearings,* Pt. 2, pp.
218–19. "Transmission of Gambling Information," *Senate Report No.
1752,* pp. 8–10. *Third Interim Report,* pp. 150–60. Schelling has raised
interesting questions as to the actual necessity of wire service information and argues that in effect it was a cover for extortion against
bookmakers who operated in violation of gambling laws. This undeveloped argument fails to account for genuine strife over the information or for control of the organization that dispensed it. While the
Committee probably overestimated the centralization in the industry,
it also failed to appreciate the ease with which the telegraph-based
Continental could be replaced by a telephone set-up. Thomas C.
Schelling, "Economics and Criminal Enterprise," *The Public Interest*
(Spring 1967), 66–69.

ver's inclination to believe in the existence of regional and even interstate criminal organizations, based largely on press accounts and crime commission reports, had been strengthened by Peterson's testimony and the weight of evidence produced in Miami and elsewhere. Drew Pearson, whose contacts in the Committee were generally reliable, indicated in a July 13 column that the senators seemed convinced of the existence of a Capone syndicate. In its interim report on Florida, submitted on August 18, the Committee made numerous references to the "Capone group" and the "Capone gang" in describing the muscle of the S. & G. Syndicate, while at the same time they acknowledged the "convincing testimony" of Peterson and Anslinger on the cooperation between groups throughout the country. After a lengthy executive session on September 9 in Washington with Campagna, Gioe, and Ricca, the three Chicago figures involved in the movie extortion parole scandal, Kefauver expressed indecision as to whether the members of the gang that centered around Capone during Prohibition still operated as a syndicate. During the executive hearings in Chicago in October, however, he argued that his group had "strong evidence" that a Capone syndicate had survived Capone and that it maintained ties with underworld groups in other regions. By late December, after six months of investigation, the Committee still appeared frustrated at its inability to produce a blueprint of the underworld and thus to determine the relationship between the Capone syndicate and other groups. At least part of this frustration seems to have been occasioned by the Senate Committee's inability to demonstrate the influence of the Capones on Continental and hence on bookmaking establishments around the country.[50]

The Committee, of course, had the material left by Ragen in which he charged his opponents in the racing-news wire war of 1946 with being backed by the Capone syndicate, headed by Guzik, Accardo, and Humphries. In addition, the Senate group had shown that the Guzik–Accardo partnership had taken a tax loss on the S. & G. Syndicate, apparently incurred through the Russell muscle operations. In Chicago the Committee attempted to strengthen the Capone angle of the S. & G. story by

50. St. Louis *Star-Times,* July 13, 1950. *Florida Interim Report,* pp. 3, 12, 13, 15. Knoxville *News-Sentinel,* October 8, 1950. Nashville *Tennessean,* October 8, 1950. Elizabethan (Tenn.) *Star,* October 8, 1950. New York *Times,* December 24, 1950.

linking William H. Johnson more closely to the Capone group on one hand and to Governor Fuller Warren and hence, the Crosby raids, on the other. At the same time, it heard testimony that W. G. "Butsy" O'Brien, head of the Florida distributor that supposedly ordered the cut-off of service to S. & G., had been active in the Trans-American operation and was a Capone pawn. To tie the main offices of Continental to the Capones, the Senate investigators hoped to obtain the records of R. & H. Publishing Company in Chicago, the alleged Guzik-dominated subdistributor with which Ragen had feuded so violently. Although the Committee failed to get the subdistributor's records, it did question Tom Kelly, McBride, and Daniel A. Serritella in connection with the Capone group's influence in the wire service.[51]

Serritella, a former scratch sheet publisher and ward politician who considered both Guzik and Ragen friends, argued that the wire service had long been subject to muscle practices and that Ragen, a tough operator bent on expansion, had been as responsible for the feud as the R. & H. group. This significant information and interpretation, however, did not find its way into the Committee reports, which ignored the previous conflicts within the wire service, concluded that the "trouble began" in 1946, and painted Ragen as an embattled entrepreneur defending his business against a takeover by gangsters. At the same time, however, the senators strongly implied that Ragen had insisted that McBride return to the ownership of Continental in 1943 so that he could gain the support of the Cleveland underworld, over which McBride had powerful influence. Aside from the obvious contradiction in a totally respectable Ragen seeking security from Cleveland gangsters, the entire attempt of the Committee to divide the gray area of the wire service war between the "good guys" and the "bad guys"—the Capone syndicate—constituted a gross oversimplification. First, it imputed a purity to Ragen and an evil to Guzik and his followers that on careful study seems less obvious. Second, it suggested the existence of a unified crime syndicate in Chicago that the Committee had never really proved.[52]

51. Crime *Hearings,* Pt. 5, pp. 984–85, 777–79.
52. Serritella testimony, Crime *Hearings,* Pt. 5, pp. 954–71. *Third Interim Report,* pp. 153, 155. Following the pattern suggested in Peterson's testimony, the Committee explored the activities of the personnel in the old Capone gang and showed that many of them were in

McBride's and Kelly's testimony reviewed much of Serritella's argument but touched more fully upon the settlement following Ragen's death and the merger of Continental and Trans-American. While the Committee never established any clear or direct influence by Guzik or Accardo on Kelly or McBride, Halley and George Robinson did extract from Kelly an admission that Continental's distributor, Illinois News Service, would not dare hike R. & H.'s very favorable service rate.

Mr. Robinson. Isn't this essentially the thing, just being perfectly frank about it? The only reason why your brother wouldn't tamper with the rate R. & H. pays to Illinois [George Kelly, brother of Tom, ran Illinois News Service] is because of the characters he knows are in back of R. & H.? Isn't that essentially the situation?

Mr. Kelly. That would be a sensible situation or argument to put up. I would say if my brother called me and I knew these people were getting the service I would never in God's world tell him to raise their rate. After all, I have a family.[53]

In Cleveland, after Counsel Joseph Nellis achieved a partial success connecting McBride with Cleveland gangsters but a weaker case in linking him to the Capone group, Halley listened with rising frustration as McBride explained the various transactions by the owners of Continental and its distributors. Continental itself, McBride explained, did not deal with illegal bookies, but only with independent distributors, for whom his company could not be held responsible. Irritated by the evasiveness of the testimony, Halley finally interrupted to announce that he was weary of McBride's denials and that, in light of the various muscles the Committee had followed and the prejudicial agreements many of Continental's distributors had entered, he was asking the Committee to report that all the title transfers and distributors were "a lot of phonies, and that Continental News is and was Arthur McBride."[54] By centralizing the responsibilities for the wire service and minimizing the autonomy of distributors and subdistributors, Halley and the Committee could argue that the various muscles throughout the nation were part of a master plan of the Capone syndicate put into effect either with the endorse-

---

the racing, slot machine, as well as policy rackets. This is not, however, the same as proving that the men operated as a syndicate. Ibid., pp. 55–58.

53. Crime *Hearings,* Pt. 5, pp. 821–22.

54. McBride testimony, Crime *Hearings,* Pt. 6, pp. 43–103.

ment or the acquiescence of McBride and Kelly.[55]

Although the Committee had demonstrated beyond doubt
that Guzik and Accardo were involved in the wire service war
and settlement, the senators never proved the presence of a
Capone syndicate in the operation, but merely assumed it. Nor
did they demonstrate just how decisive a role the syndicate
played in the wire service as a whole or in gambling in local
areas. One might argue—as the Committee almost did in one
part of its report—that arrangements with local police were
far more significant than the identity of the persons who
dominated the wire service nationally and that the Capone
gang or Continental, if they did make the local decisions as
Halley maintained, had to deal with the individual or group
who controlled the local law enforcement officials.[56] The Committee, for all its attention to the Russell muscle, never discovered whether the Crosby raids or the shut-off of service were
more important in the capitulation of S. & G. The real significance of the wire service-Capone syndicate story is not that
the Committee necessarily proved its antigambling case, the
Capone influence on Continental, or the centralization in the
wire distribution system, but that it piled up such immense
amounts of evidence that the public came to think it had established its arguments.

The Kefauver Committee had hoped to show that the racing-news wire service was the skeleton of organized crime in
America, and to do this it drew on a number of citizens' crime

55. McBride's acid-tongued attorney, William Gallagher of Washington, noted with relish that Daniel Sullivan of the Miami Crime
Commission, who had written the FCC to complain that Continental
was dominated by the Capone mob, denied first-hand knowledge of
the Capone influence when called before the FCC but rather cited a
letter from Peterson to that effect. Gallagher had previously traced the
stories that linked Continental to organized crime to Peterson. Crime
Hearings, Pt. 6, p. 103. "Transmission of Gambling Information," Senate Commerce *Hearings,* pp. 647–49.

56. *Third Interim Report,* p. 89. Wayne Coy, in his testimony based
on the 1943–1944 Federal Communications Commission study, observed that in many cases Continental did not have a free choice of
distributors and subdistributors, but did business with those who had
political connections through which to operate. Coy also thought that
in most cases the Continental subdistributors sold the information to
all buyers. The Kefauver Committee stressed the exceptions to Coy's
statements, such as the S. & G. case, and argued that they were the
developing pattern. Both, of course, noted the elements of monopoly
involved. See Coy's testimony, Crime *Hearings,* Pt. 2, pp. 5–31.

commissions, journalists, and federal agencies for evidence. The Committee did argue in a generally convincing manner that the wire service, by supplying last-minute details on a large number of races, increased the total volume of betting and in all probability increased gambling profits. Unquestionably these illegal profits contributed to the corruption of local law enforcement officials and found their way into a variety of legitimate and illegitimate ventures. More debatable was the Committee's contention that the wire service set-up allowed a Capone-dominated Continental to exploit—if not control—bookmaking around the country. Despite its assertions, the Committee never showed how extensive the influence of Guzik or Accardo really was on Continental, or for that matter, how much influence Continental had over subdistributors and local bookmaking operations. The evidence strongly suggests a much more decentralized pattern than the Committee wanted to admit. Although the racing wire service was important, the indispensable key to successful gambling operations appeared to have been influence with local law enforcement officials. In the S. & G. case in Miami Beach, in the Binaggio case in Kansas City, and elsewhere, the critical factor was local police protection for gambling, not the wire service. By searching for evidence of conspiratorial monopoly power by a Capone-dominated Continental, the Committee paid less attention than it should have to local responsibility and to the need to rationalize the often fragmented law enforcement structure. Even more important, the search for extensive conspiratorial power obscured the need for a realistic examination of the possibilities of legalization and regulation of gambling. No such study was ever made, either in Las Vegas or elsewhere, primarily because the Committee had long accepted the arguments of Peterson and the antigambling advocates of the late 1940s. The Kefauver Committee, by suggesting that local gambling was dominated by sinister outside influences, presented neither a clear analysis of organized crime nor clear alternatives for dealing with it.

5

The Mafia as Myth

Suppose you were able to prove a vast criminal
conspiracy . . .
   —Rudolph Halley, 1950

Whatever preconceived bias or overstatement the Kefauver
Committee's conclusions on gambling and the wire service
may have reflected, they were intellectually respectable and
based on substantial, if not always convincing, evidence. Such
was not true of its conclusions on the Mafia. Inadequate evidence and the necessity to reach some conclusion rushed the
Committee into fuzzy and ill-founded statements that brought
the senators sensational headlines but left an ugly popular
misunderstanding in the country.

The original concept of Mafia, at least in the United States,
had more of a cultural and socioeconomic meaning than an
institutional one. Because of ethnic isolation and newspaper
sensationalism, the connotation of the word had changed
from peasant passion and vendetta to organized criminal conspiracy by the late 1930s. Its long-time champion had been the
Federal Bureau of Narcotics, headed since 1930 by Harry J.
Anslinger. Some have been so unkind as to suggest that Anslinger used the "Mafia fear" to compete with the Cummings–
Hoover supersale of the FBI in the 1930s.[1] For whatever reason, Anslinger in 1950 was the only major federal official who
stood squarely in favor of the proposition that organized crime
was controlled by a Mafia. His advocacy of this theory ran

1. Donald R. Cressey, *Theft of the Nation: The Structure and Operations of Organized Crime in America* (New York: Harper & Row,
Publishers, 1969), p. 22. Personal interview, Rufus King, former Kefauver Committee counsel, Washington, D.C., August 7, 1969.

parallel but on a different level to Peterson's vie
bling was controlled by an interstate syndicate
fauver had adopted.

From the beginning, the Narcotics Bureau's
be seen pulling and tugging the Committee tow
that the Mafia controlled organized crime. At the Committee's
first meeting, the senators reached a decision—later ignored—
to emphasize narcotics rather than gambling in their investigation. Prior to his appearance before the Committee in a
public session on June 28, Anslinger had already held a long
executive session with the senators on June 6, and he had
supplied them with a confidential master list of eight hundred
criminals who, he argued, not only had been active in violations of the narcotics laws but in other rackets as well. When,
in public session, Halley pressed Anslinger on his concept of
the underworld structure, the Commissioner retreated into
vague generalizations not far different from those of Peterson,
and he made no mention of a Mafia.

Mr. Anslinger. I would say that all of the members of this
combine are very well acquainted with everybody else
throughout the country. The fellows in New York, Florida,
California, all know each other. Seizing their telephone lists,
they are all on there, you find. It is interlaced, and intertwined.

Mr. Halley. Do the activities in one part of the country occur
as a result of instructions given in other parts of the country?

Mr. Anslinger. No; I do not think it works on that basis. In
some sections it is pretty well organized in that particular
way, but I wouldn't say that one section of the country controls
another section.

Mr. Halley. Do they confer together?

Mr. Anslinger. They confer together, oh, yes; talk to each
other, deal with each other.

Mr. Halley. They confine their dealings pretty well to the
family; is that correct?

Mr. Anslinger. That has been our experience. They have
off-shoots. They have associates in other rackets. They make
connections for persons outside of their own combine.[2]

2. New York *Times,* May 12, 1950. Crime *Hearings,* Pt. 2, pp. 95–96.
Schedule of executive hearings, Crime Box 37, Kefauver Papers. Although the Anslinger list was supposedly not to be made public, Tobey
announced to reporters that it contained Luciano's name. The Narcotics Bureau had made much of the fact that Luciano reached Italy in
1946, the same year that a postwar increase in the narcotics traffic
began. The Bureau was seeking additional funds and personnel to
combat this activity. New York *Times,* June 7, 1950. Crime *Hearings,*
Pt. 2, p. 89.

.n the field hearings, Anslinger's local agents echoed their chief's haziness and qualifications. Agent Claude A. Follmer told the Committee in Kansas City on July 10 that he had "heard" that Binaggio was a "member of the Mafia," that the "best information" he had was that there were twenty-five to thirty members in Kansas City, that James Balestrere was "supposed" to be the local head man, that there was "supposed" to be an international head in Palermo through whom heads in other countries, including the United States, were designated. While there was "some contention" about the identity of the American head in New York, it had always been Follmer's "understanding" that it was either Vincent Mangano or Joseph Profaci. Through the New York head, state or city leaders were appointed in the United States. Follmer stated that he had never known a non-Italian member, that he understood that there were no rituals or written rules or bylaws, but that violations of a code of silence by members brought certain death. The structure of the organization, he continued, consisted of an "inner circle and an outer circle," with the inner circle holding the directing power. In later public hearings, Follmer reviewed a number of narcotics cases that ended in assassinations of informers, supposedly in Mafia style, and he played for the Committee a tape in which a suspect laughingly referred to informing on the Mafia, a reference that apparently impressed Kefauver. Follmer argued that the many Mafia-style assassinations he catalogued constituted evidence of organizational strength—a factor that might well suggest to others a lack of effective organization. Agent Thomas Edward McGuire in New Orleans provided less detail for the open hearings but did venture the conclusion that the "so-called Mafia element" was a "closely knit organization."[3]

3. Follmer testimony, Crime *Hearings,* Pt. 4-A, pp. 418–23; Pt. 4, pp. 81–100; McGuire testimony, Pt. 8, p. 281. The tone of the Follmer dictaphone conversation between two Kansas City underlings was critical of the power and money of more prestigious gang figures such as DeLuca (Ricca) and of the extravagant "protection" charged by various local officials. From the context of the tape, it is difficult to determine whether or not the statement about the Mafia was meant in a serious vein. In any event, the remark indicated that the organization was weak and dependent on the whims of local law enforcement. See ibid., Pt. 4, pp. 86–87.

Tony. Somebody must have put the finger on me, and I have a hunch who it was. How is the gambling down in Tampa now?

Narcotics Agent Charles Siragusa later in the Committee's life linked the exiled "Lucky" Luciano to the international traffic in narcotics and to the Mafia. The agent read from a statement Luciano had given the Italian police that indicated that the alleged vice king's various business ventures in Italy had failed and that his sole income was in the form of gifts from American friends.[4] Siragusa argued that some gifts, such as an American-made automobile, actually represented income from underworld ties in the United States and that the deported gangster also made substantial profits from the international drug traffic. In leading the senators through the details of a "typical" international narcotics operation, Siragusa stressed Luciano's alleged role and concluded that he was the "kingpin" of the illegal drug traffic in both the United States and Italy. Luciano, he claimed, still carried the title of "don" given to "members of the higher echelon of the Mafia" and was one of "the royal family," if not the "kingpin," of all American rackets. To Siragusa this meant that Luciano held the power to have his mandates enforced through violence and coercion.[5]

While the performance of Anslinger and his agents in public hearings was disappointing, the Committee apparently received additional confidential material in executive session. Even so, their evasive and qualified answers to the Committee's questions can only mean that the Mafia concept was vague even within the Narcotics Bureau. Unquestionably, small so-called Mafia groups had been involved in the narcot-

Joe. Hell, the Dagos couldn't do any good gambling in Tampa. The city charges, the sheriff charges, and the mayor charges. They just won't let you make any money. They used to be pretty strong out here in Kansas City, but they sort of lost out. They even asked me about the Mafia ("Laughs loud") as if I would say anything about that.

4. Crime *Hearings,* Pt. 14, pp. 346–47. Luigi Barzini maintains that the popular misconception that American underworld figures are part of the Sicilian Mafia is frequently shared by American gangsters themselves. He argues that Luciano fell into this trap and was swindled of nearly 15 million lira by his Mafia partners in a caramel factory. Luigi Barzini, *The Italians* (New York: Bantam Books, Inc., 1969), pp. 281–82.

5. Siragusa testimony, Crime *Hearings,* Pt. 14, pp. 346–58. For a devastating criticism of Siragusa's testimony, particularly his emphasis on the alleged title "don," see Giovanni Schiavo, *The Truth About the Mafia and Organized Crime in America* (El Paso: Vigo Press, 1962), pp. 15–16.

ics traffic; unquestionably, some of these had wide contacts; some were involved in other rackets; and Luciano may well have been in league with dealers in drugs as well as with managers of other vice operations. Almost certainly, however, Anslinger was guilty of overstatement in assuming any great degree of centralization of such groups in the United States or any overlordship of all American rackets by such figures. Talk of the Mafia in any but a narrow sense not only misrepresented the facts, but it actually became counterproductive when it enabled law enforcement officials to hide their failures or corruption behind an institutional bogeyman and when it separated organized crime from the broader economic and social tensions that gave it birth.[6]

Anslinger's early interest and the Bureau's list of eight hundred criminals, which he gave the Committee, quickly set the senators searching for a link between the narcotics traffic and other rackets. Casual references to a Mafia by Peterson and exposés such as that of William Drury in the Miami *Daily News* combined with the general public's interest to intensify the discussion of the Mafia and its role in the American underworld. The excitable Senator Tobey noted that Anslinger and his men had presented the "first official proof" of a nationwide syndicate of "major criminals in a variety of operations" and that the Kefauver Committee "knows who heads the combine."[7]

Kefauver adopted a more measured position on the Mafia issue and the structure of the underworld. In a pretaped radio interview with candidates, sponsored by Labor's League for Political Education, the Senator from Tennessee announced that his early investigation had led him to believe that several crime rings were operating, "some of them intertwining and overlapping, but some essentially separate in function." He was inclined neither to believe there was one national overlord of crime nor to be especially concerned about finding one. His interest lay with the economic impact and corrupting influence of organized crime and in the need to recommend legislative remedies. At least in the early summer of 1950,

6. David Bell, *The End of Ideology: On the Exhaustion of Political Ideas in the Fifties* (New York: The Free Press, 1962), pp. 127–50.
7. Nashville *Tennessean,* June 7, 1950. Peterson testimony, Crime *Hearings,* Pt. 2, pp. 132, 162, 174, 188. Miami *Daily News,* June 12, 1950. Washington *Star,* June 11, 1950. New York *Times,* July 30, 1950. Washington *Star,* June 7, 1950.

Kefauver was holding close to the official position of McGrath and McFarland on the issue of the Mafia or its less sinister counterpart, "the national crime syndicate."[8]

Although the Committee's first interim report on Florida, presented to the Senate on August 18, hedged on whether one or more nationwide syndicates operated on an extensive basis, the field hearings were already revealing substantial Committee interest in the existence of a Mafia overlordship. In the executive hearings in Kansas City, July 18–20, Halley set a pattern of questioning by inquiring whether certain underworld figures knew men in the rackets in other cities and whether they knew of or were associated with a Mafia. The Committee obviously hoped to establish through their answers the existence of a nationwide network of criminal associations similar to that already suggested by real estate and gambling ventures in Miami. Tony Gizzo of Kansas City admitted to as wide an association as any other witness, but even his admissions established very little. Gizzo acknowledged knowing the Fischetti brothers, Guzik, Accardo, and Ricca of Chicago, Dragna and "MoMo" Adamo on the West Coast, and he had met Costello in New Orleans in 1948. He recalled meeting Willie Moretti once in New York, thought he had met Joe Massei of Detroit and Joe Adonis in New York, and he had seen Pete Licavoli of Detroit and Cleveland once or twice in Chicago. On the other hand, he had never met the Capones, Santo Traficante of Tampa, or Joe Profaci of Brooklyn. Denying any business dealings with the figures he knew, Gizzo said he met them at the tracks or casually in resort areas. While one may well discount some of Gizzo's disclaimers, the essence of what he suggested was a limited, casual friendship with underworld figures around the nation, not a conspiracy. Obviously looking for a different pattern, Kefauver remarked to Agent Follmer, who testified the next day, that he was amazed at the "way he [Gizzo] knew every one of them."[9]

8. Kefauver radio interview, Labor's League for Political Education, May 26, 1950, Box 7, Hunt Papers. Washington *Post,* June 10, July 24, 1950. Unidentified news clipping, July 24, 1950, Kefauver Scrapbook IV.

9. *Florida Interim Report,* p. 15. Gizzo testimony, Crime *Hearings,* Pt. 4-A, pp. 285–305. Kefauver statement, ibid., p. 423. Gizzo freely admitted knowing Guzik and Accardo as individuals, but he denied knowing "anyone connected with . . . Continental Press in Chicago." Gizzo had extensive gambling investments in Kansas City, and if his testimony is taken at face value on this point, it could only mean that

The Committee employed the same type of questioning in pursuing the Mafia. In general, the witnesses either denied knowing anything about the Mafia or associated it with Black Hand extortion of an earlier day; invariably, they denied any personal association with such a society. Again, the Gizzo testimony is typical in terms of the answers as well as of the willingness of the Committee to slant them. Halley questioned Gizzo about James Balestrere, alleged high-ranking mafioso in Kansas City.

Mr. Halley. He is rather widely known as a prominent man in the Mafia, isn't he?

Mr. Gizzo. That is what you hear.

Mr. Halley. What do you hear?

Mr. Gizzo. The same that you said here.

Mr. Halley. Have you ever talked to Balestrere about it?

Mr. Gizzo. About what?

Mr. Halley. About his being in the Mafia.

Mr. Gizzo. No, sir.

Mr. Halley. Though you have heard it?

Mr. Gizzo. I have heard it, yes.

Mr. Halley. Are you a member of the Mafia?

Mr. Gizzo. No sir.

Mr. Halley. You know you are under oath.

Mr. Gizzo. That is right.

Mr. Halley. Do you now belong to the Mafia?

Mr. Gizzo. What is the Mafia? I don't even know what the Mafia is.

Mr. Halley. Do you know what the Unione Siciliano is?

Mr. Gizzo. No, sir.

Mr. Halley. Do you belong to any group?

Mr. Gizzo. I don't belong to any group but myself.

Mr. Halley. I will ask the question another way. Do you belong to any group which has been known or termed the "Mafia"?

Mr. Gizzo. No, sir.

Mr. Halley. Did you ever belong to any such group?

Mr. Gizzo. I never did. I never will.

Mr. Halley. Are you sure of that?

Mr. Gizzo. Positive; yes, sir.

Mr. Halley. Have you ever belonged to the Unione Siciliano?

Mr. Gizzo. No sir. My folks are Naples.

Mr. Halley. You never belonged?

Mr. Gizzo. No, sir.

---

either the Capone syndicate had little influence on Continental or that Continental and its subdistributors were more distant than the Committee argued. Ibid., p. 290.

Mr. Halley. You are sure of it?

Mr. Gizzo. Positive.

Mr. Halley. Do you know what the Unione Siciliano is?

Mr. Gizzo. No, sir, I don't know what it is.

Mr. Halley. If you don't know, why do you make the point that your folks are Naples?

Mr. Gizzo. They claim they are Sicilians, you read in the newspaper. Sicilians and Naples are different towns; different, what you call them, dialects.

Halley returned to the same line of questioning when asking about the Fischetti brothers.

Mr. Halley. Do you know whether Fischetti is a member of the Mafia?

Mr. Gizzo. I tell you, I don't know what the Mafia is.

Mr. Halley. You have heard of it, you said. It is a society; is that right?

Mr. Gizzo. All I know about the Mafia is that they had a thing happen here in Kansas City one time about 30 years ago . . .

Mr. Halley. Why do you bring this up?

Mr. Gizzo. That is what I always thought it was, that you sent a letter through the mail, Black Hand, as they call it, definition of the thing.

George White, a Narcotics Bureau agent borrowed by the Committee, who did the initial spadework in Kansas City, later attempted to get Gizzo to make a different kind of admission.

Mr. White. . . . I am just asking you if you have an acquaintance with a lot of people who are termed "members of the Mafia" by the newspapers or otherwise, whether or not that is correct? . . .

Mr. Gizzo. I don't know whether I do. I mentioned the ones I know there. If you say they belong to the Mafia, that is news to me . . .

Mr. White. Do you feel there is a basis of mutual trust and understanding between you and the people that you have said you know here, say, Tony Accardo and Joe Adonis, so that you could do business with each other and trust each other throughout the United States?

Mr. Gizzo. I have never had occasion to do any business with them. I wouldn't say that, I have never had one opportunity to do any business with any one of them. All I know is that I know them and I see them when—race horses, and stuff like that. But I never had any dealings with them.[10]

10. Crime *Hearings,* Pt. 4-A, pp. 492, 504, 508–10, 513, 519, 521, 288–89, 295–96, 299–300.

On September 28, Gizzo denied hearing about the Mafia, and Halley read him his previous testimony to the effect that he had heard that Balestrere was a prominent Mafia member.

Mr. Halley. . . . Do you remember giving those answers to those questions?

Mr. Gizzo. I might have, but I don't remember that. What you hear is what you read in the newspapers.

Mr. Halley. You at least heard that Balestrere is a prominent man in the Mafia, is that right?

Mr. Gizzo. That I couldn't tell you, Mr. Halley.[11]

Despite the obviously inconclusive nature of the testimony, the Committee cited Gizzo's hesitation as to whether he had "heard" of Balestrere's link with the Mafia as proof of the existence of such a society. To the Committee, the admission by Gizzo and others that they knew persons whom the press labeled Mafia members constituted evidence of a Mafia; the denials of membership or knowledge of such an organization by other alleged mafiosi indicated an effort to conceal the existence of the secret society. In effect, no matter what the witnesses answered, the Committee interpreted it as evidence of the existence of the Mafia and its influence in the underworld.[12]

Halley and George Robinson pursued the same line of questioning with Ricca, Campagna, and Gioe in an executive session in Washington on September 9. In general, the three admitted knowing men who were popularly thought to be associated with a Capone syndicate, but they denied the existence of such a syndicate; they also denied knowing many so-called underworld figures in other areas of the country and claimed that the only knowledge they had of a Mafia came from the newspapers. Ricca, for example, did not know Adonis, Zwillman, Massei of Detroit, Willie Moretti, Mickey Co-

11. Crime *Hearings*, Pt. 4-A, pp. 127–29.

12. *Third Interim Report*, p. 149. Gordon Hawkins, "God and the Mafia," *The Public Interest* (Winter 1969), 26. Some of the witnesses in Kansas City obviously committed perjury, as did Joseph DiGiovanni, an exasperating illiterate who reportedly earned $80,000 in 1948 through an interest in a liquor distributorship. DiGiovanni denied certain arrests and convictions in 1915 for writing a Black Hand note until presented with his actual police record, complete with photograph. After claiming that he could not recognize the picture because he had left his glasses at home, DiGiovanni later returned with spectacles and admitted his police record. Crime *Hearings*, Pt. 4, pp. 313–31, 367–75.

hen, Fred Angersola of Cleveland, "Little Augie" Pisano, Vincent Mangano, Joseph Profaci, Vito Genovese, or—significantly—William H. Johnson. While many Chicago underworld figures fled the Committee's subpoenas, the senators' counsel succeeded in questioning Jack Dragna of California, who echoed Ricca and Gizzo by denying that he knew such figures as Guzik, Kastel, Massei, and Sam Maceo of Galveston, and by claiming that he too knew the Mafia only through the newspapers. Cook County's Sheriff Walsh denied knowledge of the Capone syndicate as well as of the Mafia. United States Attorney Otto Kerner, Jr., who had, at the Attorney General's Conference in February denied having any evidence of a Capone syndicate, argued in early October on the basis of evidence he apparently had had in February that Peterson's theories were a "good probability or possibility."[13]

The Committee placed great credence in the testimony of Philip D'Andrea, a convicted member of the motion picture extortion conspiracy and former head of Unione Siciliana, the Italo-American fraternal insurance group that had reputedly been dominated at one time by Capone. D'Andrea told the senators that the fear of the Mafia or Black Hand extortion was discussed in the homes of those born in Sicily and Italy, and it would be unusual for anyone of such background to deny that they had heard of the Mafia. Kefauver seized upon this statement to show that other witnesses were lying about their knowledge of the society. He chose to ignore the main thrust of D'Andrea's testimony, however, which was that the Mafia was equivalent to the dread practice of Black Hand extortion, that D'Andrea himself, despite his association with Capone, knew no individuals as Mafia members, and that the organization—if indeed it was an organization—appeared to be decentralized and declining.[14]

Both the senators and the press persisted in elaborating on the evidence and testimony presented before the Committee in Chicago. The Knoxville *News-Sentinel* reported that Ke-

13. Crime *Hearings,* Pt. 5, pp. 41, 44, 90, 24, 93–94, 16–23, 407–37, 177, 181. *The Attorney General's Conference on Organized Crime, February 15, 1950* (Washington: Department of Justice, 1950), p. 41. Crime *Hearings,* Pt. 5, pp. 183–84.

14. D'Andrea testimony, Crime *Hearings,* Pt. 5, pp. 346–72. Humbert S. Nelli, *The Italians in Chicago, 1880–1930: A Study in Ethnic Mobility* (New York: Oxford University Press, 1970), p. 220. *Third Interim Report,* p. 149.

fauver had explained that he was convinced of the existence
of a Mafia by the admissions of Dragna and John Rosseli (Los
Angeles figures convicted in the movie extortion case), who
were supposed to have acknowledged knowing people in the
Mafia. Actually, of course, they admitted knowing persons
whom other sources linked with the Mafia, and Dragna had
specifically denied any knowledge of the society outside of
what he had read in the paper. The *News-Sentinel,* moreover,
reported that D'Andrea "sang" about the Mafia before the
Committee, certainly an overblown description of the testimony actually given. The Chicago *Tribune* reported that
Senator Wiley had claimed that the senators had "established" the existence of a Mafia and that, while Kansas City
gangsters had told them Costello was the national boss, the
Committee regarded Ricca as the "head man." Since Ricca
was on parole, however, he had temporarily given his "proxy"
to Accardo.[15] George White, a narcotics agent who was serving
as an investigator for the Committee, claimed that he had a
"pipe line" to the "inner circle" of a four-man boss board of
rackets (one man each from New York, Kansas City, Los Angeles, and Chicago) who passed on murder requests from the
underworld and occasionally commissioned a Mafia enforcement ring to do the killing. White maintained that the "full
story," on which he had been working for weeks, would appear in the Committee's final report.[16]

Meanwhile, columnist Drew Pearson and his associate, Jack
Anderson, both of whom looked with favor on the Kefauver
Committee, reprinted portions of Anslinger's testimony in the
executive hearing. In mid-October Pearson began a series of
articles, apparently based on material from the Narcotics
Bureau, stating that fifty men controlled the larger rackets in

15. Knoxville *News-Sentinel,* October 8, 1950. Dragna and Rosseli
testimony, Crime *Hearings,* Pt. 5, pp. 373–437, 410. Chicago *Tribune,*
October 1, 1950. The published transcript of the hearings in Missouri
fail to reveal any gangster's statement to the effect that Costello was
a national crime boss. Almost certainly if such a statement had been
made off the record, it would have been indicated in the Committee's
reports to the Senate, but no such claim appears in the reports.

16. Chattanooga *News-Free Press,* October 6, 1950. No new "Murder,
Inc." study appeared in the Committee's reports, and White, who pio-
neered the Missouri hearings, went on to Chicago, where he clashed
with Counsel George S. Robinson and apparently with Virgil Peterson.
The exact circumstances leading to White's departure from the Committee in Chicago are not clear. Robinson, Rice, Peterson interviews;
White to Kefauver, February 15, 1951, Crime Box 37, Kefauver Papers.

the United States; that all were members of the "mysterious Mafia"; that all but one were either Italian born or of Italo-American descent; and that Luciano, deported by Dewey for "some strange reason," directed the organization from Italy. According to a confidential memorandum from Anslinger that Pearson quoted, the Mafia had once been an honorable, if illegal, institution in Sicily, but it had lost its "spartan qualities" and had become degenerate and reactionary after Prohibition enriched its members. Cataloging a long list of underworld figures that included Costello, Adonis, Marcello, Accardo, and Profaci, Pearson concluded that the Mafia was a loose, fraternal society controlled by Luciano in Italy. To expose such an organization, Kefauver supposedly risked both personal and political safety, for the Mafia had "real political connections" that had once even attempted to gain White House influence through the "naive" Gen. Harry Vaughan. Pearson's articles, possibly written on information supplied by a Committee leak, caught Kefauver's eye and impressed him favorably.[17]

Despite the proclivities of the Committee's staff members, Tobey, Wiley, and even Kefauver, to make hasty statements to the press on the Mafia and nationwide crime syndicates, Kefauver appeared confused by the evidence and assertions. In early November he told reporters that his group had turned up no evidence of anything resembling a national crime syndicate, although there appeared to be at least an informal working arrangement among regional groups and there might still be a central organization among them. Six weeks later the Committee publicly admitted to being frustrated by its inability to draw clear lines on the national crime picture.[18]

Meanwhile, the staff prodded Kefauver toward the theory

17. Washington *Post*, August 20, October 10, 12, 13, 17, 1950. Kefauver to Pearson, October 14, 1950, Crime Box 1, Kefauver Papers. There was some fear of physical violence against Committee members. Kefauver's administrative assistant, Charles Neese, studied the possibility and concluded that an attempt on the Chairman's life was unlikely because the underworld seemed to strike out physically only against those who had once cooperated with it. Neese recalled, however, that once during the hearings, he was at a street corner in Washington with Kefauver when an automobile for no apparent reason swerved toward the Senator, barely missing him. Neese never determined whether the near-miss was actually an attempt at assassination. Personal interview, Charles G. Neese, Winchester, Tenn., July 8, 1971.

18. New York *Times*, November 12, December 24, 1950.

that the Mafia controlled the nation's organized crime. George S. Robinson, in charge of the investigation in Chicago, forwarded to the Chairman on November 24 a long report on the Mafia that apparently stressed the role of Anthony Accardo in the organization. In a memorandum a few weeks later Robinson noted that Accardo was "reported to be an influential member of the international Mafia Society although the records do not indicate that he had engaged in illicit narcotics traffic. However, he is probably one of the most influential members of the Mafia." Halley, who flew to Chicago to direct the questioning, told reporters that "from the evidence gathered thus far" Accardo appeared to be the "national syndicate boss." Then he added, "but it might be the Fischetti brothers, Rocco or Charles. They're smarter than Accardo." To Halley, who was following the advice of Pecora to find a "big man," it apparently never occurred that there might not be a "Mr. Big."[19]

Meanwhile, the Committee's chief investigator, Harold G. Robinson, in preparing for hearings on the West Coast, arranged for the appearance of inspectors Frank Ahern and Thomas Cahill, reputed Mafia "experts" of the San Francisco Police Department. In testimony broken by frequent interruptions off the record, Ahern described the interstate ties of persons who had been involved in the slaying of former Chicago gangland figure Nick DeJohn in 1947. The inspectors and their chief, James English, maintained that the details of the murder as well as the interstate background of the persons supposedly involved, established the existence of the Mafia, a loose-knit national syndicate consisting largely of Italian-Americans involved in narcotics, extortion, and legitimate business. Tobey and Kefauver were so impressed by Ahern and Cahill that they immediately appointed the inspectors to the Committee's staff, where they were charged with developing the leads on the Mafia. Halley emphasized to the men that the Committee needed not just a "story," but also concrete evidence that might help locate records or enable the Committee to seize the men and "prove the existence of the Mafia."[20] For reasons

19. Kefauver memorandum to George Robinson, December 11, 1950; Kefauver memorandum to Harold Robinson, December 11, 1950, Crime Box 5, Kefauver Papers. File memorandum on Accardo from George S. Robinson, January 5, 1950 [*sic*] Box 101, Tobey Papers. Washington *Daily News*, December 18, 1950. Rice interview.

20. Ahern and Cahill testimony, Crime *Hearings*, Pt. 10, pp. 494–503.

still not clear, the Committee apparently never seriously attempted to develop the DeJohn killing into tangible proof of a Mafia organization.

Halley, with an eye to a dramatic story, had all along been seeking to merge the theories of Peterson and Anslinger. In a memorandum to the newly created American Bar Association Commission on Organized Crime on October 27, the Chief Counsel explained that the underworld seemed to operate on two levels. First, due to "general business, social, and political connections," gangsters sought out one another for cooperation in financial ventures in a number of areas, such as Miami and South Florida. Halley asserted that these associations constituted a loose-knit organization in the same sense that violation of antitrust laws by companies operating in concert but without formal framework was "organized." On a second level, Halley noted that the Committee had "strong evidence" that many of the underworld figures loosely linked through various financial ventures belonged to the Sicilian-dominated Mafia. At first the Mafia had appeared "almost fictional" to Halley, but he noted the piling up of evidence that showed its existence. The Mafia, a continuation of the ruthless Black Hand, provided a "framework within which loose-knit criminal combinations could be controlled." Halley, Pecora's protégé, had all but merged the search for a "Mr. Big" and the quest for the Mafia.[21]

Daniel Sullivan of the Crime Commission of Greater Miami, noting "how greatly interested" Halley was in the Mafia, urged Kefauver to explore the topic in Tampa where, he alleged, Italian racketeers had only recently displaced the more numerous Latin-American and Cuban gangsters. Sullivan explained that Latin-American racketeers might testify concerning numerous gangland murders and might even implicate Santo Trafficante, reputed head of the local Mafia for twenty years. In his testimony in July, Virgil Peterson had touched on the rumored Mafia connections of certain figures

---

Kefauver thought that the Ahern and Cahill statements constituted the best collection of information the Committee had heard on the Mafia. California Attorney General-elect Edmund G. "Pat" Brown also thought that the material on the DeJohn killing showed that "all these people are associated together." Ibid., pp. 421–27.

21. Memorandum, Halley to the American Bar Association Commission on Organized Crime, October 27, 1950, Crime Box 37, Kefauver Papers.

in the Tampa underworld, and as usual, local newspapers had distorted his statement.[22]

In Tampa the Committee not only failed to demonstrate the presence of the Mafia, but it ran into new pitfalls. The senators contended that narcotics smuggling activities and about fourteen unsolved gangland slayings over twenty years in Tampa provided prima facie evidence of large-scale organized crime. The discovery of Trafficante's and local gambler James Lumia's telephone numbers among Dragna's seized effects and the tracing of murder weapons to New Orleans provided the appropriate interstate touches. In late December, however, as the Committee opened hearings in Tampa, it discovered it was unable to make an adequate investigation of the "Mafia background" of unsolved murders due to the avoidance of the Committee's subpoenas by underworld figures. "Admittedly," the Committee's report explained, "the participation of the Mafia in Tampa's series of murders and attempted assassinations is predicated on inferences."[23]

Probably one of the two most effective witnesses the Committee produced was Mrs. Anthony DiLorenzo, divorced wife of a former deputy sheriff, who testified that her husband had received money to act as a go-between for the gamblers and law officers and had known about, if not participated in, the murder of Lumia in June of 1950. The money allegedly came from Ignazio "Big Red" Italiano, an underworld figure deeply involved in the local bolita game, a variation of the numbers racket. Mrs. DiLorenzo stated that there was indeed a Mafia, although her husband, not being on the "inside," did not know who ran it and "never talked much about" it. Tampa's new chief of police, M. C. Beasley, a veteran of twenty-five years in law enforcement, agreed with Mrs. DiLorenzo that a Mafia existed, and he characterized it as consisting of southern Italians and Sicilians who had arrived in the United States in the early years of Mussolini's regime, had contributed to the rise of Capone and others, and now operated through political con-

22. Sullivan to Kefauver, November 18, 1950, Crime Box 5, Kefauver Papers. Unidentified Tampa newspaper clipping, August 8, 1950, Kefauver Scrapbook IV, p. 111.

23. *Third Interim Report,* pp. 63–64. Daniel P. Sullivan had helped organize the hearings in Tampa. The centerpiece of both the Miami and Tampa sessions was the use of charts to dramatize the testimony. This technique was to be used later in the McClellan Committee's "Valachi hearings." Crime *Hearings,* Pt. 1-A, pp. 260, 482–83.

tacts higher than himself. He assumed that the Mafia was responsible for the series of unsolved murders in Tampa "because of the circumstances that surround each one of them," and believed that the actual trigger men were "imported" so as to make apprehension more difficult. The senators reproduced in their report the portions of Beasley's testimony stating that a Mafia existed and exercised influence through political contacts, but they ignored less convincing testimony that appears on the same page.

Senator Hunt. A couple of minutes ago in your testimony you made reference to the influence the leaders of the Mafia have because of political influence on a higher level than your own. Would you designate what level and whom you have reference to?

Mr. Beasley. Well, I don't have any reference to any particular level, sir. It is all along the line, in my opinion, more or less.

Senator Hunt. Well, spell them out, if you will; name them. What levels do you have in mind?

Mr. Beasley. Well, maybe it is not the Mafia influence so much as it is the gamblers, we will say, because I can't say that the Mafia has direct influence on any politician.[24]

Although Counsels Downey Rice and Ralph Mills attempted to emphasize the Mafia's domination of local crime, the pattern that emerged was instead one of domination by local law enforcement officers with probably little reference to a Mafia. A former city policeman, whom Sullivan had mentioned as a good source of information on the Mafia, testified that rumor held that Hillsborough County's Sheriff Hugh Culbreath and Police Chief J. L. Eddings had been unable to agree on who would head the gambling syndicate. The witness also repeated as rumor the story that Trafficante had been head of the Tampa Mafia for two decades and argued that, in view of the unsolved murders, one would almost be forced to believe in such an organization. Other witnesses testified along the same line, repeating widespread rumor and speculation but generally making law officers, not the gangsters, the real arbiters of power. Mario Lounders, former associate of Jimmy Valesco, one of the murder victims, testified that he could not tell whether Sheriff Culbreath, Chief Eddings, or State's Attorney Rex Farrior was "Mr. Big." Charles M. Wall, whom Rice dubbed "an elder statesman" of Tampa gambling interests and who had recently been the object of five assassination

24. Crime *Hearings,* Pt. 1-A, pp. 167–86, 86–87.

attempts, denied knowing of any ethnic cycle of gambling domination in Tampa. Despite Rice's efforts to coach him, Wall explained that, because of his retirement from gambling almost a decade earlier, he knew nothing of the penetration of local rackets from California. Obviously, the Committee's case against the Mafia in Tampa had collapsed.[25]

In subsequent sessions, the Mafia issue reappeared, but never again was a series of hearings built around such an ephemeral theme. A local press build-up in New Orleans stressed the Committee's interest in the Mafia and Kefauver emphasized the significance of Carlos Marcello's role as a Mafia kingpin, but at the same time the Chairman admitted to reporters that "we've had difficulty in determining just what the Mafia is." In Detroit, Counsel John Burling attempted to link the Mafia to the antilabor activities of the Ford Motor Company, but with less than total success. Later on, in New York, Rudolph Halley was to devote most of his attention to identifying Costello as a "Mr. Big" but little to equating that identity with activity in the Mafia.[26]

Seeking a dramatic conclusion for its report and apparently reluctant to oppose the Narcotics Bureau's theory, the Committee gradually drifted toward a definite statement on the Mafia. Henry Patrick Kiley of Kefauver's office warned the Senator against the growing emphasis on the Mafia in the Committee's conclusions. Kiley, resentful of Halley's emphasis of the New York phase of the hearings, observed that about as many Irish and Jews as Italians appeared on the Committee's "wanted" list, and that the Senator could lose more than gain by awarding "all the oak leaf clusters" to the Italians.[27]

Halley fell ill during the final week of April and Morris Ploscowe, executive director of the A.B.A. Commission,

25. Crime *Hearings,* Pt. 1-A, pp. 137–50, 155, 236–38, 241, 242–53, 239–42, 60–71. In subsequent testimony in Washington, Culbreath and Farrior argued with some persuasion that the Committee had drawn most of its information from a local political opponent and that during their administrations there had been an actual decline in gambling and vice. Both cited local grand juries and anticrime groups that complimented their work. Culbreath, however, in particular, never explained satisfactorily the source of his unusually large income. Ibid., pp. 345–93, 395–457.

26. New Orleans *Item,* January 24, 1951. New Orleans *States,* January 25, 1951. *Third Interim Report,* pp. 82–83. Crime *Hearings,* Pt. 9, pp. 102–3, 78–80.

27. Kiley to Kefauver, n.d., Crime Box 37, Kefauver Papers.

drafted much of the widely heralded *Third Interim Report.* Kefauver maintained a close eye on the work, however, and the result reflects his own perspective as well as that of the Chief Counsel. Essentially, the report expanded the thumbnail sketch of the underworld Halley had drawn for the Patterson Commission in October.[28] The occasional joint financial ventures, telephone conversations, meetings at resort areas and race tracks, gambling transactions, wire service agreements, as well as actual admissions before the Committee established at least some familiarity among underworld leaders in all areas of the country. Through such associations almost any figure could be connected with any other in the nation. Whether or not the Committee properly gauged the degree of familiarity or concentration within the underworld either in the various cities or on the national level can be questioned. Even the inquiry into the wire service, its strongest exhibit, failed to show that the Capone syndicate, so glibly discussed, consisted of more than three or four of the many former associates of Capone in Chicago; nor did it demonstrate that the nationwide wire service alone was an effective instrument for securing local monopolies; nor, for that matter, did it prove that the so-called Capone gang dominated Continental as much as the popular press and the Committee reports suggested. While the influence of the press and local crime commissions probably prompted the Committee to exaggerate the extent and significance of casual, informal associations among gamblers around the country, there was at least some factual basis for the conclusions and some need for congressional concern.

A second level of interpretation involved the Narcotics Bureau's theory of the Mafia as the secret government that dominated the looser underworld organization Peterson had described. Here, the Committee pursued a tragic myth. Because the staff devoted most of its time to the Peterson thesis and investigation of the wire service, little time or energy could be devoted to critically appraising the scanty, inconclusive data on the Mafia or to developing historical or sociologi-

28. Personal interview, Morris Ploscowe, New York, August 21, 1969. *Third Interim Report,* pp. ii, 23, 1–5. Ironically, Ploscowe had written an excellent article in 1941 stressing the socioeconomic origins of crime in general and organized crime in particular. Morris Ploscowe, "Crime in a Competitive Society," *The Annals of the American Academy of Political and Social Sciences* (September 1941), 105–11.

cal perspectives on the problem. Having adopted a law enforcement rather than sociological view of crime, the Committee readily accepted Anslinger's contention that the narcotics traffic, gambling, and assorted vice went hand in hand;
because a Mafia headed by Luciano supposedly dominated
trade in illicit drugs, it might control other illegal activities as
well.[29] Anslinger and his allies in the press in effect constituted the only organized pressure on the Committee on this
point, and the senators moved easily in that direction. Their
acceptance of the theory that the Mafia controlled organized
crime accounts for the stunning gaps in logic in the hearings.
When the senators asked a witness if he knew certain figures
who had been identified by others as affiliates of the Mafia,
they concluded that a positive answer meant the witness knew
them *as Mafia figures,* and a negative answer meant he was
concealing a conspiracy. The records reveal an incredible nai-
vete on the part of educated and supposedly sophisticated men
who accepted as fact the repetition of common rumor by witnesses who qualified their statements to the extent of render-
ing them all but meaningless. While the Committee claimed
to have "off-the-record but convincing statements of certain
informants who must remain anonymous," its record in judging statements on the Mafia in open session is not such as to
establish confidence in its critical abilities on this issue. The
one concrete piece of evidence mentioned in its report is a
photograph of twenty-three men who were arrested in a
Cleveland hotel in 1928 in what later commentators claimed
was a meeting of the Mafia Grand Council. One of these, Joseph Profaci of New York, had been unable to explain his
presence in Cleveland at the time to the Committee's satisfaction. On the basis of such paltry evidence the Committee concluded that there existed a "Nation-wide crime syndicate
known as Mafia" with international ramifications in the narcotics traffic; that the "centralized direction and control" it
exercised over the more profitable rackets appeared to be held
by a group rather than one man; that it provided "the cement"
that bound together the Costello–Adonis–Lansky group on the
East Coast, the Capone syndicate of Chicago, as well as
smaller syndicates throughout the country; and that the
groups kept in contact with Luciano. In effect, the Committee
had accepted both the moderate Peterson and extremist Anslinger theses, simply imposing the one on the other and sug-

29. New York *Times,* March 12, 1951. Bell, *End of Ideology,* 138–41.

gesting the maximum concentration in the underworld. While admitting the difficulty in obtaining "reliable data," the Committee placed its prestige behind the discovery of the "elusive, shadowy, and sinister organization."[30]

Ironically, doubts arose among the staff and friends of the Committee sooner than among the public at large. Almost before the ink was dry on the Committee report, Rudolph Halley himself told reporter Lester Velie that had the Committee had a larger staff and more time, it "might have learned the truth about the Mafia [*sic*]." Legislative Counsel Rufus G. King, in the same year, bluntly stated that the Committee's conclusions on the Mafia were "romantic myth." On "Meet the Press," just as the Committee's report was appearing, Kefauver said the Mafia was more a way of life than an organization, and within five months he addressed the American Bar Association on "The Menace of Organized Crime" without mentioning the Mafia. Virgil Peterson, who held the confidence of Kefauver and the entire staff and whose men had access to all materials in the Committee files before it left Chicago, remained unconvinced of the proof of a Mafia's domination of organized crime in the United States.[31]

Because of their searches for dramatic and simplified analyses and because of the limited staff and time at their disposal, congressional committees frequently have endorsed conspiracy interpretations of important public issues.[32] The

---

30. *Third Interim Report,* pp. 147–50. In a report issued three months earlier, the Committee had concluded that if there was one single person acting as arbiter between the regional syndicates, it was Luciano. In the *Third Interim Report,* this statement was slightly modified and Luciano's role played down. *Second Interim Report,* p. 10; *Third Interim Report,* p. 150.

31. Lester Velie, "Rudolph Halley—How He Nailed America's Racketeers," *Collier's,* May 19, 1951, p. 82. Rufus King, "The Control of Organized Crime," *Stanford Law Review* (December 1951), 52 n4. "Meet the Press," April 1, 1951. Viewing Print in Motion Picture Division, Library of Congress. *Congressional Record,* September 25, 1951, pp. A5840–42. Peterson interview. Peterson to James E. Walker, January 5, 1955, File No. 6055, Chicago Crime Commission Records. Two knowledgeable reporters, Meyer Berger and Chambers Roberts, pointed out the exaggeration of the Mafia arguments in reviewing Kefauver's book, *Crime in America.* New York *Times,* July 15, 1951. Washington *Post,* July 15, 1951. Among the academic critics of the conclusions were Daniel Bell of Columbia University and Paul Tappan of New York University. Bell, *End of Ideology,* p. 141; Paul W. Tappan, *Crime, Justice, and Correction* (New York: McGraw-Hill Book Company, 1960), p. 232.

32. Jerold S. Auerbach, *Labor and Liberty: The La Follette Commit-*

Kefauver Committee fell into this pattern. Created in the midst of rampant fears and rumors about politico-criminal conspiracies, the Committee not so much investigated the problem as it dramatized the perspectives of the crime commissions on national crime syndicates and of the Narcotics Bureau on the Mafia. Particularly in the case of the Mafia, the senators lacked adequate evidence for their conclusions. Because such groups as the press and the academic community failed to point out the weaknesses in the Committee's overblown and unfounded statements, the public accepted them, and the popular myths and misunderstandings grew stronger, buttressed by the "proofs" of the Kefauver Committee. Sensational journalists and publishers enjoyed a field day, explaining and enlarging upon the Committee's work; gangster movies and television programs dramatized variations of the same theme; and academic and legal experts joined in echoing the Committee's conclusions.[33] Even after the initial shock and novelty of the Kefauver findings had lifted and critics began to question the more sweeping Committee statements, the public at large continued to hold to the older conspiracy view, thus making more difficult an intelligent appraisal of organized crime.[34]

---

tee and the New Deal (Indianapolis: The Bobbs-Merrill Co., Inc., 1966), p. 5.

33. Among the more popular accounts of the 1950s were Ed Reid, *Mafia* (New York: Random House, Inc., 1952), Robert H. Prall and Norton Mockridge, *This is Costello* (Chicago: Fawcett Publications, Inc., 1951), Joachim Joesten and Sid Feder, *The Luciano Story* (New York: David McKay Company, Inc., 1954), and the Lait and Mortimer volumes. For typical professional and academic acceptance, see Morris Ploscowe, ed., for American Bar Association, *Organized Crime and Law Enforcement*, 2 vols. (New York: Grosby Press, 1952–1953), and Robert G. Caldwell, *Criminology* (New York: The Ronald Press Company, 1965). Among motion pictures having a direct reference to the Committee were "Damn Citizen," "Deadline, U.S.A.," and "Hoodlum Empire." Colin McArthur, *Underworld U.S.A.* (London: Secker and Warburg, 1972), pp. 68–70.

34. In a brilliant recent anthropological study, Francis Ianni argues that the Mafia stigma has retarded Italian acculturation into American society and he cites a Harris poll, published in May, 1971, showing that 78 per cent of the American public believe that there exists "a secret organization engaged in organized crime in this country which is called the Mafia." Francis A. J. Ianni, *A Family Business: Kinship and Social Control in Organized Crime* (New York: Russell Sage Foundation, 1972), p. 194.

6

The Politics of Crime

Mr. Noonan. Senator, I know you know a certain
amount of politics.
The Chairman. We are practical politicians.
—Kansas City *Hearings,* July 19, 1950

If the Committee had good reason to think it knew the probable conclusions it would reach on organized crime, its political impact remained uncertain. The stormy political atmosphere that had first threatened Kefauver's proposals for an investigation in the spring of 1950 continued to hover over the Committee, coloring—if not shaping—its every decision. Because it was dealing with an explosive issue in an election year, the Kefauver Committee was to find that the choice of local sources, the timing of hearings in selected cities, the decision to release or to withhold executive testimony, and the need to educate the public through the popular press became political considerations.[1] During the prolonged fight over the creation of the Committee, a substantial segment of the press became increasingly convinced that powerful political forces both in and out of government opposed the revelations Kefauver might make, and many of these newspapers resolved to withhold judgment on the Committee until it demonstrated that it was free of political control and intended no whitewash.

Kefauver grasped the nature of the problems but not the depth of the feelings behind them. He had hoped to repeat the performance of the Truman Committee, cultivating the confi-

1. For the comparable experience of the La Follette Committee, see Jerold S. Auerbach, *Labor and Liberty: The La Follette Committee and the New Deal* (Indianapolis: The Bobbs-Merrill Co., Inc., 1966), pp. 81–84.

dence and trust of the Administration and his party's leaders while at the same time making political and press contacts across the country and building up a base of public support by identifying his name with a popular cause. This done, Kefauver would be "available" for higher office in 1952 or 1956. The task he set himself called for an extremely high level of political talent and luck. The Chairman understood that the Democrats controlled most of the big cities he planned to investigate, and to expose conditions there to the satisfaction of the skeptical press and the public, while at the same time avoiding unnecessary embarrassment to local Democrats and the national party, would be a delicate and demanding job. As he had explained to Senator Lucas during the debate over the creation of the Committee, he felt that failure to deal seriously with the problems presented by organized crime would cost the party grievously, while a thorough and intelligent review would redound to the ultimate advantage of the Democrats, who would receive the public credit for cleaning their own house.[2]

As the work of the Committee got under way in May, the predominant public reaction was one of skepticism. Columnist Robert C. Ruark reminded his readers of a Missouri political adage, "When it is hot in Kansas City, you can make it seem cooler by raising the temperature out of town." One persistent rumor held that Kefauver had been promised the Vice Presidency in exchange for a whitewash of the political scene in Missouri. The Senator brushed aside such speculation with the explanation that he had not had time to organize his Committee or to convince the public of his sincerity.[3] In the meantime, Kefauver was striving to establish unanimity within the Committee; he stressed the need to eschew sensationalism; and he expressed a desire to hire counsel who nourished no

2. "Quizzing Kefauver: An Interview with Senator Estes Kefauver," *U.S. News & World Report,* April 20, 1951, pp. 26–27. Kefauver to Lucas, April 4, 1950, Crime Box 37, Kefauver Papers.

3. *Christian Science Monitor,* May 10, 1950. Washington *Daily News,* June 7, 1950. Memphis *Commercial Appeal,* May 3, 1950. Knoxville *Journal,* May 21, 1950. Springfield (Tenn.) *Herald,* May 12, 1950. Nashville *Tennessean,* May 19, 1950. Chattanooga *Times,* May 8, 1950. Madisonville (Tenn.) *Democrat,* May 31, 1950. Unidentified clippings, May 16, 20, 1950, Kefauver Scrapbook, III. C. J. Gashell to Kefauver, May 10, 1950; Manley W. Immell to Kefauver, May 11, 1950; C. Guy Stephenson to Kefauver, May 16, 1950; Kefauver to Stephenson, May 20, 1950, Crime Box 2, Kefauver Papers.

active political ambitions. While explaining that the careful collection and sifting of evidence would necessarily delay the holding of public hearings, Kefauver reassured the public that the Committee would operate "on a purely non-partisan basis, without regard to politics in any form or fashion."[4] In various times and places throughout the next year, Kefauver repeated again and again that his study was free of politics, that he was "not grinding anybody's axes," and that he was allowing "the chips to fall where they may."[5] Until after the elections in November, however, many observers doubted Kefauver's claims, and in the meantime, the best the Senator could do was to keep the press from turning actively against him.

Kefauver difficulties sprang in part from the Republican challenge in the fall campaign. The impulsive Senator Tobey, whose eccentric and emotional outbursts during the hearings camouflaged a shrewd political mind, used his membership on the Committee to advance his own reelection in New Hampshire. Tobey prodded the Committee to open an investigation into gambling operations in Boston and New England, from which he might benefit; he blasted law enforcement in Saratoga and New York City; he attempted to link his New Hampshire political opponents to crime syndicates; and he dramatically called for "righteous indignation" as the proper and most effective tool against organized crime. At one point in October, he issued a half-hearted statement criticizing Kefauver for concentrating on New Jersey gambling rather than on the Harry Gross gambling scandal in Brooklyn, and he expressed disappointment at the Committee's failure to call former Mayor O'Dwyer to testify during the executive sessions in New York the same month. After making a great deal of noise about the Committee's linking Binaggio with the 1947 ballot theft in Kansas City, Tobey arrived for the hearings, ignorant of whether the stolen ballots were from a primary or a general election. Meanwhile, he had drawn fire for his appearance on the low-grade "Gang Busters" television series. Too busy in his own campaign to help Kefauver, Tobey simply

4. Undated typewritten statement of Committee objectives, Crime Box 37, Kefauver Papers. Nashville *Banner,* May 4, 1950. Kefauver radio statement, Labor's League for Political Education, May 26, 1950, Box 7, Hunt Papers.

5. Crime *Hearings,* Pt. 4, pp. 35–39. Estes Kefauver, *Crime in America* (Garden City, N.Y.: Doubleday & Company, Inc., 1951), p. 16.

grabbed for any advantage he could gain from membership on the Committee, and his enemies in New Hampshire responded by trying to show the shallowness of Tobey's claims to being a crime fighter.[6]

While providing little substantive aid to the Committee's chairman, Tobey did blunt the criticism of Republican Wiley, also engaged in a hard-fought campaign for reelection. Wiley and his administrative assistant, Julius Cahn, had proposed different Chicago attorneys to Kefauver for both chief counsel and minority counsel, hoping thereby to divert more of the Committee's work to Chicago and improve their reelection chances in nearby Wisconsin. Tobey resolutely opposed Wiley's choices and instead sponsored George S. Robinson, a native of Maine, for minority counsel. Wiley privately attacked Kefauver, Tobey, and Robinson and on one occasion threatened to resign from the Committee. In late May, while this internal controversy raged, Wiley charged in a speech over the Chicago *Tribune*'s radio station that "certain outside influences . . . connected with the Democratic political organization" were attempting to "pervert" the Committee's work. In Miami, occupied with the first set of executive hearings, Kefauver denied any such pressure.[7]

6. Boston *Daily Record,* August 1, 1950. Providence *Journal,* June 19, 1950. New York *Times,* October 12, 1950. Chicago *Tribune,* October 13, 1950. Knoxville *News-Sentinel,* July 20, 1950. Crime *Hearings,* Pt. 4-A, p. 439. Arthur J. Freund to Tobey, June 7, 1950; Halley to William Loeb, September 11, 1950, Box 102, Tobey Papers. Tobey enjoyed the thrill of detective work but did not have time for it prior to the November election. Senator Styles Bridges and the Manchester *Union*'s editor, William Loeb, backed Bridges's young administrative assistant, Wesley Powell, in the hard-fought Republican primary against Tobey. Tobey liked to think that E. H. Pauley, whose nomination as Secretary of the Navy he had blocked, was behind the Loeb–Powell campaign. The financing of Tobey's own campaign was the subject of a Senate investigation shortly after the election. Charles W. Tobey, "What Are We Going to do About It?" *The American Magazine* (April 1951), 30–31, 102–5. Washington *Post,* October 6, 1950. Tobey to John Manning, December [?], 1950; Tobey to Richard Barnard, April 7, 1951, Box 101, Tobey Papers.

7. Wiley to Kefauver, June 8, 19, 1950, Crime Box 37, Kefauver Papers. Tobey to Kefauver, May 19, 1950, Box 102, Tobey Papers. Cahn to Wiley, June 9, 1950, Series 7, Folder 4, Box 58, Wiley Papers. Robinson interview. Washington *Post,* May 28, 1950. Washington *Star,* May 28, 1950. Miami *Evening Star,* May 28, 1950. A year later Kefauver admitted that there had been certain political pressure from friends of subpoenaed witnesses, but denied any pressure from the White

A month later, Wiley, who had earlier called for "silent sleuthing" rather than headline snatching, began suggesting that the Committee was chasing "mice" when it should be pursuing the perpetrators of such crimes as the murders and ballot thefts in Kansas City. Kefauver moved to accommodate Wiley by announcing that hearings would indeed be held in Kansas City. In August, through public statements and in letters to the Washington *Post* and to Kefauver, the Senator from Wisconsin told of rumored ties between unnamed "national politicians" and "individuals representing illegitimate pursuits." To Kefauver personally he insisted that the Committee mention in its first interim report Jacksonville magnate Louis Wolfson's $150,000 contribution to Governor Fuller Warren's 1948 campaign as well as Frank Erickson's indirect contribution of $2,500 to the Democratic National Committee in 1947. Kefauver again complied with Wiley's demands. In Kansas City, Wiley interested himself more in the Mafia than in politico-criminal links, and while insisting that the Democrats were more responsible for crime because of Democratic control of the big cities, he actually defended Kefauver against alleged political "slurs" in Chicago. Wiley, burdened with other committee assignments and faced with his own reelection campaign, lacked the energy to transform the Committee's business into a distinctly partisan issue, as Ferguson or Donnell might have done. By making a series of relatively minor concessions, Kefauver had appeased Wiley and thus maintained a reasonable degree of harmony within the Committee. Meanwhile, pro-Kefauver publications reminded the Senator from Wisconsin that, since he was attending few of the hearings, his criticisms were sounding increasingly superficial, and his opposition in Wisconsin began to mock his "Dick Tracy" statements.[8]

House or the Democratic National Committee. Although Wiley did not apparently have reference to them, there is strong evidence that Senators Claude Pepper and Clinton Anderson approached Kefauver on behalf of two witnesses. There was nothing specifically improper in their doing so; probably others did likewise; and in any event, there is no reason to believe Kefauver accommodated them. "Quizzing Kefauver," *U.S. News & World Report,* April 20, 1951. Kefauver to Pepper, July 22, 1950, Crime Box 2; Kefauver to Anderson, December 15, 1950, Crime Box 5, Kefauver Papers.

8. Milwaukee *Journal,* July 6, 1950. Crime *Hearings,* Pt. 2, p. 61. Knoxville *News-Sentinel,* June 22, 1950. Washington *Post,* August 27, 1950. Wiley to Kefauver, August 9, 1950, Crime Box 37, Kefauver Pa-

Other Republicans joined Wiley and Tobey in attempts to manipulate the Committee. Indiana's Senator Homer Capehart continued to predict that the Committee would whitewash the Democratic machines in the big cities and would focus its fire upon Republican-dominated Philadelphia. The Republican congressional candidate from Lake County, Indiana, attempted to lure the Committee into his own district. Senator Daniel Brewster, chairman of the Republican senate campaign, appeared in Chicago to remind the voters of the suspected Lucas–Barkley "shenanigans" that excluded Ferguson and Donnell from membership on the Committee, and he questioned why the preelection hearings in Chicago were to be held behind closed doors.[9]

Kefauver handled Republican and press skepticism with only moderate success. He hoped to discourage those who anticipated a circus atmosphere, while at the same time he sought to awaken "the sleeping giant of public opinion" to the need for more vigorous law enforcement. The suspicion and apathy that greeted his Committee, as well as the competition for headlines by the Korean War and Fulbright's R.F.C. investigation, disappointed the Senator from Tennessee. Kefauver, nevertheless, did not panic. He postponed certain interviews, refused to be rushed into the publication of magazine articles, avoided klieg lights and the constant presence of radio micro-

---

pers. *Florida Interim Report,* pp. 8, 13. Atlanta *Journal,* August 21, 1950. Washington *Times-Herald,* September 26, 1950. Washington *Post,* October 11, 1950. Undated news clipping, Milwaukee *State Journal,* Wiley Scrapbook 26, Wiley Papers. Washington *Post,* August 19, 1950. Nashville *Tennessean,* August 27, 1950. Rhinelander (Wis.) *News,* October 30, 1950. *The League Republican,* August 28, 1950. Both Tobey and Wiley turned down appeals by Republican leaders in New Mexico and Wisconsin that they share certain politically useful inside information with the local organizations. Melvin Lencher to Tobey, July 15, 1950, Box 101, Tobey Papers. Wiley to Tom Coleman, March 7, 1951, Series 1, Folder 3, Box 30, Wiley Papers.

9. Indianapolis *Star,* September 19, 1950. Washington *Post,* June 27, 1950. Chicago *Daily Tribune,* October 6, 1950. Chicago *Daily News,* October 6, 1950. Capehart later conceded that some of his statements about the crime investigation in 1950 may have been "campaign rhetoric." Personal interview, Homer Capehart, Indianapolis, March 14, 1973. Kefauver explained that as a normal procedure the Committee gathered data and records prior to open hearings. In the rushed last months of the Committee this procedure was occasionally dropped. Unidentified news clipping, October 3, 1950, Kefauver Scrapbook V, Kefauver Papers.

phones, and on one occasion severely rebuked a reporter for the Miami *Herald* for publishing the names of witnesses who were waiting outside an executive hearing room.[10] At the same time, however, the Chairman urged his chief investigator to invite representatives of local civic groups to send witnesses or statements to the public hearings, and he prodded his staff into keeping a close tab on newspaper editorials and feature articles and into sending congratulatory letters to the writers. Through his strong ties with the Miami Crime Commission and the Knight newspaper in Miami, he attempted to convince the editor of the Knight-owned Chicago *Daily News* to withhold hostile judgments on the Committee until the Committee hearings moved to Chicago. Essentially, Kefauver sought to build a wide base of acquaintances and good will for his Committee and for himself, the same political strategy he had used against the machines in Tennessee.[11]

The Committee's dramatic debut with executive sessions in Miami in late May helped cement the already cordial friendship Kefauver enjoyed with the newspapers, radio, and civic groups of the city. Quite logically, he returned to South Florida for the first public session in mid-July. Again the Miami radio and press reported the hearings, and radio station WOAM followed the senators to Washington in August for a subsequent session on conditions in Miami. In general, the work of the Committee in Dade and Broward counties received acclaim throughout the country, but even in Miami an undercurrent of suspicion followed the Committee. Lee Hills of the Miami *Herald* warned that the favorable reaction would turn sour

10. Kefauver Speech before the National Association of Broadcasters, April 17, 1951, *Congressional Record,* April 23, 1951, pp. A2224–25. Memphis *Commercial Appeal,* July 23, 1950. Ruth Hagy to Kefauver, June 7, 1950; Kefauver to Hagy, June 12, 1950; Congressman Earl C. Michener to Kefauver, August 23, 1950, Crime Box 1; telegram from Lee Hills to Kefauver, July 11, 1950; telegram from Kefauver to Hills, July 12, 1950, Crime Box 2, Kefauver Papers. Providence (R.I.) *Journal,* July 2, 1950.

11. Kefauver to Harold G. Robinson, November 16, 1950, Crime Box 2; Kefauver to Robinson, May 30, 1950; memorandum from Kefauver to Al Klein, February 2, 1951; memorandum from Kefauver to George Martin, February 7, 1951; Kefauver to Ernest Havermann of *Life* magazine, July 26, 1950; Kefauver to B. M. McKelway, editor of Washington *Evening Star,* September 21, 1950, Crime Box 1; Kefauver to Jack R. Younger of Miami Crime Commission, September 5, 1950, Crime Box 2; Younger to Kefauver, September 11, 1950; Kefauver to Younger, September 21, 1950, Crime Box 1, Kefauver Papers.

unless the Committee followed its investigation with trials for perjury and contempt. Recognizing the problem, Kefauver sought Hills's opinion on a perjury case against Broward County's Sheriff Walter Clark and urged the newspaperman and his friends to unite behind the Junior Chamber of Commerce in its efforts to carry on the fight against crime. The president of the Crime Commission of Greater Miami, Jack R. Younger, relayed to Kefauver a "widespread rumor" that Ben Cohen, attorney for the S. & G. Syndicate, had "made a deal with a prominent member of the staff of the Kefauver Committee" to avoid testifying in Miami. Kefauver explained that it was he who had decided not to call Cohen in Miami because he was convinced that the owners of S. & G. had fled the hearings, deliberately leaving the lawyer in town as their "mouthpiece." The Chairman assured Younger that Cohen would be called at a subsequent date.[12]

Even as Kefauver's supporters in the summer of 1950 congratulated him on recent successes and urged him on to higher political office, the press continued to question his sincerity. The closed hearings at St. Louis in July stimulated both complimentary remarks and rumors implying that Senator Lucas would take care that the reputed wrongdoings of East St. Louis's City Commissioner John T. English and former City Commissioner Dougherty were "whitewashed." A close friend who was interested in the Chairman's career reported that highly rated actor-radio commentator Robert Montgomery had personally adopted a wait-and-see attitude on whether Kefauver would pursue his investigation "regardless of politics." Kefauver tried to reassure his correspondents of his nonpolitical orientation and took steps quickly to minimize obvious political temptations within the Committee.[13]

12. Jack R. Younger to Owen Uridge, August 17, 1950; O. W. McKenzie to Kefauver, July 29, 1950; Hills to Kefauver, July 25, 1950; Kefauver to Hills, July 31, 1950; Younger to Kefauver, July 20, 1950; Kefauver to Younger, July 24, 1950, Crime Box 2, Kefauver Papers.
13. Arthur Clarendon Smith to Kefauver, May 4, 1950; Frieda B. Hennock to Kefauver, August 8, 1950; Walter Humbert to Kefauver, August 21, 1950; Wade V. Thompson to Kefauver, March 30, 1951; M. C. Plunk to Kefauver, August 1, 1950; North Callahan to Kefauver, September 29, 1950; Kefauver to Plunk, September 12, 1950, Crime Box 2; Kefauver telegram to Halley, November 7, 1950, Crime Box 37, Kefauver Papers. Washington *Post,* June 24, 1950. Dougherty and English were heard in an August executive session in Washington, reportedly arranged by Lucas after they failed to appear in St. Louis.

Lee Mortimer, whom Kefauver continued to meet, advised the Senator that his isolated hearings on wire service gambling were "bad theatre," that he should work behind the scenes until he could present the story of the Mafia's growing control of both organized crime and legitimate business and that there was something to be said for Senator Joseph McCarthy's approach to committee work.[14] Meanwhile, Mortimer's partner, Jack Lait, launched a series of articles in the New York *Daily Mirror* that portrayed Kefauver as a naive do-gooder whom the Administration was grooming for the Presidency. On September 11 and 14 Lait picked up a statement, purportedly made by Thomas F. Murphy, celebrated prosecutor of Alger Hiss, to the effect that Murphy had been vetoed as the Kefauver Committee's chief counsel by the Justice Department and the Democratic National Committee, who wanted the investigation to benefit the Democrats. Lait characterized Halley as having been foisted on Kefauver by Pecora and as having served as the attorney for a railroad company in New York allegedly dominated by gangsters. The Senator rushed telegrams to Murphy, Lait, and the Chicago *Tribune,* which had carried the story, denying the allegations, pointing out that Justice and the Democratic National Committee had recommended only Murphy and had recommended him very highly, and stating that Murphy had been rejected because he lacked experience with congressional committees. Kefauver expressed complete confidence in his Chief Counsel's work and rejected any inferences that might be drawn from Lait's statement about Halley's previous clients. Mortimer, who had developed an aversion to Halley after the Chief Counsel had blocked his appointment to the Committee's staff, remained unconvinced by Kefauver's denials and made the most of Lait's charges in subsequent publications, much to the Senator's discomfort.[15]

None of that testimony was released, but English did testify in public session after the elections in February of 1951. St. Louis *Post-Dispatch,* December 6, 1950. Crime *Hearings,* Pt. 4-A, pp. 600–614.

14. Memorandum, Kefauver to Halley, July 12, 1950; Mortimer to Kefauver, July 12, August 11, 1950, Crime Box 37, Kefauver Papers.

15. New York *Mirror,* July 25, 1950. Kefauver to Z. F. Rankin, September 27, 1950, Crime Box 1, Kefauver Papers. Los Angeles *Herald Express,* September 14, 1950. Kefauver to Hunt; telegram from Kefauver to Editor, Chicago *Daily Tribune;* telegram from Kefauver to Lait, September 11, 1950, Box 27, Hunt Papers. Mortimer to Kefauver, July 12, 1950, Box 37, Kefauver Papers. Lee Mortimer, "New York

The explosive nature of the crime issue created minor political rumbles in Congress in August and September when an
ill-prepared Kefauver went before Senator Theodore Green's
Rules and Administration Committee to request an additional
$100,000 to complete the investigation. With counsel and staff
out of town, Kefauver did not have the materials on hand to
make a proper presentation, and the Rules Committee cut the
request to $50,000, with a promise of additional money when
the Chairman could show sufficient need. Although embarrassed by this failure, Kefauver felt the committee's decision
had been justified. Drew Pearson, however, charged in his
syndicated column that Republican Kenneth Wherry "had
fallen into the hands of racketeers" because he allegedly had
made the motion in executive session to reduce the funds.
Wherry, possibly believing the Kefauver staff the source of
Pearson's rumors, first taunted Kefauver for proof and then
produced a letter from Democrat Guy Gillette to the effect that
the Iowa Senator, and not Wherry, had made the original motion to slash Kefauver's request.[16]

When a witness in a black market hearing in August suggested to the Committee that a former campaign manager for
President Truman was an influence peddler, a pained Kefauver explained to the President that he and Halley had
known nothing of this angle of the story and that Senator
Tobey had developed it independently. At the noon recess the
witness identified Truman's former associate as Victor Messal. The Kefauver staff quickly reached Messal in time for him

---

Confidential: Rudolph Halley's Comet," *American Mercury* (November 1951), 87–95. The Lait articles accelerated the decay of the Kefauver–Mortimer friendship. Apparently Halley had been brought into
contact with purported gangster interests through the work of a partner in his law firm. Whatever the nature of his contacts, they did not
appear to have impeded his slashing attack on men allegedly involved
in the railroad enterprise, including Costello and Erickson. He relentlessly pursued the matter of the railroad in question during the testimony of Abner "Longie" Zwillman. On the other hand, the knowledge
of the relationship unquestionably hurt the Committee's image in
New York. Ralph W. Mills to Kefauver, June 29, 1950, Crime Box 37,
Kefauver Papers. Zwillman testimony, Crime *Hearings,* Pt. 12, pp.
605–8.

16. *Congressional Record,* August 22, 1950, p. 12968; August 30, 1950,
pp. 13803–4; September 12, 1950, pp. 14636–37; September 24, 1950, p.
15718. Memorandum from Kefauver to Halley and Harold Robinson,
August 30, 1950, Crime Box 37, Kefauver Papers.

to make what at first appeared to be a fumbling attempt to pass responsibility on to an underling in his swank Washington public relations office. A few days later, Messal located a file that convinced Kefauver that an associate had indeed handled the matter, that Messal was not deeply involved, and that in any event the $300 of which the Kefauver witness complained had been a legitimately earned fee. Kefauver felt that the Messal case was irrelevant to the hearings, and he apologized for the embarrassment the story had caused both Truman and Messal. The President expressed confidence in his former aide, blamed the development on a hostile Republican newspaper, and reassured Kefauver and Halley of his belief that the Committee was performing "good work."[17] The Messal incident revealed the perilous path the Chairman trod as he tried to placate the press and the Republicans on the one hand and a politically sensitive Administration on the other.

Kefauver found himself in an even more awkward situation early in September when St. Louis attorney Morris Shenker was appointed to the National Democratic Finance Committee. The agile-minded Shenker had accompanied several racing-news wire figures, including J. J. Carroll and William Molasky before the McFarland Subcommittee and the Kefauver Committee in Washington and St. Louis. In his attack on the appointment, Senator Wiley accused high Democratic officials of believing they could get away with "anything"; he claimed that it reminded him that a former Truman associate, St. Louis attorney Paul Dillion, had represented the alleged Capone followers in their 1947 parole case; he questioned whether Shenker's fund-raising activities for the party might not retard law enforcement against his clients; and he called upon the Kefauver Committee to look into the politico-criminal implications of the selection of Shenker. Kefauver expressed to National Democratic Committee Chairman William Boyle his disappointment at the moral and political wisdom of Shenker's appointment. Even if one discounted gossip that Molasky's $2,000 contribution to Forrest Smith's 1948 campaign had been made in expectation of having

17. Kefauver to Truman, August 24, 1950, Crime Box 37; Kefauver to Truman, August 28, 1950, Crime Box 2, Kefauver Papers. Crime *Hearings,* Pt. 3, pp. 60–64. Messal to Kefauver, September 13, 1950; Halley to Messal, September 15, 1950, Victor R. Messal Papers, Truman Library. Kefauver, *Crime in America,* 77. Truman to Kefauver, August 25, 1950, Crime Box 37, Kefauver Papers.

Shenker named to the Police Commission of St. Louis, and even if one dismissed the rumors that organized crime was reaching from state politics into national affairs, the appointment created the possibility that the Administration and the party would be embarrassed in the coming elections. When Kefauver failed to launch an investigation into the appointment, Wiley blasted the chairman's decision:

Apparently it is all right to investigate the racing wire service, but it is not all right to investigate individuals legally associated with the service, who have high-up political connections. To my mind, high-up political connections are the most sinister aspect of the whole situation.[18]

Newspaper comment and Democratic embarrassment continued even after Shenker, noting that Wiley was seeking reelection, announced that he could not accept the appointment because it might "imperil" his clients. No one explained who had committed the blunder of suggesting Shenker's name in the first place. The political repercussions of the incident continued into the spring of 1951, when the Republicans won a special congressional election in St. Louis on the issue of "Shenkerism."[19]

Far more delicate than the Shenker or Messal cases were the decisions concerning the timing of the Committee's hearings prior to the election on November 7. Kefauver, a thoroughly political animal, knew that hearings were likely to hurt the party in power, or lead to charges of whitewash, or perhaps both, and he unquestionably would have waived, if possible, the fateful decisions to go into Kansas City and Chicago prior to the elections. Unable to delay the hearings, he tried to continue balancing the established party interests with the insistent demands of the Republicans and the press for dramatic exposés. Because Congress continued in session

18. *Christian Science Monitor,* July 26, 1950. *Congressional Record,* September 11, 1950, pp. 14456–57. Kefauver to Boyle, September 11, 1950, Crime Box 2, Kefauver Papers. *Congressional Record,* September 12, 1950, p. A6455.

19. Racine (Wis.) *Journal Times,* September 13, 1950. Washington *Post,* September 13, 1950. Chicago *Tribune,* September 13, 1950. Unidentified March 7, 1951, news clipping, Wiley Scrapbook 28, Wiley Papers. *Time,* March 19, 1951, pp. 25–26. Ironically, twenty years later *Life* magazine reported Shenker's appointment to head the newly formed St. Louis Commission on Crime and Law Enforcement. Denny Walsh, "A Two-Faced Crime Fight in St. Louis," *Life,* May 29, 1970, pp. 24–31.

until late September, Kefauver had held only one out-of-town public session, the hearings in Miami in July. Amid continuing rumors that he was trying to "shy away" from public hearings in Kansas City, Kefauver announced open sessions for the President's home, the Jackson County area, when Congress recessed on September 25, and he announced that either open or closed hearings would be held in Chicago, Philadelphia, and New York prior to the election. Kefauver evidently had consulted Thomas C. Hennings, Jr., Missouri's Democratic senatorial nominee, on the hearings in Kansas City and either a misunderstanding over the dates developed or Kefauver had promised to stay out until after the election and then found he could not withstand the pressures within and without the Committee to move into Kansas City. Consequently, he went into Missouri "in order to guard his own integrity."[20]

In any event, the Committee focused its attention in Kansas City only on the wire service, gambling, and political activities of the anti-Pendergast Binaggio faction; it listened respectfully to Jim Pendergast, who downplayed his group's former associations with the slain gambler-politician. At the same time, Kefauver did not hesitate to point out that it had been Hennings's Republican opponent, Senator Forrest C. Donnell, who as governor in 1942 had pardoned Binaggio's partner, Charles Gargotta.[21] The Committee left Kansas City to a chorus of newspaper editorials that labeled the hearings as political whitewash. "If it wishes to continue to enjoy the public confidence it has enjoyed so far," warned the pro-Kefauver St. Louis *Post-Dispatch*, "it will have to do far better with its endeavors in Missouri." Kefauver wrote to Truman of the newspaper attack, and the President, a veteran target of press criticism, reportedly remarked that he was not "at all

20. New York *Herald Tribune,* July 9, 1950. New York *Daily Mirror,* September 1, 1950. Elizabethton (Tenn.) *Star,* September 26, 1950. Robert L. Riggs, "The Man from Tennessee," *The Progressive* (March 1956), 7–11. Chuck Black to Kefauver, October 28, 1950, Crime Box 1, Kefauver Papers. The unreliable Lait and Mortimer later charged that Kefauver had told them open preelection hearings would be held in both New York and Chicago, but had then "folded up like a frightened puppy" at the political situations in those cities. Public sessions in the cities were held only after the elections. Jack Lait and Lee Mortimer, *Washington Confidential* (New York: Crown Publishers, Inc., 1951), pp. 198–206.

21. Pendergast testimony, Crime *Hearings,* Pt. 4, pp. 100–108, 150, 190–91. Kefauver, *Crime in America,* 83.

Portrait of a Pensive President. Memphis *Commercial Appeal,* June 25, 1950. Cal Alley in *The Commercial Appeal,* Memphis.

surprised by the reaction in some quarters."[22]

The political woes of the Committee at its hearings in Kansas City were but a prelude to the complex problems they faced in Chicago. There, the Senate's Majority Leader, Scott Lucas, identified with the Administration despite his opposition to the President's medical care program and the Brannan Plan, was engaged in a political dogfight with former Congressman Everett M. Dirksen. Dirksen had the support of Robert R. McCormick's Chicago *Tribune;* he had campaigned vigorously since early 1949, and he took maximum advantage of the popular discontent with Truman and the Korean War, reminding voters of their "sons' bodies coming home in boxes." Lucas had the benefit of appearances by both Truman and Barkley, and he hoped to gain votes by pointing to Dirksen's inconsistencies on farm programs and foreign policy. He started late, however, and in a frenzied effort to catch up, he lost his speaking voice. Lucas also bore the heavy burden of party decay and dispute, for many downstate Democrats were displeased with Governor Adlai Stevenson's patronage policy, and Cook County's Democratic Chairman Jake Arvey remained cool to Lucas almost until election eve. Lucas obviously needed a heavy majority in Cook County to offset the expected Republican victory downstate. Unfortunately, the Democratic machine in Chicago had nominated for sheriff Daniel "Tubbs" Gilbert, long-time chief investigator for the Cook County State's Attorney and a man whose life style fed persistent rumors in the newspapers, best summarized perhaps by the *Tribune,* which dubbed Gilbert "the world's richest cop." Senator Paul Douglas, who campaigned extensively for Lucas, refused to endorse Gilbert; the usually Democratic Chicago *Sun-Times* backed Lucas and Gilbert's Republican opponent, John E. Babb. The essential question was whether Gilbert's candidacy would cost Lucas the margin he needed in Cook County to overcome the Republican lead downstate.[23] To

22. Indianapolis *Star,* October 1, 1950. New York *Daily News,* October 3, 1950. Detroit *Free Press,* October 5, 1950. Washington *Post,* October 2, 1950. St. Louis *Post-Dispatch,* October 3, 1950. Kefauver to Truman, October 9, 1950; Matthew J. Connelly to Kefauver, October 19, 1950, OF, Truman Papers.

23. Washington *Post,* November 4, 1950. Riggs, "Man from Tennessee," pp. 7–11. Chicago *Daily Tribune,* October 27, 1950. Paul H. Douglas, *In the Fullness of Time: The Memoirs of Paul H. Douglas* (New York: Harcourt Brace Jovanovich, Inc., 1971), pp. 561–62.

the extent that the Committee's activities imperiled Gilbert and the Democratic slate in Cook County, they also reduced Lucas's chance for reelection.

Kefauver sympathized with Lucas but also faced his own political dilemma. The entire logic of his investigation into Continental Press and of his findings in Miami and other cities pointed to a study of conditions in Chicago. Not to have scheduled hearings shortly in the home city of an alleged syndicate controlling the wire service would certainly have brought charges of political whitewash and might well have alienated that part of the press which supported the Committee. The preelection sessions in Chicago were, however, to be closed, and this supposedly would enable the Chairman to maintain some kind of control over press accounts of the hearings. Whether by chance or design, the scheduling or preelection hearings in Republican-dominated Philadelphia and upstate New York tended to balance the newspapers' likely censure of the parties on a national level.[24]

Kefauver's efforts to court the Administration while appeasing its critics had been strained in Kansas City, and they collapsed entirely in Chicago. After some initial indecision, Halley, in late August, dispatched Minority Counsel George S. Robinson, a veteran of the Annenberg race-news wire investigation, to explore the situation in Chicago. Robinson, despite the aid of the Chicago Crime Commission and reinforcements sent from Washington, found himself submerged in approximately a half ton of books, records, and other documents, many collected from the nearly seventy gangsters for whom the Committee issued subpoenas. Robinson, hopelessly understaffed, worked sixteen hours a day, but the volume of material and the impossibility of winnowing all of it contributed to a sense of chaos and frustration in the Committee's offices. Despairing of getting additional help from Washington, Robinson tried to locate former FBI agents in Chicago to serve on a per-diem basis as investigators and subpoena servers. Unfortunately, few such agents were available and Robin-

24. New York *Times,* July 26, 1950. Washington *Post,* July 27, 1950. Both Brewster and Dirksen suggested that someone had intervened to keep the hearings in Chicago secret. Actually, it was standard practice to keep initial hearings in any city closed until a proper public session could be arranged. In January, 1951, under the press of time, the Committee modified this practice. New York *Times,* October 4, 1950. Chicago *Daily Tribune,* October 26, 1950.

son hired at least one private investigator whose extracurricular activities included using the Committee's credentials to extort money from local tavern owners. When George White arrived in Chicago from Kansas City, he shortly began issuing statements for the Committee and clashed pointedly with the already harassed Robinson.[25]

Around this scene of political maneuvering and committee chaos circled the bizarre figure of William Drury, who had been fired from the Chicago Police Department's detective force. Drury had served as a source for Lait and Mortimer's *Chicago Confidential,* and more recently, he had been coauthor of about ten articles on the national Mafia that appeared in the Miami *Daily News.* Drury and Kefauver had corresponded about the detective's possible employment by the Committee, and although nothing came of the negotiations, Drury had transmitted to the Committee some data through his associate in the *Daily News* series, reporter Don Petit, and through Mac Lowery, Washington representative for another Miami newspaper. Drury had been collaborating with Lester Velie and with Lait and Mortimer on other journalistic projects; he had offered to provide "firsthand evidence and knowledge" on Gilbert's alleged corruption to his Republican opponent, John E. Babb, and he still hoped to solve the Ragen slaying of 1946 and to demonstrate that his dismissal from the police force had been brought about by Guzik and others.

Through an eccentric Chicago attorney, Luis Kutner (who had once represented and then quarreled with Harry Russell over the latter's refusal to appear before the Committee), Drury had apparently been attempting to arrange an appointment with Committee representatives, to provide them new information relating to Ragen's murder. Kefauver had in fact directed Robinson to talk to Drury, but in the rush of work in the Committee's offices Robinson had neglected to do so.

25. Robinson interview. Chicago *Sun-Times,* October 9, 1950. Washington *Times-Herald,* August 30, 1950. *Christian Science Monitor,* October 5, 1950. Memorandum from George S. Robinson to Kefauver, February 2, 1951, Crime Box 37, Kefauver Papers. Knoxville *News-Sentinel,* October 2, 1950. White to Kefauver, February 1, 1951, Crime Box 37, 1951, Kefauver Papers. Adding to Robinson's woes, Senator Wiley publicly lashed out at him for allowing the press to publish the names of those subpoenaed and thereby prompting their flight from Chicago. Unidentified news clipping, September 1, 1950, Wiley Scrapbook 26, Wiley Papers.

Meanwhile, the contents of a "confidential" letter Kutner had written Halley found its way into the Miami *Daily News,* which reported that Drury was to be a surprise witness before the Committee and was to relate new and startling developments. Frightened, Drury appealed through Kutner to Halley for protection against a possible attempt on his life. Late in the afternoon of September 25, Robinson called Drury's home to report that Halley had approved protection for him; Drury, however, had already been shot to death in his Cadillac outside his home.[26]

The assassination of Drury and the murder approximately three hours later of Chicago attorney Marvin J. Bas, who apparently was in contact with Drury through his work in the Babb campaign, set off a chain reaction across the country. Kefauver argued that Drury had been killed to prevent his delivery of evidence and testimony before the Senate Committee, and he vainly appealed to Attorney General McGrath to order the FBI into the case. Jack Younger of the Miami Crime Commission and Senator Wiley echoed Kefauver's request, but Director Hoover of the FBI found no jurisdiction for his agency in the case. Widespread rumors on what Drury would have told the Committee filled the press; Drury's former associates on the police force speculated that his information had more to do with conditions in Florida than with those in Chicago; and a Chicago police captain, Patrick O'Connell, suggested that the murder may have been plotted by underworld figures in Miami, Kansas City, Cleveland, or Washington in an effort to deflect the Committee's attention from their own cities and place the "heat" on Chicago. Significantly, all accounts, even those of Lait and Mortimer, held that the flight of underworld witnesses from Chicago, the silencing of Drury, and the reported closing down of all handbooks in the city indicated extensive fear of the Committee by gangster elements.[27] Drury's murder, by suggesting to the press that the

26. Miami *Daily News,* March, 2, 3, 5, 6, 7, 8, 9, 10, 12, 13, 1950. Crime *Hearings,* Pt. 5, pp. 165–71, 447–66. William J. Drury to John E. Babb, September 13, 1950, Crime Box 5, Kefauver Papers. Miami *Daily News,* July 15, September 26, 1950. Lait and Mortimer, as usual, gave a dissenting view of the Drury assassination and, as usual, found at least a semivillainous role in it for Mortimer's prime enemy on the Committee, Rudolph Halley. Lait and Mortimer, *Washington Confidential,* 202–6.

27. Telegram from Kefauver to McGrath, September 26, 1950; telegram from J. Edgar Hoover to Kefauver, September 27, 1950, Crime

underworld feared the Committee, enhanced the senators' public image; at the same time, it removed any possibility that the Committee could skip Chicago.

Aware of the political implications involved, Kefauver still attempted through his direction of the closed Chicago hearings and through his public statements to avoid embarrassing the Democratic party. He quickly ordered staff members to refrain from making public statements in the wake of the Drury–Bas murders and quickly directed the Committee's attention back to the wire service–Capone syndicate angle and away from the idea that the Committee could solve the killings. He turned over all the Committee's information on the Drury case to local officials, once it became clear that the FBI would not act. Kefauver denied that the Committee's discoveries would or should have any impact on the elections, since the gangster element apparently "played both sides of the fence." The Chairman argued before a less-than-convinced press that the law enforcement in Democratic-dominated Chicago was superior to that in Republican-dominated Cook County. The newspapers, on the other hand, suggested that Kefauver's premature praise of Mayor Martin H. Kennelly's administration would prejudice any subsequent criticism by the Committee; the *Tribune* stressed the fact that Democratic State's Attorney John Boyle had once represented Trans-American and stated that one of its reporters allegedly placed a bet with a bookie across the street from the courthouse as Mayor Kennelly testified that Chicago was clean.[28] Caught in the cross

Box 5, Kefauver Papers. Miami *Herald,* September 27, 1950. Miami *Daily News,* September 26, 1950. Washington *Star,* September 28, 1950. *Time,* October 9, 1950, pp. 24–25. Nashville *Tennessean,* September 28, 1950. Washington *Times-Herald,* September 29, 1950. Washington *Post,* September 27, 1950. Chattanooga *News-Free Press,* September 26, 1950. Washington *Times-Herald,* September 27, 1950. Washington *Star,* September 26, 1950. When the Chicago *Sun-Times* reported that Drury had intended to bring Mickey Cohen before the Committee, Cohen told the Los Angeles *Herald-Express,* "I wasn't asked to appear before the Kefauver Committee. Why goodness gracious, I just learned last week how to pronounce Kefauver." Washington *Post,* September 27, 1950.

28. Telegram from Harold G. Robinson to Halley, George S. Robinson, John Elich, and Ralph Mills, September 26, 1950, Crime Box 1, Kefauver Papers. *Christian Science Monitor,* October 5, 1950. Crime *Hearings,* Pt. 5, pp. 165–74. Nashville *Tennessean,* October 10, 1950. Washington *Post,* October 7, 10, 1950. *Christian Science Monitor,* October 9, 1950. Chicago *Daily Tribune,* October 6, 1950.

fire between a cynical press and the feeling in the Lucas and Arvey camps that as a Democrat he should have stayed out of Chicago prior to the elections, Kefauver found his fence-straddling increasingly difficult. He let it be known that he was embarrassed that other Committee members had not come to Chicago to share the burdens and political risks, and he renewed his request that Attorney General McGrath summon a federal grand jury in Chicago to sift the evidence the Committee had unearthed—and incidentally deflect some of the heat from the Committee.[29]

Sandwiched between the two sets of closed Chicago hearings of October 5–7 and 17–19 were a two-day session in New York that dealt with gambling in Bergen County, New Jersey, and Saratoga, New York, and two days of hearings in Philadelphia. In those three areas, Republican administrations came under fire. In New Jersey, Kefauver publicly stated that he was dissatisfied with the effectiveness of the local law enforcement agencies, and in Saratoga, Tobey attacked the apparently passive attitude of Governor Dewey and state and local police officials toward gambling operations. In Philadelphia the Committee discovered a large numbers racket, but because its chief witness became so totally discredited, it was unable to tie those operations to a national syndicate; it looked briefly into a reputed connection between Republican Mayor Samuel's family and the awarding of city contracts to a steel company into which a former numbers racketeer had bought; and finally the Committee left the Philadelphia situation in the hands of Max Goldschein, an old friend of Kefauver, then conducting the federal grand jury investigation in the area.[30]

29. Chicago *Tribune,* October 4, 7, 1950. Boston *Daily Globe,* October 5, 1950. Bristol (Tenn.) *Herald-Courier,* October 7, 1950. New York *Times,* October 7, 8, 1950. *Christian Science Monitor,* October 9, 1950. Hal Korda to Kefauver, n.d., Crime Box 1; telegram from Kefauver to McGrath, September 26, 1950, Crime Box 5, Kefauver Papers. Press accounts had it that O'Conor and Wiley would join Kefauver for the early October sessions in Chicago, and Wiley did send his administrative assistant, Julius Cahn. O'Conor reportedly was at his Maryland home and Hunt on a visit to his constituency in Wyoming. *Christian Science Monitor,* October 5, 1950. Crime *Hearings,* Pt. 5, pp. 111, 373. Chicago *Daily Tribune,* October 7, 1950.

30. New York *Times,* October 13, 12, 1950. Crime *Hearings,* Pt. 11, pp. 26–44, 155–206. Kefauver, *Crime in America,* p. 123. One of the main cogs in the Philadelphia story had been supplied by Assistant Superintendent of Police George F. Richardson who had written Dan-

The shaky working alliance between the Committee and the press continued on through the second series of closed Chicago hearings on October 17–19. Kefauver persisted in his scrutiny of the wire service and the Capone syndicate as the election drew nearer, but suspended all hearings for two and a half weeks prior to November 7. His effort to balance Democratic party interests with his own credibility with the press had been neither totally successful nor unsuccessful; most newspapers maintained a wait-and-see attitude. Lucas remained angry; Gilbert was enraged at what he thought was an effort to make him a scapegoat; and the Republicans suspected low-keyed duplicity. Dirksen, sharing a platform with Babb, attacked Lucas for delaying the formation of the Committee and suggested that the Kefauver Committee, like the Tydings Committee, was avoiding the issue.

People are tired of whitewash and hogwash. They want action. They want more than the perambulations of the Kefauver Committee.[31]

Enterprising reporters meanwhile sought to penetrate the Committee's secrecy. One newsman peered through windows to report the physical reactions of State's Attorney Boyle, and on October 31 an unidentified person tried to bribe Kefauver counsel Al Klein into giving him a transcript of the executive testimony of the Democratic candidate for sheriff, Daniel Gilbert. On November 1, Ray Brennan of the Chicago *Sun-Times,* posing as a new office manager for the Committee, secured from the unsuspecting reporting firm a copy of Gilbert's testimony, and the following day the transcript appeared in the

iel Sullivan of the Crime Commission of Greater Miami on July 19, 1949, that Harry Stomberg ("Nig" Rosen) since the 1930s had dominated the Philadelphia rackets, including numbers, and that Rosen had close ties with Meyer Lansky, "Longie" Zwillman, the Capone group, and various "major mobs of New York City." Apparently the Kefauver staff failed to make sufficient preparatory investigation, for at the hearings, Richardson's superior expressed lack of confidence in him; it developed that Richardson had been harassing Rosen but had possibly once accepted gifts from him; and Richardson under oath denied any present knowledge of the conditions he had related in the Sullivan letter. In his book, Kefauver stated that Richardson's testimony had been clouded by extreme wordiness, but in fact, as Halley noted, it was simply contradictory. Richardson to Sullivan, July 19, 1949, Crime *Hearings,* Pt. 1, pp. 743–45; Pt. 11, pp. 26–44, 285–301. Kefauver, *Crime in America,* pp. 119–23.

31. Robinson interview. Chicago *Daily Tribune,* October 26, 1950.

Sun-Times. Kefauver, livid with rage, promptly fired the reporting company, but the story had already been picked up by papers across the country.[32]

The Committee had been interested for some time in Chicago police officials whose income was obviously out of line with their known salaries. Although the *Tribune*'s stories had unquestionably made Gilbert the most widely discussed of several such officials, the Kefauver Committee issued merely an invitation—rather than a subpoena—to Gilbert to appear and testify. Gilbert was irate that the press had learned of the invitation and the Committee understood the veteran policeman had rejected it. Kefauver had apparently decided not to press the case against Gilbert, when the invited witness suddenly arrived outside the hearing room and asked to be heard. Gilbert proved to be a particularly inept witness, was less than clear as to the scope of his responsibilities, explained that his extensive speculation in grains and stocks brought him about $42,000 annually, and admitted making bets on football games with a La Salle Street bookmaker. A self-confessed "gambler at heart," Gilbert admitted the illegality of some of his activities, but he contended that he could nonetheless enforce the gambling laws in good faith. Dumbfounded at Gilbert's performance, Kefauver hesitated momentarily before giving the customary summary of testimony to reporters waiting outside the hearing room. He released the testimony, however, omitting at Gilbert's request certain data on grain deals.[33]

32. Chicago *Daily Tribune,* October 6, 1950. Harold B. Anderson to Kefauver, February 3, 1951, Box 102; Anderson to Tobey, November 18, 1950, Box 101, Tobey Papers. Harold G. Robinson to Combs and Alderson, November 3, 1950, Crime Box 37, Kefauver Papers. Washington *Post,* November 3, 1950. The reporting firm, which had an excellent record, including clearance to report atomic energy hearings, initiated suit, but settled with the *Sun-Times* for $12,500. They attempted to recoup their lost prestige by appealing for one more reporting job with the Committee, but the Committee refused. Kefauver later made his peace with Brennan and loaned him his personal copies of the crime hearings. Memorandum from Kefauver to Tobey, Wiley, Hunt, O'Conor, February 19, 1951; telegram from Charles Neese to Lucius E. Burch, March 9, 1951, Kefauver Papers. Criminal charges against Brennan were later dismissed on a technicality. New York *Times,* January 18, 1955.

33. Robinson interview. Kefauver, *Crime in America,* pp. 42–43. Gilbert testimony, Crime *Hearings,* Pt. 5, pp. 570–92. State's Attorney Boyle testified to the utmost confidence in Gilbert's perseverance and

Although some specific details in the stolen Gilbert testimony were new, he already had a wide reputation as a gambler and had acknowledged to the press a net worth of over $300,000. Coming as it did less than a week before the election, however, the publication of the secret testimony added new zest to the Republicans' campaign and clearly contributed to the defeat of both Gilbert and Lucas. As the Democrats had feared, Lucas failed to win the normal Democratic majority in Chicago, and the large turnout in the Cook County suburbs and downstate for Dirksen cost the Majority Leader his seat. The importance of the Kefauver Committee and the Gilbert testimony in Lucas's defeat, however, has probably been exaggerated. First, the Democrats suffered the customary off-year defeat in 1950, losing some 31 House and five Senate seats, including that of Lucas and Assistant Majority Leader Francis Myers of Pennsylvania. Second, most analysts, including Arthur Krock and William S. White in their postelection summaries, saw issues of foreign policy, reverses in the Korean War, and disagreements between Lucas and the Administration on farm and labor programs as far more important than the crime issue. Jake Arvey explained Lucas's defeat largely in terms of foreign policy, while Lucas, according to first reports, thought a quip by President Truman that any farmer voting Republican should "have his head examined" had cost him critical support downstate, where Dirksen's chances once appeared shaky. Third, while Gilbert's candidacy unquestionably hurt Lucas in Chicago, a number of voters in the city were also aroused over a controversial housing project on the Northwest Side, and while perhaps preferring to split their votes, did not understand the procedures for doing so in a number of precincts where voting machines were used for the first time. Finally, as Senator Paul Douglas later remarked, the real mistake was Gilbert's nomination, which played into Republican hands.[34] Kefauver probably could not have survived politically if he had avoided Chicago prior to the elec-

---

ability. Gilbert had offered to show his income tax records for the past ten years to the Chicago Crime Commission. Ibid., 163–64, 172, 592.

34. Kefauver, *Crime in America,* pp. 42–43. Chicago *Daily News,* October 9, 1950. Robert Griffith, *The Politics of Fear: Joseph R. McCarthy and the Senate* (Lexington: University of Kentucky Press, 1970), p. 126. New York *Times,* November 10, 8, 9, 1950. *Time,* November 20, 1950, p. 21. Otto Kerner, Jr., to Kefauver, December 5, 1950, Crime Box 5, Kefauver Papers. Robinson interview.

tion; as it was, he made every reasonable accommodation for the Democrats in that city.

The important development coming out of the Chicago hearings was less what actually happened than what Lucas and Cook County Democrats came to think had happened. A number of Lucas's campaign workers blamed the Committee's preelection appearance in Chicago for their candidate's defeat, and some apparently doubted that Kefauver and his staff were as innocent as they claimed to have been in the *Sun-Times*'s acquisition of the Gilbert testimony. Lucas, described as "blanched with anger at his defeat," became convinced that Kefauver had tried to eliminate him as a possible vice presidential contender in 1952; he upbraided Kefauver in a display of temper in a Senate cloakroom and "snarled and banged up the phone" when the Committee's Chairman called to offer his condolences. People in the Administration and a number of Democratic leaders across the country agreed with Lucas's general estimation of Kefauver, and for about three months after the election snapped viciously at the Committee.[35]

Lucas took the lead in the lameduck session of the 81st Congress in blocking Kefauver's request that the President of the Senate issue warrants of arrest and have the Sergeant-at-Arms deputize federal officials to apprehend eleven missing witnesses the Committee sought. Since the hearings in Miami in May, alleged underworld figures had fled service of subpoenas, and Kefauver and his staff became increasingly convinced that they hoped to avoid service until the Committee expired in February. When Kefauver rose, without previous

35. New York *Times,* November 10, 1950. Kefauver to Otto Kerner, Jr., December 12, 1950, Crime Box 5, Kefauver Papers. Robert S. Allen and William V. Shannon, *The Truman Merry-Go-Round* (New York: Vanguard Press, Inc., 1950), pp. 232–34. *Time,* November 13, 1950, pp. 19–20. Nashville *Tennessean,* December 10, 1950. Harry Levin to Kefauver, December 10, 1950, "General Correspondence, 1948–1955" Box, Kefauver Papers. Washington *Times-Herald,* December 11, 1950. "Whispers," *U.S. News & World Report,* November 17, 1950, p. 8. Edwin A. Lahey, "Kefauver: Underworld Nemesis," *New Republic,* February 19, pp. 9–10. Kefauver continued to maintain that his investigations had had very little to do with the defeat of Lucas. In later years, Lucas concluded that Stevenson refused to campaign for him in 1950 in the hope that he would lose and be eliminated as a presidential possibility in 1952. New York *Times,* November 13, 1950. Douglas, *In the Fullness of Time,* p. 562.

notice to the Majority Leader, on December 4 to offer his resolution for the arrest of Accardo, Humphries, the Fischetti
brothers, and others, Lucas labeled the suggestion "the most
ridiculous thing . . . in a long, long time" and capitalized on the
apparent novelty of the request to shunt it into McCarran's
hostile Judiciary Committee. Since rarely did congressional
committees encounter the problem of the evasion by witnesses and since Kefauver had offered his resolution without
notice to the leadership, some pressure for referral to the
Judiciary for legal study might have been expected. At the
same time, Kefauver did appear to have reasonable precedent
for his resolution, and the McCarran report, which criticized
the specific actions the Committee had taken to serve the
subpoenas, deserved the stinging minority report Kefauver
submitted. The only practical consequences of the Lucas–
McCarran action were to delay the authorization of arrests
and to convince certain newspapers that the Senate was punishing Kefauver by obstructing his Committee.[36]

Now that Lucas was absent from the 82d Congress and other
senators who had opposed Kefauver had been duly chastised
by the press, the Committee encountered less difficulty in the
Senate. In late January of 1951 the Chairman asked for citations of contempt from the Senate for Joe Adonis and eight
other witnesses. McCarran, in a hastily prepared speech,

36. "Report Accompanying Senate Resolution 368," *Senate Report
No. 2586,* 81st Cong., 2d sess. (1950), pp. 1–2. *Congressional Record,*
December 4, 1950, pp. 16059–63; December 5, 1950, pp. 16105–10;
December 6, 1950, pp. 16191–92. William C. Garrett to Kefauver,
December 15, 1950; memorandum from Kefauver to Halley and Har-
old G. Robinson, January 2, 1951; Kefauver to Joseph C. Duke, Senate
Sergeant-at-Arms, December 26, 1950, Crime Box 37, Kefauver Pa-
pers. *Congressional Record,* February 8, 1951, pp. 1094–96; February
21, 1951, p. 1454. Kefauver, *Crime in America,* p. 17. Washington
Times-Herald, December 5, 1950. Washington *Post,* December 5, 7,
1950. Miami *Herald,* December 7, 1950. Duluth *News-Tribune,*
December 13, 1950. Chicago *Tribune,* December 15, 1950. Arthur J.
Freund to Wayne Morse, December 5, 1950, Box 28, Patterson Papers.
As Kefauver pointed out, the Committee had already had the benefit
of official federal help in attempting to serve the subpoenas; to request
the Sergeant-at-Arms to serve the subpoenas would amount to asking
the federal officials to perform the same service they had been per-
forming for Kefauver. An arrest warrant, on the other hand, would
carry greater legal consequences for those who were avoiding the
Committee. "Judiciary Committee Report Accompanying Senate
Resolution 368 with Minority Views," *Senate Report No. 2639,* pp. 4–8.

asked that, in veiw of the Blau case decided by the Supreme
Court only a month before, the resolutions be referred to his
Judiciary group for legal study. Because of the relatively large
numbers of citations requested, the suddenness with which
Kefauver asked for their approval, as well as the Court ruling
that a witness could not be compelled to answer questions that
would provide a link in the discovery of evidence for his prosecution under the Smith Act, the resolutions might indeed have
merited study. Kefauver and Tobey argued that the Blau case
applied only to federal laws, not to violations of state laws for
which the federal government recognized no immunity. Since
the citations for contempt supposedly were based on refusals
to answer questions that might incriminate only under state
law, such as for gambling, the Blau decision would not be
applicable. Because the Senate had in September approved
the citation of Harry Russell for contempt, it had already set
the precedent that Kefauver now asked the members to follow. Angrily snapping that it would be manifestly impossible
for his Committee to carry on if obstruction continued, Kefauver wrung semiapologies and denials from McCarran and
others, and the Senate defeated McCarran's proposal to refer
the citations to the Judiciary Committee, 59 to 12. Later contempt citations came much more easily, as Kefauver and the
press focused attention on those senators who opposed the
Committee's requests.[37]

37. *Congressional Record,* January 22, 1951, pp. 499–506, 506–7, 519–
20; January 23, 1951, pp. 573–79; September 23, 1950, p. 15727; February 8, 1951, p. 1096; February 21, 1951, pp. 1453–54; March 30, 1951, pp.
3038–40. "Report to Accompany Senate Resolution 358," *Senate Report
No. 2580,* 91st Cong., 2d sess. (1950), pp. 1–24. William S. White, *Citadel: The Story of the U.S. Senate* (New York: Harper and Brothers,
1957), pp. 254–57, 261–66. Technically, in a contempt citation the
whole Senate asks the President of the Senate to certify that a given
witness has been contemptuous of the entire body by failing in some
way to cooperate with one of its committees. This citation is then by
law forwarded to the federal prosecutor in the district where the
alleged contempt occurred and is then litigated. The inability of the
Committee to grant immunity and the confusion as to what answer
might involve the admission of violations of federal laws and/or state
laws unquestionably interfered with the Committee's ability to obtain
answers to some questions. It also raised complicated legal questions
in the contempt proceedings. *Third Interim Report,* p. 17. Kefauver,
Crime in America, pp. 17–18. Joseph L. Nellis, "Legal Aspects of the
Kefauver Investigation," *Journal of Criminal Law, Criminology and
Police Science* (July–August 1951), 163–70.

The taming effects of the press on Kefauver's critics also eased the Committee's financial and working conditions. In the wake of Kefauver's defeat on the arrest problem in December, some newspapers and pro-Committee groups like the American Bar Association's Commission on Organized Crime became alarmed that additional funds or time would not be granted the special committee before it expired February 28. When Kefauver and Halley requested a lobbying campaign by the Patterson Commission on the Senate Rules Committee, the A.B.A. debated as to which of its groups should do the lobbying. By the time the A.B.A. had made up its mind, the Senate, noting the direction, if not the velocity, of public sentiment, quickly added another month to the Committee's life and gave it an additional $50,000.[38]

Although Kefauver's allies in the press had helped quiet vocal opposition like that of Lucas, McCarran, and Homer Ferguson, senatorial carping continued beneath the surface. Tennessee's senior senator, crusty old Kenneth McKellar, dared to let his personal venom against Kefauver come to a boil in floor debate on Committee measures. Texas's Tom Connally, momentarily forgetting that hearings he chaired were being covered by newsreels and radio, first noted that Kefauver was absent and then mumbled that he was "out chasing crapshooters somewhere." Regaining his presence, Connally then yelled that his remark was off the record and rushed an explanatory note to Kefauver.[39]

Although the executive branch looked askance at the Committee, it generally managed better than Congress to avoid open conflict. In mid-November, however, the Committee

38. St. Louis *Globe-Democrat,* December 22, 1950. Arthur J. Freund to Patterson, December 22, 1950; Morris Ploscowe to Bolitha J. Laws, January 10, 1951; Ploscowe to Freund, January 23, 1951; Ploscowe to Patterson, January 26, February 1, 1951; Freund to Ploscowe, February 1, 1951, Box 28, Patterson Papers. Freund to Kefauver, January 25; Kefauver to Freund, January 30, 1951, Crime Box 5; Freund to Senators McCarran, Hayden, Wherry, Wiley, Kem, and Hennings (separate letters), February 1, 1951, Crime Box 37, Kefauver Papers. *Congressional Record,* January 29, 1951, p. 716; February 1, 1951, pp. 848–49.

39. Casper (Wyo.) *Tribune-Herald,* November 24, 1950. New York *Times,* November 25, 1950. Miami *Herald,* November 25, 1950. Kefauver to Lee Hills, December, 1950, Crime Box 1, Kefauver Papers. *Congressional Record,* January 22, 1951, pp. 499–592; February 1, 1951, pp. 848–49. New York *Times,* February 17, 1951. Kefauver, *Crime in America,* p. 16.

sided with the California Crime Commission in its feud with
the Federal Bureau of Internal Revenue. In general, the Committee pointed to a lack of enthusiasm for tax prosecutions
against major racketeers and, specifically, to scandal involving agents in Nevada and Northern California. Internal Revenue Commissioner George J. Schoeneman accused the Committee of barging in just as the IRB was ready to close certain
cases, and he challenged Kefauver to produce any evidence it
had uncovered that was not then in the Bureau's hands. In
March, as the Committee made a second tour of the West
Coast, it sought to question in open session a Treasury Department intelligence agent who had been accused of improper
activities. When Acting Commissioner Fred Martin forbade
the agent to testify unless the hearing was behind closed doors
and when reports held that Secretary of the Treasury John W.
Snyder was supporting Martin's decisions, Kefauver insisted
that the agent must testify openly, as a matter of Congress's
right to investigate. Undersecretary Edward Foley the following day reversed Martin's ruling and thereby avoided a possible constitutional conflict. Newspaper accounts and rumor
held that the executive branch attempted to block the advancement of former Kefauver staff members and to ham-
string vigorous investigation in certain cities, but no convincing proof of such allegations exists.[40]

A certain level of criticism and opposition to the Committee
existed in circles outside the Congress and the executive
branch. Increasingly, witnesses refused to answer questions,
more taking the Fifth Amendment in the New Orleans hearings in late January, 1951, than in all previous sessions. This
tendency was accelerated by the acquittal of Harry Russell on
some sixty counts of contempt by a federal district judge in
Washington on February 5. Kefauver attacked the decision on
the floor of the Senate, asserting that it represented a misunderstanding of the Committee's actions and a misreading of
the Blau case, and he vowed to proceed as usual against contemptuous witnesses. More and more attorneys for witnesses
and civil liberties groups argued that the publicity given confi-

40. New York *Times,* November 15, 17, 23, 24, 26, 1950. Crime *Hear-
ings,* Pt. 10, p. 107. New York *Times,* March 3, 4, 5, 1951. Crime *Hear-
ings,* Pt. 10, pp. 1058–63, 1110–28. Kefauver, *Crime in America,* p. 132.
Unused notes from Al Ostow to Sam Armstrong of San Francisco
News, dated January 4, 1951, Crime Box 3; George White to Kefauver,
February 15, 1951, Crime Box 37, Kefauver Papers.

dential income tax information by the Committee constituted a violation of both federal law and the presidential order that opened the tax files for the Committee's inspection, a point about which legitimate doubts could be raised. Questions of immunity, on which the law was less than clear, impeded the Committee's work, as did the problem of how far into a witness's past the Committee could explore. Feeling the pressure of time, the Committee dispensed with some executive sessions when it believed it knew how the witness would testify, and it occasionally tried to take testimony in the absence of a senator —practices that prompted some adverse criticism. Suggestions that members of the Committee and Kefauver were merely seeking personal publicity issued all the way from national news magazines to the man on the street. When Senator Hunt, acting as a one-man subcommittee, abruptly ended the Tampa hearings before listening to all witnesses who evidently wanted to testify, Kefauver at first sent his congratulations to Hunt, then had second thoughts and invited the would-be witnesses to Washington and initiated a practice of explaining in later hearings that all persons whose names had been mentioned would be heard if they desired to testify. William Scott Stewart, Chicago attorney for Campagna, Ricca, and Gioe, resisted what he considered improper subpoenas by the Committee in Chicago, flew with his clients to be heard by Kefauver in Washington, and wrote a rambling, rumor-filled pamphlet on "Kefauverism," in which he repeated many of the charges that were being leveled against the Committee. This pamphlet was widely distributed to members of the A.B.A. at their convention in late February of 1951.[41]

41. Crime *Hearings*, Pt. 8, pp. 364–67. *Congressional Record*, February 8, 1951, pp. 1150–51. Kefauver to Lee Hills, February 9, 1951, Crime Box 37, Kefauver Papers. Ira Latimer, Executive Director of Chicago Civil Liberties Committee, mimeographed letter to U.S. Senators, February 23, 1951, Box 28, Patterson Papers. Crime *Hearings*, Pt. 6, pp. 134–35. New Orleans *Times-Picayune*, January 26, 1951. Telegram from Parker Fulton, attorney for Alfred Polizzi to Hunt, January 30, 1951, Box 7, Hunt Papers. Crime *Hearings*, Pt. 6, pp. 2, 15–18; Pt. 10, pp. 375, 395, 397–416. *Time*, March 12, 1951, pp. 22–26. "Kefauver Probe Stuns Cleveland," *The Christian Century*, March 21, 1951, p. 370. New Orleans *States*, January 25, 1951. Tampa *Sunday Tribune*, December 31, 1950. Kefauver to Hunt, January 2, 24, 1951; Hunt to Kefauver, January 25, 1951, Box 7, Hunt Papers. Crime *Hearings*, Pt. 6, p. 117. Memorandum from Halley to Tobey, September 8, 1950, Box 102, Tobey Papers. Washington *Post*, September 8, 1950. William Scott Stewart, "Kefauverism" (undated printed pamphlet), pp. 1–14, Box 28, Pat-

A few Kefauver critics seized upon the fact that the husband of a close personal friend and political confidant of the Senator had been arrested by Knoxville police on charges of operating a numbers game. Kefauver explained that he had received a $100 contribution to his 1948 race from the wife of the arrested man, but he denied knowing of the man's alleged gambling activities. The Chairman remained loyal to his lifelong friend, whose husband was released on a legal technicality.[42]

Because the Committee, lacking sufficient time and staff, borrowed personnel from certain local groups, it frequently appeared to be taking sides in local political squabbles. In Florida it drew largely from the Crime Commission of Greater Miami and its allied radio stations and newspapers, and soon was at dagger's point with the Commission's political enemy, Governor Fuller Warren. In California, it followed the lead of the California Crime Commission; it chastised the opponents of the Commission and Los Angeles's Mayor Fletcher Bowron, including Attorney General Fred Howser and Sheriff Biscailuz. In Chicago, the Kefauver Committee complimented the city administration, but, depending heavily on the Chicago Crime Commission, criticized opponents of certain bills the Commission was sponsoring, including one that would extend the life of the thirty-day grand jury. In Missouri, the Committee dealt almost exclusively with corruption in the anti-Pendergast faction of the Democratic party.[43]

In New Orleans, Kefauver had drawn largely upon material provided by Mayor DeLesseps S. Morrison, but he also maintained contact with Alvin Cobb, right-wing opponent of the Mayor, who disparaged Morrison's interest in crime as political expediency. When the hearings developed along lines Cobb considered unfavorable to him, he

---

terson Papers. Charles S. Rhyne to Kefauver, March 2, 1951, Crime Box 1, Kefauver Papers.

42. Kefauver to Mrs. Flora Brody, July 22, October 30, 1950; R. L. Summitt to Kefauver, January 8, 1951; Mrs. Brody to Kefauver, n.d.; Kefauver to Mrs. Brody, June 29, 1951, April 4, 1954, "General Correspondence, 1948–1955" Box, Kefauver Papers. New York *Times,* March 8, 1951. Knoxville *News-Sentinel,* July 13, 1951.

43. Crime *Hearings,* Pt. 1, pp. 234–43, 250, 213, 230, 332, 798–803, 365–66; Pt. 10, pp. 657–67, 904–6, 358, 108–32; Pt. 5, pp. 131–33, 639. New York *Times,* August 17, 1950. Kefauver, *Crime in America,* p. 129. In Kansas City, Kefauver apparently received substantial aid from U.S. Attorney Sam Wear, a friend of President Truman, Crime *Hearings,* Pt. 10, pp. 35, 37.

interrupted the proceedings with a demand to be heard. Kefauver dismissed Cobb's interests as being purely local and later confided to Senator William Langer that he felt Cobb had been "planted" to disrupt the Committee's work. Kefauver ignored pleas for a fuller investigation by other Morrison opponents, and he confidentially suggested that the Mayor help launch a citizens' crime commission before his enemies could do so.[44] While all the merits of the various local political squabbles are not clear, they did exist, and the Committee, given its limited supply of money, time and staff, was forced to pick and choose among them. By choosing staff from one side, it necessarily offended the others and perhaps on occasion demonstrated a less than frank appraisal of its friends.

The criticism that such activity would normally produce was muted by the growing press support for the Committee in the wake of the Illinois elections. Following the hearings in Kansas City, the editorial cartoonist for the St. Louis *Post-Dispatch* had feared that conditions elsewhere might be whitewashed, but was convinced after Kefauver had visited Chicago that the underworld was genuinely frightened by the investigation. While the defeat of Lucas and other Democrats had offended the Administration and the party regulars, a good portion of the press believed it to be final proof that the Committee was indeed letting the chips fall where they may, particularly when Lucas led the opposition to the arrest measure in the lameduck session of Congress. Politically, Kefauver had suffered heavily and probably unjustly in the eyes of the powers within his own party, but he had benefited immensely, also probably unjustly, in the eyes of the press, who came to depict him as something of a Saint George fearlessly slaying the dragon of crime and corruption. In the aftermath of the Chicago elections, Police Commissioner Prendergast,

44. George V. Haralson to Morrison, January 18, 1950, Box C-5, DeLesseps S. Morrison Papers, Howard-Tilton Memorial Library, Tulane University, New Orleans. Cobb to "Members of Kefauver Committee," April 21, 1950; Kefauver to Cobb, April 22, 1950, Crime Box 1, Kefauver Papers. Telegram from Cobb to Hunt, January 8, 1951, Box 7, Hunt Papers. Crime *Hearings,* Pt. 8, pp. 306–9. Kefauver to Langer, February 20, 1951; telegram from W. E. Temple, Executive Director Louisiana Citizens Action Committee, to Kefauver, February 14, 1951; telegram from Morrison to Kefauver, February 15, 1951; Kefauver to Morrison, February 19, 1951, Crime Box 5, Kefauver Papers.

Kansas City Interlude in Rat Alley. St. Louis *Post-Dispatch*, October 3, 1950. Fitzpatrick in the St. Louis *Post-Dispatch*

East Side, West Side, All Around Rat Alley. St. Louis *Post-Dispatch,* February 23, 1951. Fitzpatrick in the St. Louis *Post-Dispatch*

whom the Committee had praised, resigned preparatory to another police shake-up by Mayor Martin H. Kennelly, and the Committee received the plaudits from the press. In New Orleans, the press first condemned Sheriffs Grosch and Clancy for the conditions Kefauver exposed and then welcomed the repentant Clancy's announcement that he was going to replace the gambling dens with "belching smokestacks." In California, Kefauver expressed his appreciation for press help, including the preparation for the Committee of a thirty-page memorandum on coin machines by San Francisco *Chronicle* reporter Richard Hyers.[45] Favorable newspaper accounts paled in comparison to the sudden avalanche of praise that television brought the Committee in New Orleans in January of 1951. An especially defiant attitude on the part of New Orleans gamblers (who continued wide-open operations as the Committee began hearings) had accompanied an unusually heavy press build-up of the Committee members and of Kefauver's vice presidential possibilities. The first use of the quiet, unobtrusive cameras, which escaped Kefauver's notice until midday of the first hearing, brought overflow crowds to the courthouse, and the broadcasts reached the homes of residents in several southern states. Reportedly, the streets buzzed for days about little other than the hearings and Kefauver's sober fairness; over 90 per cent of the radio audience heard the hearings and over thirteen hundred written communications reached the television broadcasting station within three days of the session; and the local impact received nationwide coverage through such commentators as Drew

45. New York *Times, November 15, 1950. New Orleans Times-Picayune,* January 29, 1951. New Orleans *Item,* February 1, 1951. Crime *Hearings,* Pt. 10, pp. 420, 729–30, 1083–84. One exception clouded Kefauver's honeymoon with the press. During the Cleveland hearings in January of 1951, the Indianapolis *News* obtained and began publication of a confidential, unverified Committee memorandum on an alleged $10 million baseball lottery in Indianapolis. Angered at the unauthorized acquisition of the memorandum by the paper, Kefauver subpoenaed the *News* publisher and editor and "ordered" them to cease publication of the memorandum. When the Committee on Freedom of Information of the American Society of Newspaper Editors protested Kefauver's "order," the Chairman relented, apologized for the use of the word, and explained that he had only the interests of the possible innocent persons in mind. The editor of the *News* ceased publication of the Committee's material and apparently explained off the record to Kefauver how his paper obtained the memorandum. New York *Times,* January 17, 19, 20, 21, 1951.

Pearson.[46] The closing down of gambling by Sheriff Clancy in the wake of the televised New Orleans hearings did much to strengthen the Committee's credibility elsewhere.

A Detroit reporter obtained Kefauver's permission for his paper's station to televise the hearings in Michigan on February 8–10, and the public's response was similar to that in New Orleans. Eventually, two Detroit stations canceled all commercial programs, at a sizable loss of revenue, to televise the hearings, which, according to one account, attracted more attention than the championship fights of Joe Louis, a native of Detroit. Meanwhile, the St. Louis *Post-Dispatch,* whose crime reporter, Ted Link, attended the New Orleans hearings, had arranged to televise the hearings in St. Louis on February 23–24. Reports again held that the hearings attracted more people than did the World Series and dominated conversation for days after the Committee had departed. Increasingly, Kefauver's name was mentioned for higher political office.[47]

The televised hearings in St. Louis, which prompted the news media facetiously to isolate the symptoms of "Kefauveritis"—a sudden epidemic of heart attacks, high blood pressure,

---

46. Lake Charles (La.) *American Press,* January 25, 1951. New Orleans *Times-Picayune,* January 25, 1951. New Orleans *States,* January 24, 1951. Downey Rice to O'Conor, January 18, 1951, Folder 1, Box 30, Series 1, Wiley Papers. Crime *Hearings,* Pt. 8, pp. 364–67. Rice interview. Winston S. Dustin, Vice President and Sales Director of WNOE, to Kefauver, January 29, 1951; Pat Kiley to Kefauver, January 29, 1951; James A. Noe to Kefauver, January 31, 1951; Kefauver to Drew Pearson, January 29, 1951; Representative Hale Boggs to Kefauver, February 1, 1951, Crime Box 5, Kefauver Papers. Kefauver, seeking some nationwide medium to bring the various local stories together, had made arrangements for a series of magazine articles and had filmed a prologue to Warner Brothers' "The Enforcer," but he had not anticipated that television might be the most effective medium. Three years earlier, the House Un-American Activities Committee had televised some of the Hiss–Chambers hearings, but the industry was so small as to have no significant impact at that time. Kefauver Speech before the National Association of Broadcasters, April 17, 1951, in *Congressional Record,* April 23, 1951, pp. A2224–25. Jack Warner to Kefauver, November 3, 1950, Crime Box 1, Kefauver Papers.

47. Blair Moody, "The U.S. Senate," *Holiday* (February 1954), 90. *Telecasting: A Service of Broadcasting Newsweekly,* February 26, 1951. W. M. Burkhalter to Charles Neese, Kefauver assistant, March 5, 1951, Crime Box 1; Ben E. Caldwell to Kefauver, February 14, 1951, Crime Box 37; Kefauver to Link, February 5, 1951, Crime Box 5; George Fickeissen to Kefauver, March 6, 1951; Philip Steinberg to Kefauver, March 7, 1951, Crime Box 1, Kefauver Papers.

and forgetfulness among witnesses who feared the Committee
—also produced the first legal challenge to the presence of
television cameras in congressional hearings. Although Kefauver complimented the indirect lighting and physical arrangement of the television facilities, retired "betting commissioner" James J. Carroll, advised by Morris Shenker,
charged that the spectacle was a violation of his right to
privacy and refused to testify while television cameras were
in operation. Shenker argued, in effect, that the intrusion of
cameras and lights into the scene excited and disoriented the
witness and clouded his ability to answer questions, that the
stations had rescheduled their programs so as to be able to
televise Carroll's testimony while not televising others, and
that, hence, the witness was within his rights to refuse to
testify under those conditions. Kefauver retorted that he did
not control station programming, that television was merely
an extension of other media recognized in the hearing room,
and that he refused to allow the witness to dictate arrangements for Committee hearings. Carroll later withdrew his objections and testified before cameras in Washington, but the
arguments he had raised dogged the Committee for the remainder of its life.[48]

For the moment, however, the Carroll incident, like the
other questions of civil liberties raised in the winter of 1951
and the undertones of political criticism detected in Washington and elsewhere, strengthened the popular image of Estes
Kefauver as a courageous knight-errant and his Committee as

48. *Time,* March 2, 1951, p. 22. St. Louis *Post-Dispatch,* February 25,
1951. Crime *Hearings,* Pt. 4-A, pp. 751–56; Pt. 12, pp. 327–84. There
were no clear guidelines for the conduct of congressional hearings in
general nor any meaningful precedents on the presence of the media.
Radio and newsreel cameras, which caused far more noise and required brighter lighting than television, were permitted at the discretion of the committee chairmen. As early as 1948, the Association of
the Bar of the City of New York had gone on record as opposing the
presence of photographers, moving pictures, radio, or television while
the witness was testifying, but this action was only advisory. Kefauver
sought a ruling from the Justice Department after the Carroll incident; he cautioned San Francisco stations to keep the camera lights
indirect; and reportedly he expressed misgivings about allowing
television cameras in the upcoming New York hearings. New York
Times, March 4, 1951. Committee on the Bill of Rights, Association of
the Bar of the City of New York, "Report on Congressional Investigations" (New York, 1948), p. 8. New York *Times,* February 26, 1951.
Crime *Hearings,* Pt. 10, p. 962. Rice interview.

a hard-hitting investigation that exposed crime and corruption without regard to politics. Although he basked in public esteem for the moment, Kefauver would have sacrificed much of that popularity for greater approval among those who held power within his own party. They, more than the masses, held the immediate keys to political advancement. Despite denials from some of his more ardent followers, Kefauver had done everything short of tossing away his credibility to protect his own party prior to the elections. If he did so because he was fair and honorable, he also did so because it was the politically expedient thing to do. Events over which Kefauver had little control, such as the theft of Gilbert's testimony, and events over which he had no control at all—the nomination of Gilbert, Dirksen's rhetoric, the Korean War, and the Drury–Bas murders—generated a situation that Kefauver could not avoid and Lucas, the *cause célèbre* of both Committee supporters and critics, could not overcome. When Lucas turned his postelection wrath on the Tennessee senator, he took much of the Democratic leadership with him, but he also contributed to the legend of Kefauver the Dragon Slayer and he inadvertently pushed the press into the Committee's camp. The use of television, another unforeseen development, spread the Kefauver legend with unprecedented effectiveness in New Orleans, Detroit, St. Louis, and the West Coast, and it held even larger, as yet untapped potentials for the Committee's future. Meanwhile, the politics of crime, which had accompanied almost every decision the Committee had made, was raising Kefauver to a unique and uncertain position in American life. In early March, he gazed out from the cover of *Time* magazine to the coming spectacle in New York.[49]

49. *Time,* March 12, 1951, pp. 22–26.

7

The New York Crime Show

The Romans were right—there's no show like watching
people thrown to the lions.
    —Columnist Ollie Crawford, Philadelphia *Inquirer,* 1951

Chief Counsel Rudolph Halley had planned a sensational
conclusion for the Committee in New York months before the
appearance of television at the Committee hearings. The
nephew of the late Broadway producer Sam Shipman, Halley
had a knack for the dramatic flourish. His work with Hugh
Fulton and the Truman Committee had sharpened this talent,
and his old mentor, Ferdinand Pecora, veteran of the celebrated Banking Committee hearings of 1932, had advised Halley always to "go after a Mr. Big" in a congressional investigation. In the summer of 1950, Halley assigned the development
of the New York hearings to Minority Counsel George S. Robinson and explained that he himself would take responsibility
for the Committee's work in Chicago. By so doing, Halley observed that Robinson could more conveniently visit his family
in Maine and that he himself would be spared the charge of
political opportunism in New York. Approximately a week
later, Halley reversed his decision; he dispatched Robinson to
Chicago and took over the New York investigation himself.[1]

Halley's motivation remains unclear. Although Robinson
knew little about Chicago, he had worked on the 1939–1940
Annenberg racing-news wire investigation and had all along
been a logical choice to direct the Committee's study of

1. Chambers Roberts, "Crime Probe Had Precarious Infancy,"
Washington *Post,* April 1, 1951. Nellis interview. Lester Velie, "Rudolph Halley—How He Nailed America's Racketeers," *Collier's,* May
19, 1951, p. 25. Rice and Robinson interviews.

Chicago.[2] It is not improbable that Halley's decision to take command of the hearings in New York signaled the Chief Counsel's resolve to fish personally in Gotham's troubled political waters. Even if Halley was not considering his own political future, he certainly must have sensed the dramatic flavor of recent developments in New York and have been tempted to give them his personal attention.

The central figure in New York City's politics was, of course, Mayor William O'Dwyer. The eldest of eleven children born to a schoolteacher in County Mayo, Ireland, O'Dwyer studied for two years in Spain for the priesthood before migrating to the United States in 1910. In New York, O'Dwyer labored successively as a boiler-room stoker, plasterer's helper, and bartender. In 1917 he joined the police force and began the study of law at night; he made important political contacts, became a city magistrate, judge in the Kings County (Brooklyn) Court, and finally, in 1939, was elected Kings County District Attorney. O'Dwyer combined a cultivation of Frank Kelly's Democratic party machinery in Brooklyn with an appreciation of the power of the press. As magistrate he specialized in bringing together broken families, in reconciling parents and youthful offenders, and in promoting civil improvement in countless speeches before women's clubs and community organizations. His local reputation for good will and competence quickly broadened into nationwide notice when, as District Attorney, he began the prosecution of "Murder, Inc."[3]

As his fellow crime fighter Thomas E. Dewey in Manhattan cast covetous eyes on state and national offices, O'Dwyer in Brooklyn decided to challenge New York's Fusion Mayor Fiorello LaGuardia, who had dramatically cracked down on Costello's slot machines and chased Adonis into Bergen County, New Jersey, after losing the support of the two gambling figures. Defeated by the "Little Flower" in 1941, O'Dwyer left the District Attorney's office to an assistant and to his trusted political confidant, James J. Moran, in 1942 to join the Army as a special investigator. There he rose to the rank of brigadier general through his work in uncovering fraud and mismanagement in the production and delivery of

2. Robinson interview.

3. Norton Mockridge and Robert H. Prall, *The Big Fix* (New York: Henry Holt & Co., 1954), pp. 40–47.

supplies for the Army Air Force. In the promotions and plaudits coming O'Dwyer's way from Administration officials—
including Undersecretary of War Robert Patterson—little attention was paid to a clash over an investigation with a youthful counsel for the Truman Committee, Rudolph Halley.[4]
O'Dwyer had meanwhile kept a close eye on New York politics
and returned to run again for mayor in 1945.

After O'Dwyer resigned as District Attorney in August to
make the race, Governor Dewey appointed Republican George
J. Beldock to fill O'Dwyer's unexpired term. In the midst of the
fall campaign, Beldock launched a grand jury investigation
into O'Dwyer's handling of the "Murder, Inc." cases. In a preelection presentment Beldock's grand jury charged that, while
prosecuting lesser figures in the murder ring, O'Dwyer "aban-
doned, neglected or pigeonholed" cases against waterfront
boss Albert Anastasia, Joe Adonis, and other alleged heads of
the conspiracy. Specifically, the grand jury found that, despite
O'Dwyer's claim that he had a "perfect murder case" against
Anastasia through the testimony of Abe "Kid Twist" Reles, he
never presented the case to a grand jury in the twenty months
he had Reles in custody. In November, 1941, when Reles mysteriously plummeted to his death from a sixth-floor hotel suite
while supposedly being protected by six police guards, O'Dwyer lost his "perfect murder case." Despite this loss, O'Dwyer
appeared as a "defense witness" for the policemen in a depart-
mental trial in which the six men claimed to have fallen
asleep simultaneously. Beldock's grand jury charged, moreover, that O'Dwyer had protected Anastasia in another case by
sabotaging a waterfront investigation by John Harlan Amen,
a special prosecutor appointed by Governor Lehman in 1939.
Finally, the grand jury alleged that O'Dwyer's close personal
friend and political adviser, Chief Clerk James J. Moran, had
lifted the "wanted" notice on Anastasia from the police files,
thereby impeding the apprehension of the waterfront boss.
O'Dwyer's Republican opponent joined Beldock in claiming
that O'Dwyer knew Adonis and Irving Sherman, thought to be
a go-between for Costello, and that O'Dwyer had called at
Costello's apartment during the war. Costello's name, of

4. Mockridge and Prall, *The Big Fix,* pp. 77–78. Charles Garrett, *The
LaGuardia Years, Machine and Reform Politics in New York City*
(New Brunswick, N.J.: Rutgers University Press, 1961), 271–73. Patter-
son to Secretary of Defense Louis Johnson, August 2, 1950, Box 38,
Patterson Papers. Crime *Hearings,* Pt. 7, pp. 1386–87, 1369, 1380–81.

course, since the 1943 Aurelio case, had become synonymous with charges that gangsters dominated Manhattan's Tammany Hall.[5]

O'Dwyer explained that, since New York law required at least one independent corroborating witness in a murder indictment and since he was of the opinion that a conviction of Anastasia and the actual triggerman would necessitate the use of the testimony of a "delicate" young boy, O'Dwyer did not press the first case against Anastasia. He denied that his actions had sabotaged Amen's waterfront prosecutions or that Moran's removal of Anastasia's "wanted" notice had any significance. Whatever mistakes had been made, he argued, resulted from his preoccupation with the "Murder, Inc." cases and from actions taken in the District Attorney's office after he took leave of absence in June of 1942. O'Dwyer angrily charged that the grand jury presentments, as well as his opponent's charges, were politically motivated. After O'Dwyer won the election, the presiding judge of the Kings County Court ordered both the preelection presentment and a subsequent one, in December of 1945, expunged from the record, on the grounds that they violated technical rules of secrecy for grand juries and that they were indeed politically motivated. Subsequently, Beldock, seeking bipartisan backing for a judicial election, explained that none of his findings reflected on "the personal integrity and honesty" of O'Dwyer.[6]

Despite his overwhelming victory and the expunging of the grand jury statements, O'Dwyer began his administration under a cloud. While launching an impressive building program and expanding city services, O'Dwyer also cultivated the image of independence from Tammany; he played one faction against another while making some concessions to get cooperation. He particularly valued the political friendship of New York County's (Manhattan) District Attorney Frank Hogan whose renomination he had forced upon the Democratic orga-

5. Garrett, *LaGuardia Years,* pp. 297–99. Crime *Hearings,* Pt. 7, pp. 1525–27. Mockridge and Prall, *The Big Fix,* pp. 111–12.

6. O'Dwyer testimony, Crime *Hearings,* Pt. 7, pp. 1349–51, 1344–45, 1520–24, 1358–60, 1362–63, 1367–68. New York *Times,* March 29, 1951. When Halley asked why O'Dwyer had stated during the proceedings for the second presentment that the first was "fully justified," O'Dwyer explained that he had meant it was justified on the basis of the facts Beldock told the grand jury but that he had not told them all the facts in the case. Crime *Hearings,* Pt. 7, p. 1529.

nization in 1945. Despite frequent weariness and irascibility,
O'Dwyer became a popular mayor. His personal warmth as
well as domestic events—the death of his first wife and his
subsequent courtship and marriage to a highly publicized
model, Sloan Simpson—attracted to him a sizable public following.[7]

In early 1949, O'Dwyer, suffering from a thyroid condition
that plunged him frequently into fits of depression, announced that he would not run for reelection; he apparently
gave his private blessings to at least three possible successors,
one of whom was Frank Hogan. Bronx Democratic leader Ed
Flynn prevailed upon O'Dwyer to reverse his decision and
seek reelection; Hogan became alienated, and the LaGuardia
Fusion groups united behind Newbold Morris, whose supporters vainly resurrected the 1945 grand jury presentments and
again charged O'Dwyer with involvement with Costello. Returned to an office he did not want, O'Dwyer sought relief in
extended Florida vacations, in flights to his brother's California ranch, and in thoughts of resignation. When Miles Mc-
Donald, who had defeated Beldock in 1945 for the Brooklyn
District Attorneyship, launched his inquiry into gambling and
police corruption in late 1949, O'Dwyer reacted impetuously,
angrily defended the police department, and labeled McDonald's investigation a "witch hunt." Flynn, evidently frightened
by McDonald's activities and O'Dwyer's increasing instabil-
ity, interceded with the White House to have the Mayor appointed Ambassador to Mexico. Just as McDonald's men were
arresting Harry Gross, who admitted to paying police officials
$1 million annually for protection and who claimed to have
handed Moran $20,000 for O'Dwyer's two campaigns, the Sen-
ate, with only slight hesitation, approved O'Dwyer's nomination as ambassador.[8]

7. Garrett, *LaGuardia Years,* p. 309. Crime *Hearings,* Pt. 7, 1553–54.
Lester Velie, "William O'Dwyer—The Man Who Won't Come Home,"
Collier's, August 7, 1953, pp. 19–23; August 21, pp. 30–34. Mockridge
and Prall, *The Big Fix,* p. 211.

8. Velie, "William O'Dwyer," August 21, 1953, pp. 30–34. Garrett,
LaGuardia Years, pp. 319, 311. Mockridge and Prall, *The Big Fix,* pp.
230–32. "Getting 'the Hogan Treatment,'" *The Nation,* July 23, 1949,
pp. 70–71. Daniel Bell, *The End of Ideology: On the Exhaustion of
Political Ideas in the Fifties* (New York: The Free Press, 1962), p. 162.
Congressional Record, September 18, 1950, pp. 14996–15011. "Ambassador O'Dwyer," *Newsweek,* September 18, 1950, p. 38. O'Dwyer's
knowledge of Spanish, his Catholicism, and his wife's interest in

The special elections that followed, as columnist Walter Winchell quipped, constituted the "only dirty show in New York." Acting Mayor Vincent R. Impellitteri, running independently when denied the Democratic nomination, charged that Tammany-backed Ferdinand Pecora was actually supported by Costello. Impellitteri "revealed" that Tammany had attempted to buy him off with a $28,000 judgeship, while Pecora retorted that the slow-witted "Impy" must have requested four judgeships. The Republican candidate, Edward Corsi, agreed that Pecora had Costello's support, but added that the Acting Mayor was backed by Erickson and an underworld figure, Thomas Lucchese ("Three Finger Brown"). In a last-minute telegram, Corsi urged the Kefauver Committee to complete an investigation on the alleged underworld ties of his opponents.[9]

Republicans on the state level also tried to link the Democrats with the developing crime-and-corruption issue, but found themselves frequently on the defensive. Lieutenant Governor Joseph R. Hanley, in failing health and deeply in debt, had wanted to run for governor, but he agreed to seek Lehman's seat in the Senate when Governor Dewey announced for a third term. To ease Hanley's disappointment, Dewey promised him that if he agreed to oppose Lehman he would be guaranteed financial security regardless of the outcome of the election. Hanley explained the agreement in a letter to Republican Congressman Kingsland Macy, an intraparty opponent of Dewey, who made its contents public, much to the embarrassment of both the Governor and Hanley. Dew-

---

bullfighting and his own interest in the Cuban or Mexican Embassy made him a logical choice for the appointment, although some questioned why he should take a salary cut and leave a more prestigious job in New York. Flynn also apparently hoped to stimulate a large turnout for the state Democratic slate by staging a special election in New York at the same time. Democratic Senator Herbert Lehman probably would have won regardless of Flynn's actions. Unidentified Robert C. Ruark column, August 29, 1950, Kefauver Scrapbook V, Kefauver Papers; Mockridge and Prall, *The Big Fix*, p. 235; Willard Shelton, "Notes from Capitol Hill," *The Nation*, August 26, 1950, p. 181. Allan Nevins, *Herbert H. Lehman and His Era* (New York: Charles Scribner's Sons, 1963), p. 329. "Lucky Billo," *Time*, December 8, 1952, pp. 23–24.

9. *Time*, November 6, 1950, pp. 23–24. "New York's Big Wheel," *Newsweek*, October 23, 1950, p. 28. New York *Times*, November 3, 1950.

ey's Democratic opponent, Representative Walter A. Lynch, charged that the Governor's 1946 commutation of Luciano had been a response to pressure brought by Costello and was not the result of Luciano's reputed wartime services, as the State Board of Paroles and Dewey claimed. Finally, when the Republicans pointed to gambling scandals in Democratic New York City, the Democrats asked about the illegal gambling that had gone on for years in the Saratoga area without interference from the state Republican administration. Although Lehman easily won reelection, the Democrats lost to Impellitteri in New York City and failed to oust Governor Dewey.[10]

While the Kefauver Committee stayed clear of New York City prior to the November election, it did dabble around the edges of crime in the metropolis. In the closed hearings held in the city in October, the Committee, armed with information from Hogan's office, looked into gambling in New Jersey and at Saratoga. The Committee showed that Republican law enforcement in Bergen County was lax. Tremendous sums of money were lost by New Yorkers in the plush casinos across the George Washington Bridge. Hogan had hoped to jar complacent Bergen County officials with his indictment of Max Stark in 1948 for conspiracy. Stark had been accused of cashing checks in a New York bank, checks that had been written for gambling losses incurred in New Jersey. New Jersey officials experienced unexplained but consistent difficulty in locating the operations Hogan's men had so easily discovered. Kefauver, angered at the Republican officials' irresponsibility, threatened to call Governor Alfred Driscoll unless the law enforcement agencies of New Jersey began to act against gambling, and he quickly obtained the cooperation of special prosecutor Nelson Stamler, who aided the Committee in finding Adonis and Jerry Catena and who launched a major investigation of his own.[11]

10. Nevins, *Herbert H. Lehman,* pp. 330–31. New York *Times,* October 15, November 4, 1950. Undated columns by Jack Lait and John Lardiner, Kefauver Scrapbook IV, pp. 158, 165, Kefauver Papers.

11. Crime *Hearings,* Pt. 7, pp. 35–243. *Second Interim Report,* pp. 3, 12–13. Fred J. Cook, *Two Dollar Bet Means Murder* (New York: The Dial Press, 1961), pp. 98–116. Kefauver to Senator Robert C. Hendrickson, June 15, 1953, Crime and Corruption Box 1; Stamler to Kefauver, September 25, 1950; telegram from Kefauver to Stamler, September 26, 1950, Crime Box 2; Kefauver to Stamler, October 30, 1950, Crime and Corruption Box 1, Kefauver Papers. New York *Times,* November

Also on the basis of Hogan's material, the Committee began a study of gambling in upstate New York, where they discovered that Adonis and Detroit-based interests owned sizable shares in certain Saratoga casinos. This investigation, which prompted a preelection blast at Dewey by Senator Tobey, marked the first round in an escalating squabble between the Governor and the Committee.[12]

Meanwhile, O'Dwyer, who understood that a congressional investigation reflected the perspective of its sources, took steps to cultivate Kefauver and counter anti-O'Dwyer influences. Although he could not expect the Committee to endorse his proposal to legalize off-track betting on sporting events, he did seek to establish favorable contact with Kefauver through the appointment of a special liaison officer and through a promise of full cooperation with the Committee. Prior to his nomination as ambassador, O'Dwyer, using U.S. Attorney Morris Fay as an intermediary, dined with the Senator from Tennessee at the Carleton Hotel in Washington and expressed his own general views of the crime problem. When McDonald's inquiry into gambling attracted increasing attention, when Halley appeared to be relying on Hogan and McDonald for information, and when Tobey urged that the former mayor be called for the executive hearings in New York in October, O'Dwyer again requested through Fay that the Committee hear his views. A "very disturbed" O'Dwyer talked at length with Chief Investigator H. G. Robinson in October prior to leaving for Mexico. He asserted that certain police officers he thought honest had actually been in the pay of the gamblers and that the resulting scandal threatened to tarnish his entire career. He defended his conduct as District Attorney and as investigator for the Air Corps. The Amen investigation, he told Robinson, as well as the recent Gross gambling case had been misinterpreted by the press. The study of gambling activities by his commissioner of investigations, John Murtagh, and the presenting of Murtagh's evidence to Hogan and New Jersey officials belied, he contended, the charge that his administration coddled

---

1, 13, December 13, 1950. For an account of Stamler's prosecutions and his dismissal in 1953, see either Cook, *Two Dollar Bet* or the same author's *The Secret Rulers: Criminal Syndicates and How They Control the U.S. Underworld* (New York: Duell, Sloan and Pearce, 1966).

12. New York *Times,* October 12, November 4, 1950. *Third Interim Report,* pp. 106–7. Estes Kefauver, *Crime In America* (Garden City, N.Y.: Doubleday & Company, Inc., 1951), p. 147.

gamblers; indeed, his proposal for legalized off-track betting was intended not only to develop a new source of revenue for civic projects but also to divert money that, under existing circumstances, was flowing into illegal channels. Finally, he suggested that the Committee take up an investigation on Wall Street manipulations by gamblers, that they resurrect a study along these lines that LaGuardia had allegedly suppressed, and that they reexplore the "Murder, Inc." cases through confidential material he volunteered to make available.[13]

Although Robinson seemed impressed, Halley and Kefauver remained uncertain about O'Dwyer, who shortly departed for residence in Mexico City. After the elections, Kefauver announced that the Committee would explore the rumored influence of organized crime on Tammany Hall, then torn by a feud between Mayor Impellitteri and Tammany head Carmine De Sapio. Halley began to drift into the anti-O'Dwyer faction; before deciding on the date for additional closed hearings in New York, Kefauver and Halley conferred with the new mayor, his police commissioner, Thomas F. Murphy, and District Attorneys Hogan and McDonald. McDonald reiterated his intentions of calling O'Dwyer to testify before the Kings County grand jury, but Kefauver expressed uncertainty as to whether the Ambassador's testimony would be needed by the Committee. After the Cleveland hearings in which Halley explained his official position on the wire service, Kefauver announced that the Chief Counsel would devote his attention exclusively to the hearings in New York and that he would be assisted by two former LaGuardia aides, Reuben A. Lazarus and Louis E. Yavner. Both men were steeped in New York politics and held a strong affection for the late LaGuardia. Yavner had been both an old friend and investigating partner to Halley during his work with the Truman Committee. Halley openly expressed an admiration for the "Little Flower" and his investigators and declared that they could show him "where the bodies are buried."[14]

13. New York *Times,* July 13, 1950. Kefauver to Lester Velie, June 27, 1953, "General Correspondence, 1948–1955, C" Box, Kefauver Papers. New York *Times,* August 15, October 12, 13, 1950. Memorandum from H. G. Robinson to Kefauver and Halley, October 19, 1950, Crime Box 37, Kefauver Papers.

14. New York *Times,* November 27, 1950; January 13, 23, 24, 1950.

William O'Dwyer, sensing a growth of skepticism toward him in the press and in the Committee, decided that he, too, might know where some "buried bodies" lay. In early February he asked to be allowed to testify before the Committee and requested Halley to send a representative to Mexico to review some constructive recommendations he might make. After advising Kefauver to accept, Halley dispatched the pro-LaGuardia Yavner to Mexico City. Yavner questioned the Ambassador for about twenty-five hours and reported to Halley that O'Dwyer had woven his story with unsought denials and had repeated previous statements stressing his own poverty. Although Yavner and Halley insisted to the press that the Ambassador was not "under suspicion," in fact he was under the gravest suspicion. In three marathon days of closed hearings in mid-February, Halley, assisted by Lazarus and the Hogan staff, quizzed Costello for a total of thirteen hours on his gambling activities, the sources of his income, and his political contacts. The Committee also called a number of former O'Dwyer aides, including Moran and Frank Bals, who had risen rapidly in the police department despite the fact that he had been the supervisor of the six "sleeping" police guards the night of Reles's death. Halley took care to avoid upsetting Costello with needless harangues, and he publicly praised the gambler for his "forthright" testimony. Beyond the obvious fact that he was questioning a number of O'Dwyer associates —some about a meeting in 1942 between O'Dwyer and Costello, the Chief Counsel made no open attempt to link the two men. Even Kefauver did not fully understand that Halley in-

Velie, "Rudolph Halley," p. 78. A day after the Lazarus–Yavner appointments, Halley added James D. Walsh and David I. Shivitz, both former city officials, to his New York staff. Boris Kostelanetz, who since October had headed a team of investigators who were concentrating on the New York–New Jersey area, resigned when Halley took over personal direction of the study in New York. Previously Kostelanetz, an old Kefauver associate whom the Senator had wanted as chief counsel, had completed a survey of possible links between the American and European underworlds. With the exceptions of Luciano's mysterious income and an attempt by a New York-based gambling group to purchase the casino at Monte Carlo in 1949, Kostelanetz found little evidence of contact between the American underworld and European crime or gambling. Washington *Post,* October 7, 1950. New York *Times,* October 6, 1950, January 23, 31, 1950. Kostelanetz to Kefauver, September 25, 1950, Crime Box 37, Kefauver Papers.

tended to make the supposed ties between Costello and O'Dwyer the very keystone of the New York hearings.[15]

Meanwhile, newspapers began to speculate that the back-stage jostling between Halley and Governor Dewey had sparked Dewey's approval of a legislative investigation into gangster influence in Tammany Hall. Allegedly, Dewey had become angered over the Kefauver Committee's suggestions that he was ultimately responsible for suppressing gambling in Saratoga and over Senator Guy Gillette's Committee on Election Expenditures' continuing interest in the possibility that Dewey's letter to Hanley in 1950 (the "Macy letter") constituted violation of federal election laws. The Governor supposedly hoped to deflect public attention with a Republican-sponsored investigation into Costello's influence in Manhattan's Tammany Hall. Regardless of Dewey's motives, Halley continued to develop the picture of Republican-tolerated gambling in Saratoga, and he supposedly frightened prominent state figures by requesting the payroll records of the entire state legislature. Kefauver, questioned in St. Louis about Halley's reported request, explained that, while he was not conversant with all the details of Halley's work in New York, he knew the Committee was looking for specific data and that the newspaper reporters must have misunderstood the scope of the Chief Counsel's inquiry. While Kefauver retained broad policy-making decisions, Halley clearly exercised wide latitude in developing the investigation in New York.[16]

In an obvious attempt to expand the already extensive pub-

15. New York *Times,* February 13, 16, 14, 15, 17, 1950. Velie, "Rudolph Halley," p. 78. *Time,* February 26, 1951. Kefauver to Velie, June 27, 1953, "General Correspondence, 1948–1955, C" Box, Kefauver Papers. Rising skepticism about O'Dwyer led Pennsylvania Congressman Hugh D. Scott, who had recently visited the American Embassy in Mexico City, to praise O'Dwyer and to urge his detractors to let him get on "with the good work he is doing." *Congressional Record,* January 22, 1951, p. 536.

16. New York *Times,* February 7, 14, 15, 23, 24, 25, 1951. Crime *Hearings,* Pt. 7, pp. 401–527. Apparently, Halley either made the sweeping statement about the legislative records to frighten the Republicans or else he was indeed misunderstood. The Committee was interested in the recent appointment to a legislative staff position of a Tammany-backed candidate and had developed the interest through a lead furnished by the Impellitteri camp. New York *Times,* February 27, 1951.

licity the inquiry in New York was receiving, Halley fed the press small pieces of advance information about the public hearings scheduled to open March 12. Virginia Hill, mistress of the late "Bugsy" Siegel and party hostess for a number of underworld figures, was to testify. Both Costello and O'Dwyer were to appear and the resulting revelations were expected to be "sensational." The Committee expected to explore the Mafia, the waterfront rackets, gambling, the narcotics traffic among teenagers, the gangsters' infiltration into legitimate business, and politicians' ties with criminals. Halley insisted that the hearings be "live" in the sense that the alleged under-world figures and politicians were to tell their own stories rather than have investigators or so-called crime experts do the testifying. New Yorkers, according to *Time* magazine, "could hardly wait."[17]

Ironically, it was not Halley, but Kefauver, who made the decision to televise the hearings. Reports of the unprece-dented public response to the televised hearings in New Or-leans, Detroit, and St. Louis and on the West Coast reached representatives of independent station WPIX, owned by the tabloid New York *Daily News,* in the winter of 1951. Executive producer Walter D. Engels approached Halley in late Febru-ary about televising the hearings in New York and Halley, who had not attended any of the previous televised sessions, referred the request to the federal judges in charge of the Foley Square Courthouse. In keeping with their long-standing tradition, the New York judges refused to permit the presence of television, radio, or press photographers in their court-rooms. After attempting to plant the idea in Kefauver's mind that the judges were thereby interfering with the Senate's investigative prerogatives and after suggesting that WPIX would be willing to hire the ballroom of the Biltmore for the Committee if necessary, Engels approached Halley again but found the Counsel's position unchanged. At Engels's sugges-tion, however, Halley telephoned the Chairman who, despite some reservations about the continued use of television fol-lowing the hearings on the West Coast, now was determined to have live television coverage in New York. The judges, pre-sented with the awkward dilemma forced upon them by Kefauver's decision, reversed their traditional position

17. New York *Times,* February 13, 15, 23, 27, 1951; Velie, "Rudolph Halley," p. 79. *Time,* February 26, 1951, p. 24.

against the presence of photographers and television cameras, but they did shunt the proceedings off to a small 28th-floor courtroom.[18]

Although both Kefauver and Halley expected that the sessions in New York would be the most dramatic of the hearings, neither anticipated the enormous impact of television. Unlike the earlier televised sessions, the hearings in New York, through a pooling agreement with WPIX, were picked up by three national networks as well as several independent stations and broadcast to over twenty cities dotting the eastern half of the country. Although the number of homes with television sets had risen dramatically during 1950, daytime programming was generally dull. *Time* magazine, hoping to combine a public service with relatively inexpensive advertising, decided to sponsor the hearings over one network, and a considerable number of other stations canceled their regularly scheduled programs to cover the more promising Committee sessions. Public response to the hearings exceeded even the most optimistic predictions: Seventeen times as many people viewed the morning telecasts as watched the usual programs and over 80 per cent of those who watched television observed the crime hearings. An estimated 20 million to 30 million people viewed the hearings across the nation.

In Chicago people stared at the television screens through store windows, shifting their chilled feet in 15-degree weather, and in Minneapolis, spectators crowded early in the morning into bars and restaurants that were equipped with television sets. New Yorkers all but deserted the department stores and movie houses during "Kefauver hours" and "gawked like a country boy looking at a painted woman for the first time." Two movie houses relayed the televised proceedings onto their screens and invited the public to view them without charge. So fascinated by the hearings were the majority of citizens that Senator Hunt observed that at the rush hour, there was no rush; Kefauver interrupted the testimony to remind Red Cross blood donors that the blood supply was desperately low due to the demands for plasma in the

18. Ellsworth Scott Bryce, "The New York Hearings of the Kefauver Crime Committee: A Rhetorical Analysis" (Master's thesis, Indiana University, Bloomington, 1963), pp. 15–16. Walter D. Engels to the author, May 25, 1970. Rice interview. Harry W. Kirwan, *O'Conor: The Inevitable Success* (Westminster, Md.: Newman Press, 1962), p. 451.

fighting in Korea; and the Brooklyn Red Cross Chapter, yield-
ing to popular demand, installed a television set among its
cots, found that its blood donations increased 100 per cent, but
that it then had the problem of shooing away large numbers
of donors who already had given their pint. Although a number of schools dismissed students to watch the hearings, the
majority of viewers were housewives who could convert afternoon canasta or bridge sessions into so-called "Kefauver Parties" or who could easily combine ironing and cleaning chores
with television watching. One group of women in Queens
formed shopping–listening clubs in order to purchase necessary items quickly during intermissions; grocers and butchers
reportedly were swamped with customers when the Committee recessed at noon. Children at play mimicked the senators,
counsel, and witnesses in endless variety of make-believe
hearings. Husbands viewed the one live evening session and
nightly reviews of each day's proceedings. In one week national sales of Pops-Rite popcorn for home popping increased
112 per cent.[19]

The impressive public response through television, far out-
stripping the interest in the World Series and necessitating
the addition of a giant generator by Consolidated Edison Company, quickly overcame any lingering opposition to the presence of cameras in the courtroom. During the first two days,
the Committee was crowded in the small, narrow room the
judges had chosen for the hearings, along with over sixty
newsmen and photographers, two WPIX cameras, radio
equipment, lights, microphones, newsreels, witnesses and
spectators. Kefauver complained of the hot and cramped conditions and on the third day the Committee moved with its
assorted followers and paraphernalia to a larger room on the

19. New York *Times,* March 8, 12, 1951. Joseph Bruce Gorman, *Kefauver: A Political Biography* (New York: Oxford University Press,
1971), pp. 91, 87. *Time,* April 2, 1951. Hunt to Tracy McCracken, March
26, 1951, Box 7, Hunt Papers. "Biggest Show Stopped New York's
Clock," *Business Week,* March 24, 1951, p. 21. Hunt to Arthur Kline,
April 17, 1951, Box 7, Hunt Papers. Crime *Hearings,* Pt. 7, p. 1241. New
York *Times,* March 21, 14, 20, 1951. Mildred E. Bodin to Hunt, April
9, 1951, Box 7, Hunt Papers. Bryce, "New York Hearings," p. 6–7. Alex-
andria (La.) *Daily Town Talk,* March 30, 1951. Bryce, "New York
Hearings," pp. 11–12. James Stewart-Gordon to Kefauver, May 14,
1951, Crime Box 1; telegram from Jim Blevins, "Mayor" of Popcorn
Village, Nashville, to Kefauver, March 20, 1951, Crime Box 2, Kefauver Papers.

third floor. Although WPIX then added two cameras, it maintained straightforward broadcasting with little extraneous explanation from Harry T. Brundige, WPIX commentator and former crime reporter in St. Louis. Rejecting such visual tricks as split screens or fade-in focuses, the station shifted its broadcast picture quickly between the witness and the Committee during testimony, intensifying the suggestion of two sides in some moral Armageddon.[20]

Television, however, merely intensified an already dramatic situation. Halley had carefully planned the appearance of witnesses so as to relate a live, orderly story with fresh daily sensations. He had originally hoped to call O'Dwyer first, with the expectation that the former mayor's self-defense would necessarily introduce political and underworld figures as well as set the stage for questioning on the gambling situation in New Jersey, rackets on the waterfront, the operations of the Mafia, and the growing narcotics traffic. O'Dwyer, however, suffered an acute attack of bronchitis and pulmonary congestion in early March, and Halley necessarily rearranged his schedule and postponed the Ambassador's testimony a full week.[21] Due to the press of time, moreover, the Chief Counsel devoted little attention to the problems in New Jersey or on the waterfront, but concentrated on the alleged links between crime and politics in New York City. By focusing first on Costello as an arbiter of underworld and political activities and then on his supposed associations with O'Dwyer, Halley actually achieved a greater impact than if he had pursued a greater range of questions.

On the first day, Halley began the pursuit of Frank Costello, the Committee's "Mr. Big." The Chief Counsel had acquired about 90 per cent of his information on Costello, including a number of wire taps, from District Attorney Hogan. To demonstrate Costello's influence and activity in the underworld, Halley called as his first witness an attorney, George Morton Levy, who was president of the Nassau Trotting Association,

20. Bryce, "New York Hearings," pp. 5–6, 11–12, 14–15. *Rocky Mountain News,* March 21, 1951. G. W. Tasker, Research Director, Cunningham and Walsh, to Kefauver, April 4, 1951, Crime Box 1, Kefauver Papers. *Business Week,* March 24, 1951, p. 21. New York *Times,* March 22, 1951. *Electrical World,* April 2, 1951, p. 6. Gilbert Seldes, "New Concepts of Television Technique Will Result from the Kefauver Show," *Printers' Ink,* April 20, 1951, pp. 33–35.

21. Velie, "Rudolph Halley," p. 78. New York *Times,* March 6, 8, 10, 1951.

which operated harness racing in the Roosevelt Raceway. Levy had begun receiving persistent complaints in 1946 from the head of the New York State Harness Racing Commission that bookmakers in large numbers were frequenting the race meetings and thereby endangering the license of the trotting association. Levy mentioned the matter to his frequent golfing companion, Frank Costello, and asked if he could help reduce the number of bookies at the races. Costello did not know how he could help Levy, but he agreed to mention the plight of his friend and the threat to the trotting association in his daily rounds of bars and restaurants. Although skeptical that bookmakers in any number had ever operated at his races, Levy was so relieved when complaints from the Commission ceased that he insisted on paying Costello $15,000 yearly, a practice he continued until 1949, when the Bureau of Internal Revenue refused to allow the payment as a business expense.[22]

Costello corroborated Levy's bizarre testimony; both men agreed that prior to 1946 they had never discussed Levy's concerns with horse racing. Following these statements Halley submitted a wire tap Hogan had made in 1943 on Costello's phone, which indicated that at least one such conversation between the two men had taken place prior to 1946. Although the manually recorded tap obviously referred to bookmaking activities and to a contract with the Pinkerton Detective Agency, the exact wording was not clear. The Committee interpreted one sentence by Levy to mean he was favorable to illegal bookmaking at the Yonkers trotting meeting in 1943, and on that basis the Committee attacked the witness's veracity in its report. After the Committee had expired, Levy presented additional evidence and character references, and the senators thereupon acknowledged that they had misread the recorded Levy–Costello conversation. The over-all impression, however, of Costello as a man of influence among bookmakers had been measurably strengthened.[23]

Costello's associations with other underworld figures also

22. Lester Velie, "Crime Busting is Right Up Hogan's Alley," *Collier's,* July 7, 1951, p. 66. *Third Interim Report,* pp. 113–14. Levy testimony, Crime *Hearings,* Pt. 7, pp. 758–810.

23. Crime *Hearings,* Pt. 7, pp. 775–77; Costello testimony, pp. 941–60. *Third Interim Report,* pp. 114–15. "Memorandum in re George Morton Levy" from James D. Walsh and David I. Shivitz to Kefauver, April 22, 1952; Kefauver to O'Conor, Hunt, Tobey, Wiley, June 6, 1952; Hunt to Kefauver, June 13, 1952, Box 7, Hunt Papers. New York *Times,* March 13, 14, 15, 1951.

attracted the Committee's attention. His supposed efforts to obtain the release of Luciano, his reported presence at the going-away party given Luciano in 1946, his meeting with the deported vice king in Cuba a year later, all became part of the testimony. The Committee explored Costello's joint enterprises and investments with such figures as Lansky and Adonis in the Saratoga Springs Piping Rock Casino in 1933, in the Beverly Club near New Orleans in the 1940s, as well as their later legitimate business venture into the sale of television sets. Such ties illustrated more complex interlocking associations of what the Committee perceived as an Eastern crime syndicate dominated by Costello, Adonis, and Lansky and paralleling that of the Midwestern Capone group in Chicago. Through a series of such associations, Costello could be linked to almost any underworld activity in the nation during the preceding two decades. To dramatize Costello's position in the underworld, Halley produced from the Hogan office grand jury testimony and wire-tapped conversations that, he argued, showed that Costello had ordered an ailing and talkative Willie Moretti to stay in California and to be less garrulous before investigators. Costello and Moretti had been close friends since childhood, and Costello had served as godfather to Moretti's first child. The Hogan tapes showed that Moretti referred to Costello as "Chief," but Costello explained that the word had often been tossed about in conversational banter for some time between the two men, a statement Halley said was unsubstantiated by the tapes. Costello maintained he had merely encouraged his old friend to remain quiet in California for the sake of his health, while Halley argued that the tone was more of an order.[24]

24. *Third Interim Report,* pp. 118–21. Crime *Hearings,* Pt. 7, pp. 965–72, 1017–19. Costello denied that his associations were as close or his position as authoritative as the Committee found. Unquestionably, his authority over Moretti appeared to be stronger than one might expect, and Costello certainly had been in contact for years with a number of other East Coast underworld figures, but these circumstances did not necessarily reveal a syndicate with a chain of command. Moretti had earlier entertained the Committee with a rambling discourse explaining that "everything is a racket today," and that a mob was "anybody . . . who makes 6 percent more on money." He knew a larger number of the underworld figures and insisted that he met many such "well-charactered people . . . automatically" at the race tracks. There was, of course, a certain truth in what Moretti said about meetings at tracks and resort towns; big-time gamblers shared

Costello failed in his effort to create a positive image before the Committee. Although he refused to state his net worth before the senators, he did give answers, however evasive or perjured, to other questions rather than to plead the Fifth Amendment. When his counsel, George Wolf, objected to the spectacle that television was making of Costello, Senator O'Conor, presiding at the hearings, ordered the cameras to turn away from the witness. Unknown to the senators at first, the WPIX cameramen focused alternately on the Committee and on Costello's hands as he crumpled a handkerchief, interlocked and picked at his fingers, grasped for a glass of water, stroked his eyeglasses where they lay on the table, and "rolled a little ball of paper between his thumb and index finger." The picture of the gambler's nervous, sometimes twitching hands suggested immense conspiratorial power and, more than any other single episode, caught the dramatic quality of the hearings in New York. At the nightly rebroadcasts, television drew material from the newsreel cameras, which had not been ordered to turn away from Costello's face, and they showed the gambler's sleepy-eyed, almost furtive countenance as his sun tan paled and as he "mopped his brow, wet his lips, opened his mouth from time to time as if to increase his intake of oxygen, and simultaneously seemed to . . . [chew] a corner of his tongue."[25]

As Halley pressed Costello to explain contradictions in previous statements that affected his naturalization applications in 1925, in the dates in which he engaged in bootlegging, in his present liquor interests, in his night-club operations in Louisiana, in his efforts to protect his phone from wire taps, Costello's public credibility plummeted. In fact, Costello could not be expected to remember all the details of his statements before

---

the popular postwar interest in gambling, and such meetings could be expected to be automatic. Moretti, caught up in the gambling scandals in New Jersey, was murdered, gangland style, in October of 1951. Cook, *Secret Rulers,* pp. 288–95.

25. Bryce, "New York Hearings," p. 84. Costello testimony, Crime *Hearings,* Pt. 7, pp. 877–78, 1170–75. Eric Goldman, *The Crucial Decade and After, America, 1945–1960* (New York: Vintage Books, 1960), p. 192. "The Biggest Show," *Newsweek,* March 26, 1951, p. 52. New York *Times,* March 14, 1951. Costello justified his refusal to give his net worth on the fact that the Committee had drawn harsh and unfriendly judgments toward him in its *Second Interim Report,* issued after the witness had testified in executive session, and promised to supply a net worth statement. Crime *Hearings,* Pt. 7, pp. 878–84.

earlier grand juries and liquor authorities, but his evasiveness, the presence of television and newsreel cameras, and the sheer volume of material Halley asked him to explain, all contributed to a popular feeling that the gambler must be guilty of grievous misdeeds. As a final blow to Costello's respectability, the Chief Counsel attempted to show that his legitimate interest in Wall Street real estate, in Texas oil lands, in a newly developed infra-electric broiler were insignificant, since they required only a minimum amount of his time and attention. To an amused press, Halley disclosed that Costello's earlier legitimate interests included the manufacture of chocolate-covered ice-cream cakes and the production of Kewpie dolls as prizes for punchboards.[26]

The witness became increasingly weary and testy before the aggressive Halley and the peering reporters and cameramen who recorded and interpreted his every movement. On the third day of his appearance before the Committee, after testifying for over seven hours in open hearings, Costello complained of the heat, lights, and confusion of the courtroom, which he claimed interfered with his right to counsel and with his ability to testify lucidly and consistently. He asked for a postponement of his testimony until he could recover from a severe throat inflammation and laryngitis. When Kefauver, Tobey, and Halley implied he was merely seeking to delay testifying until the Committee expired at the end of the month and insisted that he continue until his inability to talk became more obvious, Costello and his attorney walked from the hearing room. The following day, Costello repeated his walk-out before television cameras. After haggling with the Committee over various physicians' analyses of his throat condition—from which he had suffered for eighteen years—Costello returned to testify, refreshed by a weekend of rest. His voice, "midway between the speaking voice of Eddie Cantor and the death rattle of a seagull," held out, and he answered questions for a shortened period of time each day.[27]

26. Crime *Hearings,* Pt. 7, pp. 883–936, 960–65, 976–1015, 1066–82. *Third Interim Report,* pp. 111–12.

27. Crime *Hearings,* Pt. 7, pp. 1170–80, 1258–62. New York *Times,* March 17, 18, 20, 21, 1951. *Time,* April 2, 1951. "A Gambler's Luck Holds Out," *Life,* January 28, 1952, pp. 22–23. There was some speculation that Costello's gravelly voice was the result of an earlier operation for cancer of the throat. Actually, as Costello explained shortly before his death in 1973, a physician in the early 1930s had unintentionally singed the gambler's vocal cords while removing polyps from his throat by a burning process. The striking similarity between Costello's

A beaten man, Costello admitted knowing political leaders in ten of Manhattan's sixteen districts, but he attempted to minimize his political interests, once prompting laughter from the audience when he argued that a meeting between himself, Carmine De Sapio, and other political leaders was to discuss a benefit for charity and to obtain use of Madison Square Garden for its staging. Symbolically, WPIX commentator Harry Brundige got Kefauver's attention at the end of Costello's testimony and rushed to the witness stand to ask the witness directly to "smile a little bit" for the television audience. A bedraggled Costello managed a weary smile for the cameras.[28]

For a change of pace, the Committee called Virginia Hill Hauser, thirty-five-year-old former mistress of the murdered Benjamin "Bugsy" Siegel. One of ten children born to a marble cutter and horse trader in a small village near Bessemer, Alabama, Miss Hill had, in the mid-thirties, run away to Chicago, where she shortly became the companion of and hostess for a wide assortment of underworld personalities, including one of the Fischetti brothers, Joe Adonis, and Siegel. The recipient of substantial gifts and cash from these figures, Miss Hill traveled widely and spent extravagantly. Newspaper speculation made the striking Miss Hill into an Alabama heiress, a budding movie personality, and transporter of large sums of money and intelligence for the underworld. One account held that she knew the true story behind Siegel's death and had "insured" herself by recording it and arranging for the information to be available to law enforcement officers in the event that she met with foul play. In the meantime, however, she had married an Austrian-born ski instructor.[29]

Lee Mortimer, carrying on a petty feud with the "gangster

---

voice, broadcast by radio and television in 1951, and that of Marlon Brando's "Godfather" in 1972 is in all probability more than coincidental. New York *Times,* February 27, 1973.

28. New York *Times,* March 20, 21, 1951. Crime *Hearings,* Pt. 7, p. 1676. *Time,* April 2, 1951. Joe Adonis (Doto) felt that Costello, who frequently lapsed into broken English and Brooklynese, had made a serious mistake in attempting to answer Halley's questions. Adonis, a much more articulate man than Costello, had appeared twice before the Committee and in a cold, metallic monotone, refused to answer questions. Velie, "Rudolph Halley," p. 24. Crime *Hearings,* Pt. 7, pp. 280–316, 847–65.

29. Dean Jennings, *We Only Kill Each Other: The Life and Bad Times of Bugsy Siegel* (New York: Prentice-Hall, Inc., 1967), pp. 91–94, 112–14, 138–40, 238–40. Crime *Hearings,* Pt. 10, pp. 717, 719.

moll," had suggested in the summer of 1950 that the Committee look into the source of her income. After locating Miss Hill in Bar Harbor, Maine, in the fall, the Committee postponed her appearance until the hearings in New York in order to give her ample time to recover from the birth of a child. During closed preliminary questioning by the Committee, Mrs. Hauser had become hysterical, and Associate Counsel Joseph Nellis pointed out to Halley that she could add nothing to the testimony to be developed, and he suggested that she not be called. Halley quipped that she would make a good show but, fearing that she might become abusive in the witness chair, he and Kefauver questioned her with extreme delicacy, dealing almost exclusively with the large sums of money she had obtained from underworld friends rather than on the details of her personal associations with the men. Apparently expecting a vigorous cross examination, Miss Hill arrived for the hearing tardily and in bad humor, threatening to "throw something" at the cameramen unless they quit annoying her. Kefauver, noting that she was "right nervous," ordered the photographers to cease their harassment. During the open testimony, Mrs. Hauser, a puffy, slightly overweight woman in a tight black dress, silver-blue mink stole, and broad-brimmed black hat, maintained that she knew nothing of the activities of the men who had given her the money. When she was in residence at Siegel's Flamingo, for example, she often stayed upstairs alone, away from the cactus, to which she was allergic. She also knew nothing that would help to solve the Siegel murder. Although remarking that her story appeared "impossible," Halley took pains not to disturb her temporary equanimity on the stand. Her testimony completed, Mrs. Hauser sipped from a glass of water, smiled for the photographers, lifted her stole, and began her exit to scattered applause from the spectators. Again encountering the insistent press, she kicked one reporter on the shins, slapped Marjorie Farnsworth of the New York *Journal-American,* and shouted her hope that "the atom bomb" would fall on each of them.[30]

30. Memorandum from Kefauver to Halley, July 12, 1950, Crime Box 37, Kefauver Papers. Washington *Times-Herald,* October 1, 1950. Washington *Post,* October 3, 1950. Knoxville *News-Sentinel,* October 3, 1950. Velie, "Rudolph Halley," pp. 78–79. Nellis interview. Kefauver, *Crime in America,* pp. 156–58. Goldman, *Crucial Decade,* pp. 195–96. Crime *Hearings,* Pt. 7, pp. 1144–70. New York *Times,* March

The Committee also publicly stated its case against Governor Dewey. In addition to showing that local officials in Saratoga not only tolerated but also profited from the illegal casino gambling during the legal racing season, the Committee developed what it considered a case of laxity on the part of the state government. During the summer of 1947 Superintendent of State Police John A. Gaffney, anticipating an upswing in gambling activity in Saratoga County, ordered a police survey. A report detailing the ownership, location, and description of several wide-open gambling establishments promptly reached Gaffney, who remarked that it appeared to be "a sizable operation." He then, however, filed the report, claiming that he could take no action until the governor or local officials requested it. Illegal gambling meanwhile continued undisturbed for the next two years, until the scandal and publicity prompted state police to close down the operations prior to the 1950 season. Tobey upbraided Gaffney for not bringing the report to Dewey's attention; one Committee counsel argued that Gaffney was legally responsible for supervising the conditions regardless of the governor's knowledge; and Halley attempted to establish that Dewey's office had actually seen the report. Dewey admitted that the law enforcement by the Saratoga police had been grossly inadequate, that a rigid observance of precedent on the part of state police had led to an embarrassing situation, but at the same time he found no evidence of impropriety on Gaffney's part. Indeed, he insisted that, with its limited size, the state police could not possibly enforce local laws, and he called for a review of the dangerous precedents that might have been set by the state troopers' actions in the 1950 season.[31]

The Committee sparred with Dewey over his responsibilities and his knowledge of the facts prior to 1950; it invited him

16, 1951. Miss Hill ran into serious tax problems in the wake of her Kefauver Committee testimony; her home in Seattle was sold by the government, and to avoid prosecution, she took up residence in Europe, where she died, financially broken, of an overdose of barbiturates in 1966. Ibid., July 7, August 3, 21, 1951. Jennings, *We Only Kill Each Other*, pp. 239–56.

31. *Third Interim Report*, pp. 106–9. Crime *Hearings*, Pt. 7, pp. 426, 1246, 1244, 1255. Report, Lawrence E. Walsh, Counsel to the Governor, to Dewey, March 28, 1951; Press Release by Governor Dewey, March 28, 1951. Ibid., pp. 1732–34.

to appear as a witness and, when he pleaded a virus infection and countered with an invitation to the Committee to hear him in Albany, the senators sneered, said they had already set up shop in New York City, and declined his offer. Regardless of his awareness of the Gaffney report, it is all but inconceivable that, prior to 1949, Dewey, a veteran crime fighter, did not know in general of the flagrant conditions in Saratoga, a perennial problem for New York governors. At the same time, the Governor, a precise and logical administrator, understood that with a force of seven hundred men he could not possibly police the entire state; practical, if not political, considerations suggested that he follow precedent and hope for more effective action by local authorities. Dewey asked the New York State Crime Commission, which he appointed in the wake of the Kefauver Committee's activities, to explore the problems inherent in the division of law enforcement between state and local officials.[32]

Picking up an old campaign issue of 1950, the Committee expressed doubts that Luciano's parole could be justified by any vital information on Sicily or the New York waterfront that he might have channeled to federal officials. The full details, however, were unavailable to the Committee; Dewey, who also may not have had access to all the facts, appeared in any event to be effectively insulated from attack by the State Board of Parole, and the Committee, unwilling to go to Albany to hear the Governor, questioned the wisdom of the parole and then dropped the matter.[33] As Kefauver had promised, the

32. *Third Interim Report,* pp. 1325, 1549, 1695. Kefauver, *Crime in America,* pp. 149–50. Dewey Press Release, Crime *Hearings,* Pt. 7, p. 1732. In Illinois, Governor Adlai Stevenson had a similar but perhaps more widely dispersed problem with gambling. He tried to persuade local officials to take action, but at the same time he reorganized the state police to act, in the event that the local officers did not comply. Finally, he reluctantly ordered state troops in a number of local gambling areas. Stevenson testimony, ibid., Pt. 5, pp. 209–19.

33. *Third Interim Report,* p. 119. Kefauver, *Crime in America,* pp. 29–30. Frederic Sondern, Jr., *Brotherhood of Evil: The Mafia* (New York: Farrar, Straus and Cudahy, 1959), pp. 111–12. Sid Feder and Joachim Joesten, *The Luciano Story* (New York: David McKay Co., Inc., 1954), pp. 169–74. Joesten later repudiated his pro-Dewey book, and Congressman Macy, whose leadership in Suffolk County was being challenged by Dewey's political allies, remained in contact with Kefauver and carried on the attack on the parole in 1951. Kefauver's office remained convinced of skulduggery in the matter of parole, but

Committee heard testimony on the Macy letter and on the charges and countercharges concerning influence by gangsters in New York City politics growing out of the 1950 elections. The evidence on the famous letter was taken in executive session and never released; neither Pecora nor Impellitteri responded to the Committee's invitations to appear, and the testimony of Republican Edward Corsi was so lacking in proof that Kefauver publicly voiced his dissatisfaction with it.[34]

The appearance of Virginia Hill and the testimony on Saratoga gambling and Luciano's parole were mere sideshows for the main attraction, the attack on O'Dwyer. While the Ambassador partially recovered from his pulmonary bronchitis and flew to the city for the St. Patrick's Day Parade, the Committee began setting the stage for his testimony. From a former Democratic politician and undersheriff, the Committee learned that Brooklyn political figures of the 1930s frequently met in the restaurant of Joe Adonis, where they exchanged information and made deals and frequently got money from Adonis. O'Dwyer and a number of his later appointees were among those observed at Adonis's establishment. A gossipy Republican friend of O'Dwyer, Charles Lipsky, told the senators that he had carried a message to Tammany from the new mayor in 1946, asking for a change of leadership and certain structural reforms; when his request met with opposition, however, O'Dwyer did not carry out his threat to "starve out" Tammany. Lipsky also told of his belief in the political power of Costello over Tammany. Frank Bals, a close friend whom O'Dwyer had appointed Seventh Deputy Police Commissioner despite his failure in supervising the policemen guarding Reles in 1941, brought laughter and hisses from the spectators with his theory that Reles had fallen from the sixth-floor window in an attempt to sneak to the floor below his suite and then reappear outside his room and surprise his guards. (Tobey ridiculed the proposition as

no balanced study of the incident has ever been published. Joachim Joesten, *Dewey, Luciano, and I* (Great Barrington, Mass.: Limited mimeographed pre-edition, 1955). Telegram from Kefauver to Halley, April 4, 1951, Box 37; Macy to O'Conor, July 25, 1951, Box 27, Hunt Papers. Memo from Henry Patrick Kiley [?] to Kefauver, October 14, 1955, Crime Box 3, Kefauver Papers.

34. Crime *Hearings*, Pt. 7, pp. 504, 1580–85, 1619.

the "peek-a-boo" theory.) James J. Moran, admitting to a "certain amount of gutter wisdom," was all but trapped in a perjury charge over the number of times he had been visited by a well-known policy dealer.[35]

O'Dwyer appeared with a prepared statement in which he gave his views on the development of organized crime since Prohibition and stressed the value of his work in the "Murder, Inc." cases and his extensive building programs as mayor. For over an hour O'Dwyer talked as Kefauver expressed concern that his voice would fail; the television audience, bored, called in to demand that his soliloquy be stopped. When Halley began to ask his questions, many of them referring to events a dozen years earlier, O'Dwyer appeared stunned by the extent of the Counsel's preparation. Because his answers generally lacked the studied detail of Halley's questions and because he invariably tended to blame subordinates or political foes for his failures, O'Dwyer's answers seemed evasive or quarrelsome. Aided by copies of the 1945 Beldock grand juries reports obtained through a court order from Brooklyn Judge Samuel Leibowitz, Halley quizzed O'Dwyer in great detail about the failure to prosecute Adonis and Anastasia, the removal of the "wanted" cards by Moran, the seemingly cavalier attitude O'Dwyer had adopted toward Bals and the sleeping policemen after the death of Reles, and the alleged sabotage by O'Dwyer's office of Amen's waterfront investigation. The Ambassador, impressively dressed in a blue pencil-striped suit, answered defensively, sometimes indignantly, while his deep tan reddened in anger and strands of well-groomed gray hair occasionally fell to his forehead, accenting the image of an embattled, aging man.[36]

Perhaps the major thrust of the questions was oriented toward puncturing O'Dwyer's image as an enemy of Tammany Hall. The former mayor explained that as a Brooklyn Democrat he had not been in the debt of the Manhattan organization and had earnestly sought to democratize its procedures and to rid it of gambling and gangster influences. He understood, however, that money brought immense power within the organization to such figures as Costello. "It doesn't mat-

35. New York *Times,* March 16, 1951. Crime *Hearings,* Pt.7, pp. 869–77, 831–47, 1098–1129, 1282–1320.

36. Bryce, "New York Hearings," pp. 76–84. O'Dwyer testimony, Crime *Hearings,* Pt. 7, pp. 1326–1401, 1491–1580.

ter," he elaborated, "whether it is a banker, a businessman or a gangster, his pocketbook is always attractive." O'Dwyer, in fact, vacillated between statements about forthrightly fighting Tammany and about more discreet efforts merely to control its direction. The Kefauver Committee, acting out of a pro-Fusion, LaGuardia bias, viewed his attitude as hypocritical.[37]

O'Dwyer, for example, related how in 1942 he had gone to Costello's apartment to question him about a rumor relating to a contract for war materials and had found a cocktail party in progress, with Tammany leader Michael Kennedy and several lesser political figures as guests. The Committee implied that O'Dwyer's presence may have been more political than he admitted, and it pointed out that, despite his highly publicized posturing against the sinister gangster influence in Tammany and the indelible imprint the meeting had on him, he had never before found occasion to inform the public of the incident. Prior to his race in 1945, O'Dwyer not only cultivated Irving Sherman, whom he knew to have contacts with Costello and other underworld figures, but he later supported Kennedy in his effort to regain his former leadership role in Tammany. Indeed, O'Dwyer appointed to civic offices a number of persons who had been associated with Costello or other underworld figures. He named Hugo Rogers, a close friend of Costello, to the traffic board, a brother-in-law of Willie Moretti to the Department of Hospitals, and a cousin of Irving Sherman to a city marshalcy. O'Dwyer declared that his association with the mysterious Sherman gave him hints into underworld activities for his wartime investigations and that, while Sherman had been enthusiastic about O'Dwyer's candidacy, he had never asked for political favors. O'Dwyer had supported Kennedy as the lesser of two evils; Rogers, he felt, was both competent and conscientious; he did not know of Sherman's connection to his appointee until he read it in the paper; Moretti's relative, he conceded, had been appointed to get the necessary political "cooperation." O'Dwyer recalled casually meeting Adonis once in the past and acknowledged that some of his good friends and appointees, including his onetime law partner Judge George Joyce, Lipsky, Brooklyn district leader Kenneth Sutherland, and Fire Department Commissioner

37. Crime *Hearings*, Pt. 7, pp. 1517–20, 1536.

Frank Quayle were also Adonis's friends.[38] The impression
left by the questioning was that O'Dwyer's administration had
been riddled with politicians who were responsive to gangsters.

The Committee pointed out, moreover, that despite
O'Dwyer's knowledge of conditions on the waterfront, little
had been done to control or improve them during his terms in
office. The Ambassador admitted that bookmaking had pro-
ceeded on a large scale while he was in office, but he argued
that he had appointed the best men he knew to head up the
police department and had ordered John J. Murtagh, Commissioner of Investigations, to conduct a study of bookmaking and
the resulting corruption of police. Kefauver had previously
heard about Murtagh's study, based on the accumulation of
records of telephone calls to and from known bookie establishments, and he acknowledged its thoroughness. Murtagh and
the Committee differed, however, over the practical benefits
of the study. Murtagh maintained that it had led to massive
discontinuance of telephone service to bookies in New York,
that it had enabled him to supply the sluggish New Jersey
officials with information on a number of large wire rooms in
their state, and that indirectly it had led to the conviction of
Erickson. Halley and Yavner stressed the contributions of federal agents and the McFarland Subcommittee in getting New
Jersey to act and in bringing about Hogan's arrest of Erickson.
They also wondered aloud why Murtagh's study had not
brought to light the Gross bookmaking ring and its massive
corruption of policemen. Murtagh replied that there must
have been information in his files on Gross and that while his
office believed there had been dishonesty in the police department, it could never prove it. These developments, plus a series of questions that elicited an apology from O'Dwyer for
labeling McDonald's inquiry a "witch hunt," left the impression that his administration had been singularly inept and lax
in fighting organized crime.[39]

38. *Third Interim Report*, pp. 136–40. Crime *Hearings*, Pt. 7, pp.
1554–67. The mysterious Sherman, who reportedly moved more freely
and openly between the underworld and political figures than did
Costello, was at one time Halley's "number one New York objective."
He was missing at the time of the hearings in New York and was being
sought by the FBI. Velie, "Rudolph Halley," p. 79.
39. *Third Interim Report*, pp. 132–36. Robert Wohlforth to Kefauver,
April 3, 1950; Kefauver to Wohlforth, April 6, 1950, Crime Box 2, Kefauver Papers. Murtagh testimony, Crime *Hearings*, Pt. 7, pp. 1401–19.

In singling out O'Dwyer, the Committee not only reflected a distinct pro-LaGuardia, pro-Fusion bias, but it also blurred the picture of the gambling and corruption in the larger cities. LaGuardia at one time had had the support of Costello and Adonis and launched his campaign against Adonis after the latter had backed his opponent in 1937. O'Dwyer, lacking the non-Democratic backing of the "Little Flower," could hardly afford to destroy Tammany; as he allegedly told Mrs. Eleanor Roosevelt in 1945, since her husband had not been able to reform Tammany as governor and President, it was surely an overly ambitious task for a mayor. A product of Brooklyn's Democratic political life, he would obviously know and occasionally deal with political figures who had known Adonis or Costello.[40] LaGuardia, despite his verbal blasts at the "tinhorn" gamblers and gangsters, had not solved the conditions on the waterfront and had indeed bemoaned the growing gambling and police corruption in his own administration. The very figures for scratch sheet sales the Committee received from McDonald's office that showed gambling to be widespread in O'Dwyer's tenure revealed the increase coming under LaGuardia and an actual decline, however slow, under O'Dwyer. The fact that wire service rooms and other operations essential to gambling might have physically moved across the Hudson to New Jersey in the early 1940s could serve as good an excuse for O'Dwyer as for LaGuardia.[41]

By suggesting, in its focus on O'Dwyer's career, that the existence and toleration of racketeering and gambling were the product of one man's political expediency, the Committee was not only personally unfair, but it was also obscuring the fundamental truths that these conditions transcended reform cycles and that they sprang from certain basic problems in defining law and morality and perhaps government itself. In

40. *Newsweek,* November 21, 1949, p. 31. Bell, *End of Ideology,* pp. 145–46, 197. Lipsky testimony, Crime *Hearings,* Pt. 7, p. 832.

41. Garrett, *LaGuardia Years,* p. 162. McDonald testimony, Crime *Hearings,* Pt. 7, p. 1040. By obtaining secret testimony before the grand jury, the Committee in the final phase of its hearings was able to show a direct contradiction between O'Dwyer's testimony and that of John P. Crane, head of the Firemen's Union, who claimed he had personally handed the Mayor $10,000 for a political campaign. Although the matter was investigated with the hope of establishing perjury, no case was proved against O'Dwyer, who after appearing before Hogan's grand jury returned to Mexico. Crane testimony, ibid., pp. 1676–90. New York *Times,* March 22, 1951. Velie, "William O'Dwyer," August 7, 1953, pp. 19–23.

scapegoating Tammany, Costello, and O'Dwyer, moreover, the Committee fell into the old American pattern of seeing vice and crime as things set apart, imposing themselves on the broader community only through political corruption. To dramatize its case against a "Mr. Big," the Committee needed to show his influence on a political figure of some importance. By suggestion and repetition, its charges linking Costello and O'Dwyer, although never proven, gained a high level of public acceptance.[42]

As the senators moved toward their final statement on O'Dwyer and Costello, the public response to their revelations mounted to unprecedented frenzy. No precise count of letters and communications to the Committee was kept, but a total of a quarter of a million would be a reasonable estimate. *Time* magazine received 100,000 to 130,000 letters within three weeks of the hearings in New York; Senator Tobey's office received over 15,000; Kefauver's, probably 30,000; Halley, over 1,000; and most senators, although they were not members of the Committee, received a number—one as many as 1,000. Probably 95 per cent were favorable to the Committee; one compared the immediate reaction to the Committee's work to the public outrage that followed the attack on Pearl Harbor, and another declared that the hearings were the greatest drama he had ever witnessed. The creator of the *Superman* comic series wrote to President Truman; Fran Striker, originator of the "Lone Ranger" radio series, explained to Tobey that the Committee served the same function as his "Robin Hood" character in the early West; a few expressed anger at television comedian Milton Berle's spoof of the senators' work.[43] In 1952 *Look* magazine, in its second annual

42. Bryce, "New York Hearings," pp. 90–97. Bell, *End of Ideology,* p. 141.

43. Gerald Broidy to Tobey, June 8, 1951, Box 104, Tobey Papers. *Congressional Record,* April 13, 1951, pp. 3821–23. Tobey to (Claremont, N.H.) *The Daily Eagle,* February 20, 1953, Box 106, Tobey Papers. "No Stampede," *The New Yorker,* April 21, 1951, pp. 21–22. Senator Joseph O'Mahoney to F. L. Ralston, April 11, 1951, in "General Legislations, A–Z, 1951" Box, O'Mahoney Papers, University of Wyoming Library, Laramie. Senator James P. Kem to Mrs. George Alexander, April 17, 1951, Kem Papers, Western Historical Manuscripts Collection, University of Missouri, Columbia. "Letter from the Publisher," *Time,* April 16, 1951, p. 13. *Variety,* March 16, 1951. Edward Petersen to Hunt, March 26, 1951, Box 7, Hunt Papers. Jerry Siegel to Truman, May 17, 1951, Box 101, Tobey Papers. Fran Striker to Tobey, March 20, 1951; O. H. Langhaus to Hunt, March 21, 1951, Box 7, Hunt Papers. Telegram from Hildegard and Arthur Gillis to Tobey, March

television awards survey, honored the Kefauver hearings for special achievement and as the best public affairs program of the year. The Academy of Television Arts and Sciences awarded the hearings an "Emmy" for special achievement "for bringing the workings of . . . government into the homes of the American people."[44]

Although much of the massive response sprang from the novelty of television, not a little resulted from the inherently dramatic nature of the story unfolded by the Committee. Contemporary journalists and letters to the Committee members suggest that very few citizens could not identify with someone on the Committee. A persistent, occasionally sarcastic inquisitor glaring at witnesses through his dark horn-rimmed glasses, Halley spun a complex series of questions like a web to entrap the unwary witness. In a monotonous, singsong lisp, he presented the same question in a variety of forms, only to pounce like a spider on the smallest inconsistency in answers and hopefully extract some larger truth from the testimony. The architect of the hearings in New York, Halley was to emerge from the proceedings as the new hero of the Fusion movement in New York City.[45]

Although he contributed virtually nothing to the questioning, Senator Tobey expressed the gut reaction of much of the public. Occasionally wearing the green eyeshade of the country editor, the bespectacled, balding Tobey listened intently to the witnesses and then erupted in scathing wrath. He mocked Costello's claim to respectability and patriotism by asking what the gambler had ever done for his country, wringing the lame reply that he had paid his taxes. He mercilessly upbraided Bals, the Saratoga officers, and the state police for their apparent laxity. He needled the thin-skinned O'Dwyer so relentlessly on the circumstances of Reles's death, the Anas-

28, 1951, Box 103, Tobey Papers. A counsel for the Committee estimated that 75 per cent stated that they had a different perspective after seeing the television hearings than they would have gotten from newspaper accounts; and 45 per cent mentioned that they had never written a government representative prior to the Kefauver Committee. Memorandum from Larry Goddard to Kefauver, n.d., Crime Box 1, Kefauver Papers.

44. Gorman, *Kefauver*, p. 102.

45. John Crosby column, Minneapolis *Morning Tribune,* March 23, 1951. *Time,* March 26, April 2, 1951. Alan Barth, *Government by Investigation* (New York: The Viking Press, Inc., 1955), pp. 67–80. New York *Times,* March 16, 1951. Velie, "Rudolph Halley," pp. 24–25, 78–80, 82.

The Greatest Show on Earth. Cleveland *Plain Dealer*, March 21, 1951.
Ed Kuekes, *The Plain Dealer*

tasia prosecution, and the Costello–Tammany association that O'Dwyer exploded with the innuendo that the bookmakers at Bretton Woods supported Tobey. The Ambassador charged that the Senator sent for tainted money from New York during his recent reelection campaign and asserted that he carried a letter in his pocket to document his charge but would show it only to Tobey. After some delay and hesitation, the Committee asked for the letter which, as it developed, was only a bread-and-butter note to a New Yorker associated with the National Committee for an Effective Congress. Kefauver praised the liberal group, and O'Dwyer, in an apologetic tone, admitted that his charge had been made in a fit of passion. Tobey, on center stage, then delivered a homiletic eulogy on his own poverty and freedom, so moving that he brought himself to tears and the audience to applause. Earlier, he had recited John Greenleaf Whittier's "Problems" upon hearing District Attorney McDonald tell of the peddling of narcotics in the Brooklyn public schools; this recitation had drawn cheers from the courtroom spectators and almost universal praise from the television audience. Although Tobey encountered a spate of criticism when he read into the record a letter that some interpreted as a slight on the Italian community, the majority of people heartily approved of his actions. Like a "Greek chorus singing its lines from Bartlett's *Familiar Quotations*," Tobey voiced the frustrations and impatience of America's heartland at what had transpired in New York.[46]

New York, however, had given her heart to Senator Ke-

46. New York *Times,* March 15, 1951. Crime *Hearings,* Pt. 7, pp. 1668, 1117–19, 1244–45, 1341–43, 1570, 1536, 1376, 1534, 1576–77, 1039–40. Tobey to H. L. Seldon, April 3, 1951, Box 191, Tobey Papers. Crime *Hearings,* Pt. 12, pp. 432, 767. Syracuse (N.Y.) *Herald-Journal,* March 16, 1951. Tobey to George C. Sololsky, March 17, 1951, Box 101; Luigi Criscuola, Chairman of Italian-American Congress, to Tobey, March 28, 1951; Vincent R. Impelliterri to Tobey, April 4, 1951; Tobey to Impelliterri, April 5, 1951; Tobey to Fortune R. Pope, April 4, 1951, Box 102, Tobey Papers. Tobey to Vincent Zavett, April 2, 1951, Crime *Hearings,* Pt. 12, p. A1829. Ray Tucker column, Grand Rapids (Mich.) *Herald,* March 29, 1951. "Rise of Senator Legend," *Time,* March 24, 1952, pp. 20–24. A group of Tobey's critics filed a resolution in the New Hampshire legislature to send the weeping Tobey a supply of bandannas. Tobey received a number of threatening letters, which he transmitted to the FBI. Boston *Herald,* March 21, 1951. Representative John W. McCormick to Tobey, March 17, 1951; Tobey to Grenville Clark, March 28, 1951, Box 102; Tobey to J. Edgar Hoover, March 29, 1951; Hoover to Tobey, April 3, 1951, Box 101, Tobey Papers.

fauver, who, as calm, low-keyed mediator of the hearings, presented a different image than the relentless Halley or sanctimonious Tobey. His quiet Southern drawl and spontaneous, jack-o'-lantern smile helped Kefauver rule the proceedings with benign understatement. Commentator Quentin Reynolds remarked that Kefauver the man literally dominated comment on the Committee because he alone seemed to recognize the pain and fright of the witnesses and to be less openly prejudiced against them. From proceedings that alternately resembled a carnival sideshow, a medieval morality play, and a revival camp meeting, Kefauver emerged "a sort of Laurence Olivier with a briefcase." In the pioneering days of television, he had captured the essence of what Marshall McLuhan would later call the "cool" personality.[47]

In the wake of the hearings in New York, Kefauver's name began to appear regularly in speculation about candidates for the Presidency and Vice Presidency. From 20 to 25 per cent of those who wrote to the Committee referred directly to his election as President in 1952, and 60 per cent indirectly suggested that he become a candidate. Noting the strength of his support for higher office, long-time Kefauver followers such as George R. Dempster of Knoxville and Judge Will Cummings and Carl F. McAfee of Chattanooga began encouraging Kefauver to declare his candidacy; others warned him against being trapped into accepting the nomination for Vice President. Porter Warner, as he launched his Kefauver-for-President Club in Chattanooga, began receiving encouraging reports from the press in Washington. Although obviously pleased by the groundswell, Kefauver played the traditional game of innocence, kept open all options by cultivating influential journalists and other public figures, and tried to exploit his popularity to push remedial legislation through Congress.[48]

47. *Time,* March 26, 1951, pp. 22–24, 80–81; April 2, 1951, pp. 62–63. Grand Rapids *Herald,* March 29, 1951. Barth, *Government by Investigation,* pp. 67–80. Bryce, "New York Hearings," pp. 19–21, 97–99. Tape of Quentin Reynolds radio broadcast between March 22–28, 1951, Kefauver Papers. Harriet S. Lazarus to Tobey, April 2, 1951, Box 101; Thomas L. Stokes, column for March 27, 1951, unidentified newspaper, Crime Scrapbook, Tobey Papers. Kenneth Stewart and John Tebbel, *Makers of Modern Journalism* (New York: Prentice-Hall, Inc., 1952), pp. 36–38. John Crosby article, Minneapolis *Morning Tribune,* Box 100, Tobey Papers. "Playboy Interview: Marshall McLuhan," *Playboy* (March 1969), 56, 61.

48. "Friends Hand Harry Misery Aplenty," *Newsweek,* April 2, 1951,

In one sense, Kefauver's strategy of seeking national exposure and political availability through the crime issue had worked too well. The clang and bustle and hoop-la of the news media—and particularly the all-seeing eye of television—had lifted him from the obscurity of early 1950 to the dizzying heights of national attention in New York a year later. Public cynicism and political opposition had temporarily paled before him. Kefauver understood, however, the fickle nature of his support and hoped to translate it into legislative monuments before his following dispersed and his critics returned to do battle.

---

p. 17. Memorandum from Larry Goddard to Kefauver, n.d., Crime Box 1; Worth M. McCown to Kefauver, March 27, 1951; H. D. Thompson to Kefauver, May 14, 1951; Dempster to Kefauver, April 6, 1951; Will Cummings to Kefauver, March 29, 1951; McAfee to Kefauver, March 27, 1951; Hillsman Taylor to Kefauver, March 28, 1951; N. Key Hart, *U.S. News & World Report,* to Porter Warner, April 30, 1951; Hart to Kefauver, April 30, 1951, Crime Box 2; telegram, Walter Winchell to Kefauver, April 13, 1951; Kefauver to Marquis Childs, March 31, 1951; Kefauver to Drew Pearson, March 31, 1951; Kefauver to Walker S. Buel, Cleveland *Plain Dealer,* April 6, 1951; Kefauver to Ray Tucker, April 9, 1951; Kefauver to Charles Bartlett, March 17, 1951; memorandum from Martin Fay to Kefauver, March 27, 1951, Crime Box 1; Kefauver to Dinah Shore, April 18, 1951; Kefauver to Billy Graham, Crime Box 2, Kefauver Papers.

8

The Decline of the Committee

Already the pendulum of crime is starting in
the swing back against the reform wave.
  —Alexander Wiley, August 1951

Despite the unprecedented successes in New York, the Committee faced serious problems in translating its findings into legislation. In Congress the polite smiles barely concealed a bitter opposition born in part of jealousy and in part of the fear that the Committee's exposures would critically damage the Democratic party; in Senate cloakrooms, Kefauver reportedly had the appeal of a "skunk at a lawn party." The Administration, having already suffered the Committee's barbs over the Internal Revenue Bureau, now was embroiled in an embarrassing outcry for O'Dwyer's resignation. Kefauver, who had shaken off periods of weariness during the grueling year's work, was now nearing physical exhaustion; Halley, who enjoyed boundless stamina, labored relentlessly on the Committee's final report until the sudden onset of a kidney ailment forced him into Roosevelt Hospital for emergency surgery; the staff, driven for months by the tireless Kefauver and Halley, was numb with fatigue.[1]

1. New York *Times,* March 25, 1951. Memorandum for weekly press conference, David E. Bell to George M. Elsey, March 27, 1951, George M. Elsey Papers, Truman Library. Mrs. Preston Blair to Truman, May 19, 1951. John Doremus to Truman, March 22, 1951; Marjorie Grabhorn to Truman, June 30, 1951, OF, Truman Papers. Samuel Ungerleider to Charles Neese, January 16, 1951; Neese to Ungerleider, January 20, 1951; Ungerleider to Kefauver, March 26, 1951; Kefauver to Ungerleider, April 2, 1951, "General Correspondence, 1948–1955" Box, Kefauver Papers. Lester Velie, "Rudolph Halley—How He Nailed America's Racketeers," *Collier's,* May 19, 1951, pp. 78–80. New York *Times,* April 8, 1951. Unpublished Executive Session Minutes

To meet the March 31 deadline set by the Senate, the Committee attempted to hold final hearings and write its report simultaneously, an enormous task that was complicated by the disorganization of the voluminous files during the hearings in New York. Fearing that efforts by Tobey and Wiley to extend the Committee would only diffuse public interest, Kefauver hoped to focus attention and support on his proposal for the establishment of an independent Federal Crime Commission. The cornerstone of Kefauver's legislative program, the proposal had reached the Senator almost a year earlier and had been privately supported by Special Justice Department Prosecutor Max Goldschein, an old friend and associate of Kefauver. While the Senator from Tennessee tried to mobilize support for his proposal, public opinion strongly endorsed the Republicans' argument that the Committee's assignment had not been completed and that the Committee should be continued. From 90 to 95 per cent of those who wrote to the senators favored an extension for six to twelve months; members of the Junior Chamber of Commerce of Ypsilanti, Michigan, flew to Washington with a petition that bore 18,000 signatures asking for a continuation of the Committee; a few sent small amounts of money to support further Committee investigation. Columnist Walter Winchell argued that pressure from the White House and Senate accounted for Kefauver's reluctance to continue the Committee, and an increasing number of letters implied that a widespread reaction against the Committee would follow its death under such circumstances. Senators Hunt and O'Conor remained undecided about continuing the Committee until Attorney General McGrath and FBI Director Hoover, testifying in the final days over national television, urged extension of the Committee's life and blasted the establishment of a Federal Crime Commission as a first step in the creation of a dread national police force. Kefauver finally consented to a temporary agreement to ask for a thirty-day extension, and the Senate's Democratic majority, unwilling to be branded with a procrime label, readily agreed.[2]

---

of Committee Meeting, March 29, 1951, Box 3, Kefauver Papers
  2. Unpublished Executive Session Minutes of Committee Meeting, March 29, 1951. "Final Report of Special Committee to Investigate Organized Crime in Interstate Commerce," *Senate Report No. 725,* 82d Cong., 1st sess. (1951), p. 14. New York *Times,* March 24, 25, 26, 30, 1951. Frank J. Wilson to Kefauver, April 16, 1950; Kefauver to Wilson,

The month's extension provided additional time for the mobilization of the forces pushing for further continuation and opposing Kefauver's Federal Crime Commission idea. Although Kefauver, Hunt, and Halley proposed to use the additional time for drafting the Committee's report, O'Conor and the two Republicans urged that it be spent in holding hearings. Associate Counsel John L. Burling left the Committee in protest against the rush to write the report, and other staff members, who expected the Committee to expire shortly, began to seek employment elsewhere. In the period of indecision, Wiley publicly criticized Senate Sergeant-at-Arms Joseph C. Duke for arranging low bond for three laggard Chicago witnesses, Charles and Rocco Fischetti and Murray Humphries, and also reprimanded the Committee for not holding hearings to take their testimony. The Committee's on again–off again plans to hear the mysterious Irving Sherman brought a mild censure from FBI Director Hoover, who had been trying to help locate the witness.[3] At first the exhausted Kefauver argued adamantly for an end to the Committee, pointing out that the broad picture of organized crime had been surveyed, that little could be gained by gathering additional documentation, that public opinion was ideally recep-

---

April 21, 1951, Crime Box 1; Kefauver to O'Conor, April 18, 1951; Kenneth Colegrove to Kefauver, March 21, 1951; Ed Wimmer to Kefauver, March 28, 1951; Senator George A. Smathers to Kefauver, March 26, 1951, Crime Box 2, Kefauver Papers. Henry A. Wallace to Tobey, March 17, 1951; C. P. Shallenberger to Tobey, March 23, 1951, Box 100; Henry Elliot Williams to Senators Spessard Holland and George Smathers, March 27, 1951, Box 104, Tobey Papers. Clinton (Ia.) *Herald,* March 27, 1951. Washington *Religious Review,* March 19, 1951. Mr. and Mrs. G. Harold Haus to Hunt, March 29, 1951; telegram from Adolf A. Berle, Jr., to Hunt, March 29, 1951, Box 7, Hunt Papers. Memorandum, Larry Goddard to Kefauver, n.d.; Neese to Walter Winchell, March 29, 1951, Crime Box 1, Kefauver Papers. McGrath testimony, Crime *Hearings,* Pt. 12, pp. 511–12. *Congressional Record,* March 29, 1951, p. 3305. Charleston (S.C.) *Daily Mail,* March 27, 1951. "Keeping Kefauver," *Newsweek,* April 9, 1951, p. 18.

3. Unpublished Executive Session Minutes of Committee Meeting, March 29, 1951, Box 3, Kefauver Papers. New York *Times,* March 30, April 1, 4, 5, 8, 24, 1951. John L. Burling to Tobey, April 5, 1951; Tobey to Burling, April 9, 1951, Box 101, Tobey Papers. Burling to Hunt, April 5, 1951, Box 7, Hunt Papers. *Final Report,* p. 13. Tobey to Joseph Nellis, April 7, 1951, Box 101, Tobey Papers. Joseph C. Duke to Kefauver, April 23, 1951; J. Edgar Hoover to Kefauver, April 6, 1951, Box 37, Kefauver Papers.

tive to legislative remedies, that further hearings might entail errors that would damage the Committee's prestige and retard its program, that they would lead to too great local dependence on federal law enforcement, and that they would keep members of the Senate from devoting attention to other problems, such as his own Atlantic Union proposal. With Senator Hunt, he explained that he wanted to be relieved of further service if the Committee was continued. The public at large, prodded by Wiley and Tobey, refused to accept Kefauver's arguments and suggested that a sinister bargain had been struck to kill an extension of the Committee.[4]

Realizing that he was now the object of the same type of public pressure he had directed against Lucas and McCarran a year earlier, Kefauver stole away to "Homestead," his Hot Springs, Virginia, home for rest and reflection. There he rethought his position, considered alternatives, and modified his strategy. His administrative assistant, Charles Neese, proposed the creation of an extraordinary national grand jury, to remain in continual session and ferret out organized crime in any of the forty-eight states. Although he rejected Neese's plan, Kefauver adopted a proposal put forth by Investigator Henry Patrick Kiley for the establishment of a joint House–Senate watchdog committee, and he persuaded Senator O'Conor to take the lead in drumming up support for the idea. For encouragement, he informed the Maryland Democrat that he wanted him to take over the chairmanship regardless of whether subsequent action established a joint committee or continued the old special Senate Committee. At the same time Kefauver noted some support for his still vague proposal for a Federal Crime Commission, and he doggedly determined to push it despite opposition from the Justice Department and the FBI.[5]

4. Edward J. Meeman, editor, Memphis *Press-Scimitar,* to Kefauver, March 24, 1951; Kefauver to Meeman, March 29, 1951, Crime Box 2; memorandum from Martin F. Fay to Kefauver, n.d., Crime Box 37, Kefauver Papers. Hunt to Mrs. Dorothy Kellogg, April 17, 1951, Box 7, Hunt Papers. Ruth Hagy [?] of Philadelphia *Bulletin Forum* to Kefauver, April 5, 1951; Clarence Kolwyck to Kefauver, April 13, 1951; Hugo T. Bennett to Kefauver, March 27, 1951; Judge T. W. Bethea to Kefauver, April 2, 1951, Crime Box 2, Kefauver Papers. Bremerton (Wash.) *Sun,* April 26, 1951. Arthur L. Jackson to Tobey, April 9, 1951, Box 100; Tobey to Vernon L. Strempke, April 16, 1951, Box 101; Lillian Finck to Tobey, April 3, 1951, Box 104, Tobey Papers.

5. "The Neese Plan," undated proposal; Kiley to Kefauver, n.d.; Kefauver to O'Conor, April 9, 1951; Congressman Charles R. Howell to

The Chairman picked up some support for his proposal at a joint meeting of the Committee and the American Bar Association Commission, but this was partially negated by counsel's comment that large areas of crime such as narcotics, sports fixes, auto theft, juvenile delinquency, and organized interstate murder remained unexplored and might more effectively be investigated by something stronger than a "watchdog" committee. Meanwhile, Senator Wiley, pointing to the confusion within the Committee, its uncompleted work, and delay in writing the report, introduced for himself and Tobey a resolution (S. Res. 129) extending the Committee until January 15, 1952, and granting it $150,000. He argued that the creation of a Federal Crime Commission would be an abdication by Congress of its investigative responsibilities, that a commission with subpoena power might abuse its power and one without it would be useless. A watchdog committee, he maintained, would be a toothless guardian—powerless when compared to a special committee armed with full investigative authority. Implying that Kefauver could be replaced, Wiley warned Majority Leader McFarland and other Democrats that any senator who delayed a decision would have to "account to the American public." On the prompting of Kefauver, O'Conor countered the Wiley–Tobey resolution with the proposal that the Committee's work be carried on by either a joint watchdog committee or, preferably, by a three-man Federal Crime Commission appointed by the President and operating with limited subpoena power. After a long, heated session, the Senate Democratic Policy Committee first determined that the Wiley–Tobey measure could not be defeated and then struck a bargain with the Republicans, cutting the appropriation to $100,000 and the extension date to September 1. A dispirited Kefauver, who had finally consented to continue as a member, expressed the hope that legislation rather than accumulation of new evidence would occupy the Committee's attention. O'Conor, meanwhile, had agreed to take over the chairmanship for the last four months.[6]

Kefauver, March 30, 1951; Kefauver to Howell, April 6, 1951; telegram from William J. Donovan to Kefauver, April 14, 1951; telegram from Kefauver to Donovan, April 21, 1951; Kefauver to O'Conor, April 18, 1951, Box 37, Kefauver Papers.

6. Telegram from Kefauver to Robert P. Patterson, April 9, 1951; telegram from Patterson to Kefauver, April 10, 1951, Box 28, Patterson Papers. Unpublished Minutes of Joint Committee Meeting with the

The squabble within the Committee over its future signaled its decline as a distinct entity and its absorption into the emerging "corruption issue" of the 1952 campaign. The *Third Interim Report,* which appeared May 1, was almost anticlimactic. Although in the rush and confusion a number of factual errors found their way into the document, the report was a classic statement of prevailing views on organized crime. It found, of course, two major syndicates and a number of lesser ones held together by the Mafia, and it maintained that illegal gambling, stimulated by the wire service, constituted the financial backbone of such enterprises. Such dramatic conclusions tended to overshadow the Committee's limited reform program. Perhaps its most constructive work had been the documenting of widespread corruption at the local and state level and the exposing of attempts by law enforcement officials to conceal their malfeasance or ineptitude behind the maze of conflicting, overlapping jurisdictional boundaries. Indeed the senators' recommendations for renewed local and citizen vigilance and for comprehensive state-wide reviews of their law enforcement structures fitted in logically with the evidence the Committee had actually uncovered. Unfortunately, the senators' preoccupations with interstate associations and ethnic conspiracies diverted its own and the public's attention from these constructive suggestions as well as from consideration of broad policy alternatives, such as legalization and regulation of public gambling. Ignoring the social and economic causes of organized crime, the Committee advanced the simple law enforcement–conspiratorial perspective that would dominate public opinion for a generation.

Given the enormous conspiracy that the Committee claimed to have discovered, its remedies at the federal level seemed modest in the extreme. Specifically, the senators recom-

American Bar Association Commission, April 16, 1951, pp. 15, 40–41, Box 3, Kefauver Papers. *Congressional Record,* April 13, 1951, pp. 3813–14; April 17, 1951, pp. 3953–55; April 18, 1951, pp. 4053–55. Kefauver to O'Conor, April 21, 1951, Box 7, Hunt Papers.*Congressional Record,* April 23, 1951, pp. 4139–40; April 24, 1951, pp. 4272–75. "Kefauver Findings," *Newsweek,* May 7, 1951, p. 27. New York *Times,* April 25, 1951. So chaotic were the Committee offices that a memorandum, dated April 12, apprising Tobey of the joint meeting with the A.B.A. on April 16, reached the Senator on April 21. Memorandum from Al Klein to Tobey, April 12, 1951, Box 101, Tobey Papers.

mended the enlargement of the rackets squad in the Justice Department; the creation of a Special Frauds Squad in the Bureau of Internal Revenue; closer scrutiny of gamblers' tax returns; a bill similar to the earlier Attorney General's proposal, which was designed to regulate the flow of gambling information through interstate commerce and to obstruct Continental Press; the outlawing of the transmission of bets and wagers through interstate commerce; expanded authority for wire tapping by federal agencies; expansion of the Johnson Slot Machine Bill of 1950; an increase of personnel for federal enforcement agencies; imposition of heavier penalties for narcotics violations; and a number of less important proposals related to regulation of immigration and deportation, penalties for perjury, and the activities of underworld figures in the alcoholic beverage industry. Most of the proposals excited little enthusiasm either in Washington or in the hinterland because of their complexity, because they promised no quick solution to the problem, and because other events, such as the controversial firing of Gen. Douglas MacArthur by President Truman in April, diverted public attention away from the Kefauver Committee. A number of administrative changes in the Justice Department and the Bureau of Internal Revenue followed the Committee's suggestions, but in most cases bureaucratic jealousy (as in the controversy between the Federal Communications Commission and the Justice Department over the wire service bill), resentment against the Committee, as well as the lack of time, precluded any serious consideration of the legislation. Kefauver's proposal for establishment of a Federal Crime Commission encountered opposition from Wiley and the American Bar Association Commission, and it died in committee.[7]

The inability of the Committee to sustain public enthusiasm or to achieve rapid legislative remedies resulted in a quickening of public frustration and apathy; according to one survey taken in the summer of 1951, a small percentage of New Yorkers actually thought the televised hearings had worsened the problem of organized crime. Critics, consequently, hesitated less in attacking the Committee openly. President Truman,

7. Buckley M. Byers to Kefauver, May 23, 1951, Crime Box 2, Kefauver Papers. "No Evidence," *Business Week,* May 26, 1951, p. 21. *Third Interim Report,* pp. 5–20, 181–83. Morris Ploscowe, ed., *Organized Crime and Law Enforcement,* 2 vols. (New York: Grosby Press, 1952–1953), I, 64–66.

who snapped that he only watched television when his daughter Margaret was a featured singer, stoutly defended Ambassador O'Dwyer as a "fighter" and asserted that his Administration, through the Attorney General's Conference and the various Justice and Treasury Department programs, had for some time been pursuing "vigorous . . . actions against organized crime." Kefauver, in presenting the Committee's report, found himself awkwardly half defending and half attacking O'Dwyer and the Bureau of Internal Revenue.[8]

Meanwhile, the methodical, diplomatic Herbert R. O'Conor had moved into the chairmanship. Because Halley and most of Kefauver's appointees had resigned in April and May, O'Conor needed to assemble a staff quickly. To serve as chief counsel he selected Richard G. Moser, a junior partner in the New York law firm of Judge Robert Patterson, head of the A.B.A. Commission on Organized Crime. Kefauver and Tobey had considered Moser when they first staffed the original Committee but had passed over him in favor of the more experienced Halley. With Republican Moser heading the staff, the senators hoped to lessen congressional fear that the investigation was being used as a political stepping-stone by Kefauver and others. A product of Harvard Law School, the forty-one-year-old Moser had dabbled briefly in New Jersey politics and had become active in the Bar Association work. Lacking the flair or investigative background of Halley, Moser frequently appeared ill at ease, and his efforts at the dramatic flourish generally either backfired or failed. In addition, he made a number of unfortunate choices in staffing the Committee.[9]

O'Conor and Moser sifted a number of proposals for investigation, including the vote theft in Kansas City in 1947, labor racketeering, the interstate organization of prostitution, and

8. G. D. Wiebe, "Responses to the Televised Kefauver Hearings: Some Social Psychological Implications," *Public Opinion Quarterly* (Summer 1952), 179–200. New York *Times,* March 21, 30, May 4, 1950. "Outline of a Message on Crime," April 7, 1951, in Elsey Papers, Truman Library. *Congressional Record,* May 1, 1951, pp. 4572–81.

9. *Final Report,* p. 13. New York *Times,* May 11, 1951. Tobey to Kefauver, June 8, 1950, Crime Box 37; Moser to Kefauver, May 19, 1950, Crime Box 2, Kefauver Papers. Moser to author, April 16, 1973. Rice interview. Personal interview, James Hepbron, Administrative Assistant to O'Conor Committee, Baltimore, November 1, 1969. Telephone conversation, Col. Thomas S. Smith, Committee Investigator loaned by the Maryland State Police, Baltimore, October 27, 1969.

the fixing of sports events. While assigning Counsel Rufus King to draft the Committee's legislative proposals, Moser and O'Conor opened investigations into the narcotics traffic and into the crime pattern in medium-sized cities; they also planned to assess the results of the previous Committee's investigations in Florida, Kentucky, and New Jersey.[10] O'Conor hoped to hold public attention long enough, through a series of "quickie" investigations, to ensure that Congress would consider the Committee's legislative program.

While the inquiry into the narcotics traffic was the broadest study to be completed under O'Conor and attracted the widest praise to the Committee, the perspective of twenty years opens it to severe criticism. Kefauver had expressed some passing interest in the illicit drug problem early in his chairmanship and Halley had planned to introduce the topic at the New York hearings, but for both men other considerations precluded any serious study of the traffic in narcotics. Meanwhile, other groups, such as the New York State Crime Commission appointed by Governor Dewey and the office of District Attorney McDonald, had begun investigations of the problem. Moser and O'Conor based their study on testimony taken from staff members and patients at the United States Public Health Service Hospital at Lexington, Kentucky, from prisoners at two institutions near Baltimore, and from personnel of the Narcotics Bureau. Indeed, the Narcotics Bureau loaned the Committee one of its agents, Charles Siragusa, as chief investigator for over three months.[11]

Almost without exception, the Committee reflected the Nar-

10. Rock Springs (Wyo.) *Miner,* April 29, 1951. St. Louis *Globe-Democrat,* April 29, 1951. *Congressional Record,* May 1, 1951, p. 4580; May 23, 1951, p. 5714. Tobey to O'Conor, May 29, 1951; O'Conor to Tobey, May 31, 1951, Box 101; Rose V. Russell to O'Conor, May 3, 1951; O'Conor to Walter Shults, n.d., Box 102, Tobey Papers. Kefauver to Maple T. Harl, May 19, 1951; Melvin J. Richards to Kefauver, April 9, 1951, Crime Box 2, Kefauver Papers. New York *Times,* May 11, 1951. O'Conor to Kefauver, May 24, 1951, Crime Box 37, Kefauver Papers. Symbolically, the Kefauver Committee ran a deficit of over $20,000, which reduced O'Conor's available funds to less than $80,000. O'Conor to Wiley, May 24, 1951, Folder 7, Box 9, Series 4, Wiley Papers.

11. Harry W. Kirwan, *O'Conor: The Inevitable Success* (Westminster, Md.: Newman Press, 1962), pp. 455–56. New York *Times,* May 12, 1950. Ray Erwin, "Reporter Sparks Anti-Dope Drive," *Editor & Publisher,* February 3, 1951, pp. 14, 47. New York *Times,* June 14, 1951. *Final Report,* pp. 24, 14. O'Conor to Hunt, June 6, 1951, Box 27, Hunt Papers. Personal interview, Charles Siragusa, Chicago, July 20, 1970.

cotics Bureau's perspective on drugs. Significantly, the Committee ignored the direct testimony by the hospital's staff and an overwhelming number of patients and prisoners that marijuana created no physical dependency; it completely missed strong implications that the relationship between marijuana and drugs like heroin was one of marketing and misinformation rather than a natural progression of addiction. Lumping all "drugs" together, the senators emphasized the agony of addiction, and they advised the public to avoid drug abuse "like the plague."[12] The Committee made no apparent effort to explore the thesis of the LaGuardia Report of 1945 that marijuana had no permanently harmful effects, but simply accepted the position of the Narcotics Bureau's Director, Harry J. Anslinger (which was supported by the *Journal of the American Medical Association),* that the Report had materially contributed to addiction among teenagers. Wiley brushed aside the suggestion of one young inmate that use of drugs be legalized for addicts under a physician's care, thereby removing the profit from the traffic and reducing its volume.[13]

At the same time, the O'Conor Committee accepted Anslinger's argument that the illicit traffic in drugs could best be controlled by an expanded appropriation for the Narcotics Bureau and by the passage of legislation for mandatory sentences for violation of the narcotics laws. Eventually, the Committee drafted two bills for mandatory sentences, one a companion to the House Boggs bill, which attracted immense public and official support and became law despite opposition from the American Bar Association's Commission on Organized Crime.[14] Having based their view of drug use on infor-

12. Crime *Hearings,* Pt. 14, pp. 119–20, 244, 73, 81, 83, 91–92, 101, 109, 84–85, 94, 105, 271–81, 153–226. *Final Report,* pp. 24–37. O'Conor's claim that many teenaged addicts in Washington were introduced to drugs in high school brought a strong denial from Anslinger, who maintained that only in New York were the high schools involved. New York *Times,* June 15, 18, 1951. Kirwan, *O'Conor,* p. 456.

13. Mayor's Committee on Marihuana, *The Marihuana Problem in the City of New York: Sociological, Medical, Psychological and Pharmacological Studies* (Lancaster, Pa.: The Jaques Cattell Press, 1945), pp. 24–25. Crime *Hearings,* Pt. 14, pp. 426–32, 215–16.

14. *Final Report,* pp. 35, 90–91. Acting Secretary to the Treasury E. H. Foley to Kefauver, July 17, 1951, Crime Box 37, Kefauver Papers. Truman statement, New York *Times,* August 25, 1951. Mrs. Smith Eads, Jr., to Tom Connally, August 25, 1951; Mrs. A. A. Luckenback to

mation from the Narcotics Bureau, Moser and O'Conor linked
the traffic in heroin to the Mafia and denied the claims of
underworld gambling figures that they held moral compunc-
tions against illicit trade in drugs. After superficially acknowledging that addiction was a "disease" which required
medical and psychological treatment, the Committee then accepted Anslinger's law enforcement position on the narcotics
problem even more readily than it accepted the antilegalization position on the gambling issue. In neither case did it
seriously examine the basic issue of public policy—that is,
whether or not major changes in the law, such as decriminali-
zation or legalization and regulation might not be more effective tools in dealing with the problems. No one can, of course,
establish with absolute certainty that the results of the law
enforcement approach to these problems has been more in
error than the regulatory approach might have been. At the
same time, however, no one can deny that the Committee promoted the law enforcement alternatives on less than an objective appraisal of all facts at their disposal.[15]

Even if tragically in error in the long run, the O'Conor Committee's work in narcotics received almost universal approval
in its own time—something less true for its work on other
problems. The Committee, for example, returned to a number
of areas it had visited earlier, in an effort to assess the progress
that was being made in the antigambling crusade. In Miami,
Moser and Counsel Downey Rice attempted to show that gangsters financed publications that advocated legalization and
opposed Kefauver. One such publication that attracted the
Committee's attention was the *Morning Mail,* a prolegaliza-

Connally, n.d.; R. E. Knight to Connally, August 3, 1951, Box 296, Tom
Connally Papers, Library of Congress; Ploscowe, ed., *Organized Crime
and Law Enforcement,* I, 53–55. The Bar Association objected to the
Boggs Bill primarily because it failed to discriminate between the
addict and the peddler and permitted equal punishment for both. The
Committee proposed a 20-year minimum sentence for selling narcotics to minors under seventeen. Senator Everett Dirksen drafted legislation calling for the death penalty for such offenses. Ibid.; New York
Times, June 20, 1951.

15. The Committee noted the arrest of former bootlegger Irving
Wexler (Waxey Gordon) for pushing drugs in New York and argued
that Luciano was directing an international narcotics ring from Italy.
Here again the Committee assumed that the underworld was a distinct group of immoral men who shifted their operations solely for
profit. *Final Report,* pp. 28–37.

tion newspaper that had operated for forty-eight days in late 1949 and early 1950. The Committee's *Final Report* implied that the journal had operated as a front for gangster influence when in fact the Committee's principal witness, the divorced wife of a brother of Chicago underworld figure Anthony Accardo, testified that the publisher had solicited funds from her former husband in the vain hope of getting the physical as well as the financial support of the Chicago underworld in an advertising campaign. The facts of the case appear to parallel those which showed that local politicians and law enforcement officials exploited both local and interstate gamblers as much as gamblers exploited local officers. In attacking a *Morning Mail* editorial of January 26, 1950, which had welcomed Costello to South Florida, Moser first tried to suggest that the New York gambling figure had contributed to the newspaper. Failing to establish that, Moser then claimed that the editor and publisher had been irresponsible in publishing the article without knowing all the "facts" about Costello. In reaction to unfavorable editorials about Kefauver and the personnel of the Miami Crime Commission, the Committee subpoenaed the financial records of the shaky Miami *Life,* a weekly. The senators then called the writer of the editorials before its television cameras and pointed out to the audience his criminal "record," which included many arrests that were not followed by convictions. In publicly chastising its enemies within the press and thereby trying to protect itself from additional attack, the Committee became entangled in the vicious Miami press wars, raised doubts as to its respect for freedom of the press, and certainly appeared to be petty and quarrelsome.[16]

The Committee's principal objective in returning to Miami was to check on progress made in controlling gambling since the previous hearings. Daniel Sullivan of the Crime Commission of Greater Miami reviewed what he regarded as less than optimal energy on the part of local prosecutors. Sullivan also condemned Governor Fuller Warren's controversial reinstatement of Dade County Sheriff James "Smiling Jimmy" Sul-

16. New York *Times,* June 21, 22, 1951. *Final Report,* p. 74. Crime *Hearings,* Pt. 16, pp. 44–52, 186–98, 236. Miami *Life,* June 10, 1950, p. 76, Kefauver Scrapbook IV; Jack Younger to Kefauver, April 26, 1951; Kefauver to Younger, April 30, 1951; Senator George Smathers to Kefauver, May 7, 1951; Kefauver to Smathers, May 12, 1951, Crime Box 1, Kefauver Papers. Crime *Hearings,* Pt. 16, pp. 59–74.

livan and the failure of the State Racing Commission to deal
vigorously with the supposedly illegal contribution of race
track owner William H. Johnson to Governor Warren's 1948
campaign. Both matters involved certain complex legal questions, but Daniel Sullivan appeared to have had an especially
strong case for his argument that, under the law, the governor
was not required to reinstate the sheriff. In any event, the
Governor's actions had invited the attack of the Kefauver
Committee in its *Third Interim Report* and had prompted
bitter criticism in the state legislature and the press, with the
Miami *Herald* calling for Warren's impeachment. The Governor retorted that the charges were based on "latrine gossip,"
accused Kefauver of political opportunism, and encouraged
the state legislature to investigate two of his persistent critics,
the Miami *Herald* and the Tampa *Tribune.*[17]

Although Sheriff Sullivan resigned when the Committee returned to Miami, O'Conor continued to press the Governor
with urgent invitations to appear before the Committee to
discuss organized crime in the state. Warren, weary from the
almost continual fire he had been under since taking office,
withdrew to an undisclosed hideaway, pleaded physical exhaustion, and telegraphed his denials to the Chairman. In an
effort to regain the initiative, however, he charged the Crime
Commission of Greater Miami with improperly accepting a
large sum of money to finance their antigambling crusade.
O'Conor then issued the subpoena for the Governor, which the
Committee had considered even before the latest hearings. A
Duval County solicitor, an appointee of Warren, responded by
subpoenaing O'Conor, and the Governor challenged the new
chairman to a debate with him in Miami on the subject of
gambling in Florida, Maryland, and the District of Columbia
and on the Committee's alleged "suppression of embarrassing

17. Daniel Sullivan testimony, Crime *Hearings,* Pt. 16, pp. 13–21.
Third Interim Report, p. 36. "Storm over Miami," *Newsweek,* April 23,
1951, p. 41. "Protestant Churches Lead Revolt Against Gambling," *The
Christian Century,* April 25, 1951, p. 515. Knoxville *Journal,* June 29,
1951. New York *Times,* May 3, 1951. St. Petersburg *Times,* May 3, 1951.
A. F. Lorenzen to Kefauver, May 4, 1951, Crime Box 2, Kefauver Pa-
pers. Miami *Herald,* May 4, 1951. "Relentless Probing Fails to Keep
Tourists Away," *Editor & Publisher,* May 12, 1951, p. 9; "Miami *Herald*
Smears Fail to Win Support," ibid., June 2, 1951, p. 10; "Reporter Feud
Tied to Florida Anti-Press War," ibid., July 7, 1951, p. 14. Miami *Her-
ald,* July 30, 1950.

evidence."[18] Warren, moreover, at first claiming "states' rights," refused to leave Florida to testify before the Committee, but when O'Conor extended the time of the subpoena and offered to return to Tallahassee to take his testimony, the Governor announced that he would not testify under oath in any circumstance. Meanwhile, South Carolina's Governor James Byrnes, a former senator and associate justice of the Supreme Court, accused "overzealous counsel" of responsibility for the Senate's subpoena of Warren; in his opinion, the Committee could not legally compel the presence of the Governor of Florida in Washington, and he urged Warren not to respond to the subpoena. O'Conor insisted that the Committee had such subpoena power, but in view of Warren's refusal to testify under oath, he dropped the matter altogether. Clearly, both the Governor and the Committee had suffered embarrassment from the squabble.[19]

Florida provided the most interesting, and perhaps the least fortunate, area hearings. Reports that illegal gambling continued in northern Kentucky brought the Committee back into the Covington–Newport area, where public officials were then engaged in a summer election campaign. Observing that gambling operations halted only when the grand jury was in session and that by custom the grand juries did not scrutinize noncurrent conditions, the Committee nonetheless noted that some progress had been made toward control of criminal activities but that still more should be done to suppress gambling.[20] In three medium-sized cities, Reading and Scranton, Pennsylvania, and Atlantic City, New Jersey, the O'Conor

18. Rice interview. Crime *Hearings,* Pt. 16, pp. 230, 217–18. New York *Times,* June 21, 22, 24, 27, July 1, 3, 1951. Telegram from Jack R. Younger to Wiley, June 18, 1951; telegram from Wiley to Younger, June 18, 1951, Folder 6, Box 30, Series 1, Wiley Papers.

19. New York *Times,* July 8, 11, 15, 20, 1951. "Heat on Governor Warren," *Newsweek,* July 16, 1951, pp. 24–25. *Time,* July 16, 1951, pp. 18–19. Governor Byrnes later refused to leave South Carolina when the House Un-American Activities Committee, investigating the Harry Dexter White controversy, issued subpoenas for former President Truman, Supreme Court Justice Tom Clark, and Byrnes, who had been Secretary of State at the time White was appointed to the International Monetary Fund. Telford Taylor, *Grand Inquest: The Story of Congressional Investigations* (New York: Simon & Schuster, Inc., 1955), pp. 223–25.

20. Telegram from R. L. Age to Kefauver, May 1, 1951, Crime Box 2, Kefauver Papers. *Final Report,* pp. 42–52. Crime *Hearings,* Pt. 15, pp. 223–24.

Committee found tight local partnerships between gambling interests and politicians. The Committee chose to emphasize the only interstate links of note—the facts that daily Treasury Department figures and the racing-news wire service came through interstate channels and that slot machines were generally purchased from out-of-state suppliers. No convincing evidence that outside interests dictated policy or controlled the operations emerged in any of the three cities. In Maryland, O'Conor's home state, the Committee found evidence of an active racing-news wire operation that was tied into the Continental chain.[21]

The youthful and inexperienced staff made a number of embarrassing mistakes during the last four months of the Committee's life. In Reading, the Committee subpoenaed the records of the Democratic candidate for District Attorney when he would have turned them over voluntarily, and in Jersey City the staff issued a subpoena for the assistant corporation counsel under similar circumstances. The most conspicuous mistake, however, involved Ambassador O'Dwyer, who had survived the Committee's attack on his record and a subsequent determined effort by Republicans to force his resignation. Senator Tobey had received an anonymous postcard during the hearings in New York concerning a mysterious million-dollar check in O'Dwyer's name that had circulated between New York and Mexico City. Since O'Dwyer had constantly stressed his poverty, and no one had ever proved he received monies improperly, the development of the lead might have established the necessary evidence to destroy completely the Ambassador's credibility. O'Conor dispatched Moser to Mexico City to inquire about the check at approximately the same time the New York *Daily News* and several other respected newspapers published reports that the Committee was investigating the rumor. A few days later, the State Department explained that the controversial bank transaction did not involve O'Dwyer personally at all, but had merely been the first installment on Mexican lend-lease repayments. O'Dwyer, apoplectic with rage, thundered that the Committee had been part of a concerted conspiracy to destroy his reputation, and he demanded that O'Conor identify the original source of his information and explain why he

21. *Final Report,* pp. 37–42, 52–62, 76–83. Crime *Hearings,* Pt. 19, pp. 2–10, 23–45.

sent Moser out of the country before first making quiet in-
quires in Washington and New York about the bank draft. The
O'Conor Committee meekly accepted the State Department's
explanation and in effect admitted an error that could easily
have been avoided.[22]

In its final stages the Committee failed to develop sufficient
background information prior to hearings and therefore suffered further humiliation. It attempted to show, for example,
that Abner "Longie" Zwillman, who had made a fortune in the
Reinfeld bootlegging syndicate during Prohibition, had invested heavily in legitimate business and took an active,
though clandestine, part in New Jersey politics. Moser's argument that the forty-seven-year-old Zwillman exercised influence in state politics rested largely on the testimony of a journalist biographer, Jim Bishop, who had worked for the 1949
Democratic gubernatorial candidate. The Chief Counsel
sought more forcefully to demonstrate Zwillman's political
power in Newark. Among those he questioned was Hugh J.
Strong, former Newark policeman and at the time mayor of
Kennilon Borough, a Newark suburb. Strong voiced the opinion that some of Zwillman's reported influence in Newark's

22. *Congressional Record,* June 25, 1951, pp. A3856–57. New York
Times, July 30, 1951. "The Summing Up," *Time,* May 14, 1951,
pp. 26–27; April 2, 1951, p. 17; April 9, 1951, p. 20. "The Luck of
Bill O'Dwyer," *Newsweek,* May 14, 1951, p. 30. Anonymous note to
Tobey, postmarked March 23, 1951, Box 104, Tobey Papers. *Congressional Record,* August 2, 1951, p. 9461. "L'Affaire O'Dwyer," *Newsweek,* August 13, 1951, pp. 15–16. New York *Times,* August 4, 1951.
Moser to author, April 16, 1973. The unhappy O'Dwyer continued on
as ambassador through the 1952 elections, quarreling with reporters,
refusing to return for more testimony before the grand jury in New
York, fighting demands for his recall, and eventually experiencing
the breakup of his marriage. Staying on in Mexico several years after
resigning, O'Dwyer did some legal work and spoke of returning to
New York to vanquish his tormentors and to accept the applause of
the "little people" in a gigantic reception in Ebbets Field. Throughout
it all, O'Dwyer protested that he had been "jobbed" by Kefauver and
Halley in order to promote their own political ambitions. A Kefauver
investigator admitted: "Let's face it, the cards are stacked against the
witness." O'Dwyer did in fact return to New York in 1960 and died
there in 1964. "Lying Bastard," *Time,* August 11, 1952, p. 42; "People,"
ibid., January 26, 1953, p. 36. "First Job for a New President," *Collier's,*
May 17, 1952, p. 82. Henry Oliver, "A Mayor in Exile," *The American
Mercury* (September 1954), 98–102. Lester Velie, "William O'Dwyer—
The Man Who Won't Come Home," *Collier's,* August 7, 1953, pp. 19–23;
August 21, 1953, pp. 30–34. New York *Times,* November 25, 1964.

Third Ward was in fact the result of a Jewish ethnic vote
rather than a reflection of Zwillman's personal power. When
Strong expressed contempt for Zwillman and denied any close
personal contact with him, Moser suddenly produced telephone company records, which showed several calls between
Strong's home and that of Zwillman in 1946. For a moment
spectators expected a dramatic break in the story, but instead
they heard Strong's explanation that at the time of the calls he
had operated a kennel, and Mrs. Zwillman, who had purchased a dog from him, had telephoned several times to inquire about methods for housebreaking the animal. When the
laughter in the courtroom subsided, O'Conor granted Strong a
"clean bill of health," and the Committee—having failed to do
its homework—looked decidedly less awesome than it had
during the March hearings.[23]

Mistakes in the preparation or conduct of hearings were
only partially responsible for the difficulties encountered by
the O'Conor Committee. With the crime issue having to share
increasing amounts of the public and official attention with
such issues as the MacArthur debate and the Committee having to devote more time to the infinitely more complex and
controversial issue of legislation, a decline in public support
and enthusiasm was inevitable. The failure to deliver quick
results following the hearings in New York, moreover, created
an atmosphere that was receptive to a thousand rumors and
recriminations. Some citizens criticized the Committee for
failing to look for the broader causes of crime; some de-
nounced its failure to pursue additional avenues of inquiry or
to call certain witnesses; others criticized specifics of the Committee's legislative program. In addition, the Committee was
bedeviled by crank letters that complained of overcharges on
electricity bills, of chiropractors' ability to win lawsuits, or of
local clerks' snubbing of persons who advocated impeachment of President Truman.[24]

23. "Longie Zwillman: Big Business and/or Gangster?" *Newsweek,*
August 27, 1951, pp. 23–25. *Final Report,* pp. 65–73. Crime *Hearings,*
Pt. 18, pp. 871–78. New York *Times,* August 18, 1951.

24. H. Hofmeister to Tobey, April 2, 1951, Box 104; Miss H. F. Lovejoy
to Tobey, April 5, 1951, Box 101, Tobey Papers. Percival E. Jackson to
Hunt, April 17, 1951, pp. 3396–98. Undated Westbrook Pegler column,
Box 100; "A Native New Yorker and a Democrat" to Tobey, March 24,
1951, Box 103, Tobey Papers. *Congressional Record,* July 6, 1951, pp.
A4171–72. Chicago *Daily News,* May 3, 1951. J. A. Melendez to Hunt,
March 22, 1951; John G. Thomas to Hunt, March 22, 1951, Box 7, Hunt

Meanwhile, Lait and Mortimer wrote *Washington Confidential,* which was published on the eve of the hearings in New York and which portrayed Kefauver as ambitious for the Vice Presidency and as having sold out to a corrupt Administration. Most of Lait and Mortimer's charges contained only the smallest grain of truth, but their repetition in Mortimer's daily column and in a series of articles in *American Mercury* disturbed the senators greatly and contributed to a growing— and in most cases, unjustified—skepticism about the political implications of the Committee.[25]

Some of the Committee's own publicity gimmicks backfired as well. To arouse the public to crime as a nationwide problem and also to advance his own political fortunes, Kefauver in pretelevision days had begun negotiations for a book and a series of articles on the Committee's work. A professional writer, Sidney Shalett, joined Kefauver in drafting the book, *Crime in America,* as well as a four-part series for *Saturday Evening Post.* Although a few people criticized Kefauver for thus benefiting financially from his work with the Committee, a substantially larger number condemned the publication of the *Post* series before the *Third Interim Report.* Kefauver explained that the *Post* had originally scheduled the articles to appear after the Committee's report, but that the thirty-day extension granted the Committee in late March, which he opposed, had delayed the appearance of the report but not of the magazine piece, which could not be postponed for techni-

---

Papers. Joseph W. Eck to Tobey, May 24, 1951; Brenton S. Ayers to Tobey, April 30, 1951, Box 100, Tobey Papers.

25. Jack Lait and Lee Mortimer, *Washington Confidential* (New York: Crown Publishers, Inc., 1951), pp. 72, 154, 194–206. New York *Mirror,* March 25, 1951. Lee Mortimer, "Senator Tobey Confidential: Sin in the White Mountains," *American Mercury* (July 1951), 64–71; Mortimer, "Frank Sinatra Confidential: Gangsters in the Night Clubs," ibid. (August 1951), 29–36; Mortimer, "Maryland Confidential: The Crusading Senator O'Conor," ibid. (September 1951), 28–34; Mortimer, "New York Confidential: Rudolph Halley's Comet," ibid. (November 1951), 87–95. Jack Lait and Lee Mortimer, *U.S.A. Confidential* (New York: Crown Publishers, Inc., 1952), pp. 16–19, 352–53, 100–105, 253–57. Tobey to Thomas A. Watson, April 1, 1952; Tobey to Kate Smith, April 1, 1952, Box 71, Tobey Papers. H. J. Hamlin to Kefauver, May 24, 1951; Kefauver to Hamlin, May 28, 1951, Crime Box 2; telegram from Kefauver to William Bradford Huie, April 20, 1951, Crime Box 1, Kefauver Papers. Detroit *Free Press,* March 23, 26, 1951. Flint (Mich.) *Journal,* March 24, 1951. Telegram from Francis J. Myers to Kefauver, November 3, 1951, Crime Box 3, Kefauver Papers.

cal reasons.[26] Kefauver also related in the first article an attempt by a wealthy "Mr. X" to "buy" him during the hearings by contributing a sum in six figures to the Democratic National Committee. When readers throughout the country suggested that Kefauver was violating the law by failing to report the identity of the unsuccessful briber, the Senator hastily took refuge in the contention that as a lawyer he considered "Mr. X's" suggestion an effort to create a favorable atmosphere and not an attempt at bribery.[27]

26. *Congressional Record,* April 23, 1951, p. A2224. Malcolm Fooshee to Kefauver, April 4, 1951, Crime Box 1; John Fischer, Harper and Brothers, to Kefauver, October 30, 1950; Shalett to Kefauver, November 10, 1950; Ellen Walpole to Kefauver, February 11, 1951; Kefauver to Judge John J. Langenbach, August 3, 1951, "Crime in America" Box; W. D. Weatherford to Kefauver, September 28, 1956; draft of letter from Henry Patrick Kiley to Weatherford, October 8, 1956, Crime Box 4, Kefauver Papers. Kefauver had earlier refused the request of one magazine that he withhold certain public information until an article on it had been published. While there is some evidence that an overzealous "representative" of Kefauver may have promised Shalett that some material would not appear in the Committee's report, little of importance appeared in the article that was not in the report. Supposedly, the "representative" of the Senator claimed Kefauver would attack J. Edgar Hoover for his lack of cooperation with the Committee and possibly "the man with the medals" in the White House. Kefauver, in any event, made no such references in either the report, the article, or the book. David Brown to Kefauver, November 30, 1950; "Report on Book and Article Possibilities" to Doubleday and Company [?] from Shalett, n.d., "Crime in America" Box, Kefauver Papers. Estes Kefauver, "What I Found Out in the Underworld," *The Saturday Evening Post,* April 7, 1951, pp. 19–21, 71–72, 76, 79.

27. Kefauver, "What I Found Out in the Underworld." Washington *Times-Herald,* April 6, 1951. C. C. Sheppard to Kefauver, April 6, 1951; Herbert Breed to Kefauver, April 19, 1951; Kefauver to Breed, April 27, 1951, Crime Box 2, Kefauver Papers. New York *Times,* April 18, 1951. Kefauver received requests to do prologues and epilogues to a spate of gangster movies that were being produced at the time. On one occasion he filmed a prologue for Warner Brothers' "The Enforcer," but was so dissatisfied with the movie that he asked that his portion be withdrawn. Eventually, he made a commentary for Aspen Production's "The Captive City" and substituted for regulars Halley and O'Conor on the popular "Crime Syndicated" television series. The monies went to the Cordell Hull Foundation, which provided scholarships to an international student exchange program. Telegram, Kefauver to George Dorsey, February 19, 1951, Crime Box 1; Kefauver to Frank E. Houston, January 14, 1952; telegram from B. A. Babb to Kefauver, March 13, 1952; Winston S. Dustin to Kefauver, March 11, 1952; Kefauver statement on CBS, October 2, 1951; "General Correspondence, 1948–1955" Box, Kefauver Papers.

Thorniest of all the criticisms to plague the dying Committee was the broad question of civil liberties. The sensational nature of the investigation and the public questioning of underworld figures about their personal affairs strongly suggested a judicial proceeding although few of the guarantees accorded a defendant in a trial were available to the people who were called before the Committee. (O'Conor once inadvertently referred to Costello as a "defendant.") The immunity laws, as they affected congressional hearings, were not at all clear, and although the right to counsel was accorded witnesses by the Committee, the right to cross-examine was less than absolute and occasionally unavailable. When John P. Crane testified concerning his alleged $10,000 campaign contribution to O'Dwyer, serious questions immediately arose as to possible bribery and perjury on the part of the Ambassador, but O'Dwyer, not being present, had no opportunity to cross-examine the witness. He did, however, have the right to file a statement in rebuttal, and had he insisted, would probably have been heard again by the Committee. In effect, while the Committee's rules, which the senators drafted, were quite advanced in comparison with those of other committees of the time, the nature of the matter under investigation and the decision to call underworld figures rather than "crime experts" created the atmosphere of a public trial and almost inevitably led to abuses of the witnesses' rights.[28] These abuses were intensified by the presence of television, particularly the hearings in New York.

Indeed, the controversy over the use of television displaced the central problem, which was how to deal with at least semijudicial matters in supposedly legislative hearings. New York's highly respected construction coordinator, Robert Moses, wrote that, by exposing its witnesses to television, the Committee had created a widespread and unjustified impression that large numbers of public servants were corrupt. Arthur Garfield Hays (an attorney for Zwillman) of the American Civil Liberties Union and Labor Party leader Dean Alfange joined a conservative observer of events on Capitol

28. Crime *Hearings,* Pt. 7, pp. 877, 1676–96. New York *Times,* March 22, 23, 1951. While O'Dwyer complained to reporters that he would have liked to cross-examine Crane, he made no request to appear again before the Committee, and his telegram of protest simply denied the charge and submitted a large number of favorable editorials on his public career in New York. Ibid. Crime *Hearings,* Pt. 12, pp. 502–3.

Hill, William S. White, in decrying the Committee's taste for free publicity and the "hippodroming" impact of television. The pro-Kefauver Cleveland *Plain Dealer,* while confessing its fascination with the role of television, admitted a certain possibility for abuse; *The Catholic World* thought the abuse had already occurred. Walter Lippmann suggested that the new medium should be banned from congressional hearings until it "proved itself," and Westbrook Pegler advised witnesses simply to refuse to testify before television cameras. Thurmond Arnold argued that, regardless of the technical distinctions between courts and congressional committees, the Kefauver hearings were semijudicial and the televising of them had destroyed judicial objectivity and had led to a state of "mutual excitement" between the senators and the viewing audience that amounted to "mob justice."[29]

The Committee, however, along with such commentators as Jack Gould, radio and television editor of the New York *Times,* Eric Sevareid, and Attorney Telford Taylor, defended the presence of television. Taylor argued, in effect, that the investigative function of Congress involved in many cases an informing function for the public. The people, as well as Congress, needed information on which to form judgments about contemplated legislation, or the legislative process could not reflect the public will. Television merely extended the observation by other accepted media in the hearing room, including photographers, newspaper reporters, radio, and newsreels, and to exclude it on the basis that it reached more people would be both unjust and unwise. This line of thought played down the judicial nature of the Committee hearings and maintained that if embarrassment had resulted from the proceedings, it was in the nature of the facts developed, not in the presence of the television cameras that broadcast them. Kefauver recognized that some abuses had occurred and that under certain circumstances the presence of television and

29. New York *Times,* August 13, 1951. Joseph J. Cassidy to Hudson Motors, March 26, 1951, copy in Box 103, Tobey Papers. New York *Times,* August 10, 1951. William S. White, *Citadel: The Story of the U.S. Senate* (New York: Harper and Brothers, 1957), pp. 245–46, 252. *Congressional Record,* August 10, 1951, p. 9799. "Kefauver's Court: Trial by Television," *The Catholic World* (May 1951), 81–85. Washington *Post,* April 2, 1951. "Newspapers Praised for Anti-Crime Help," *Editor & Publisher,* March 31, 1951, p. 8. *Congressional Record,* August 10, 1951, pp. 9794–95.

other news paraphernalia could be both unfair and counterproductive, if, for example, they really did distract or disorient
the witness, or if they only scheduled or presented one point
of view. He discovered after the hearings in New York were
in progress that in some cases local stations had commercial
sponsorship in addition to the monitoring by *Time,* and he
took steps to terminate such practices. In the *Third Interim
Report* and in *Crime in America,* he called for a legal clarifi-
cation of the rights of witnesses before committees, for a code
of conduct for hearings, and for technical improvements to
reduce the glare, sound, and heat, which were generated more
by newsreel cameras than by the television equipment. He
also supported Senator Wiley's resolution for a study by the
Rules Committee on the use of television by committees in
general. Kefauver, personally, favored expanded use of television on the floor of the House and Senate, but he agreed that
reasonable limits would have to be drawn there as well as in
committee hearing rooms.[30]

The attempt of a legislative committee to deal with
semijudicial matters in public raised these questions rather
than did the presence of television; the basic conflict would
have existed—although admittedly on a smaller scale—in the
absence of the new medium. The Committee, recognizing that
roving photographers were especially bothersome to witnesses during their delivery of testimony, ordered them to take

30. New York *Times,* March 23, September 20, 1951. Eric Sevareid,
In One Ear (New York: Alfred A. Knopf, 1952), pp. 183–85. Memorandum from Kefauver to "All Members of the Staff," March 23, 1951; A.
J. Rechlin to Kefauver, March 24, 1951; Kefauver to Rechlin, March
30, 1951, Crime Box 1; Kefauver to John Chester Simmons, Jr., February 9, 1953; "General Correspondence, 1948–1955, O-S" Box, Kefauver
Papers. Crime *Hearings,* Pt. 12, pp. 499–500. *Third Interim Report,* pp.
24–25. Estes Kefauver, *Crime in America* (Garden City, N.Y.: Doubleday & Co., Inc., 1951), pp. 165–66. *Final Report,* pp. 99–103. *Congressional Record,* April 13, 1951, pp. 3812–13. Few could seriously agree
with Halley that the presence of television had a sobering effect on
Committee members and counsel, and some have gone as far as to
suggest a similarity with the motives of Senator Joseph McCarthy.
Decision to use television coverage has been generally a prerogative
of committee chairmen in the Senate, but a House rule, born partly
out of the hostility of Speaker Sam Rayburn, forbade television coverage of that body until very recently. New York *Times,* September 20,
1951; June 25, 1951. William F. Buckley, *McCarthy and His Enemies:
The Record and Its Meaning* (Chicago: Henry Regnery Company,
1954), pp. 285*n,* 289.

flash exposures only before and after the actual questioning, but the photographers repeatedly violated the order. In a number of instances, counsel interrupted witnesses before they had completed their answers, a practice that O'Conor refused to tolerate. Occasionally, witnesses were intimidated by the supposed authority of the Committee into turning over incriminating evidence or into making certain statements that later, due to the confusing immunity laws, resulted in legal difficulties for them in the courts; this same development had occurred, however, in the case of Frank Erickson's admissions before the McFarland Subcommittee, where no television cameras were present. Unquestionably, television contributed to a certain circus atmosphere and Tobey and some counsel reacted to it, but it was the sensational nature of the problem being investigated, the understandable contradictions between the legislative and judicial process, and the presence of older, already accepted media in the hearing room that created the real basis for civil libertarians' objections to the Committee's procedures.[31]

Slowly, the Committee itself retreated on the issue of television and other media. During the testimony of James J. Carroll in St. Louis in early March, a perplexed Kefauver, sitting alone, concluded that the presence of the television cameras was not oppressive to the witness and he moved for contempt charges when Carroll refused to testify before them. O'Conor, however, had second thoughts and persuaded the Committee to adopt the "Costello rules" in New York, whereby television coverage could continue but the witness would not be televised over his objection. Carroll returned to testify under these rules, but two Cleveland gamblers, Morris Kleinman and Louis Rothkopf, pleading a right to privacy, refused to testify until television, and all other media as well, were cut off and removed from the hearing room, a demand that the senators firmly rejected. When Kefauver moved for contempt proceedings, a small group of senators, led by Washington's Republican Harry Cain, launched a spirited attack on the Committee's use of the media, particularly television. Kefauver and O'Conor argued that, since television had actually been cut off from one of the witnesses who still refused to talk, the issue

31. Crime *Hearings,* Pt. 16, pp. 2, 7, 36, 44, 95, 97; Pt. 19, pp. 17, 175, 203; Pt. 15, pp. 26–46. Alan Barth, *Government by Investigation* (New York: The Viking Press, Inc., 1955), pp. 76–79.

was not really the presence of television but that of the other media, long accepted in committee hearings. Cain and Herman Welker of Idaho pointed out that the cameras had continued to focus on the senators and that the other media, particularly the still photographers, had annoyed the witnesses and given them an excuse to refuse to testify. Welker asked why not, if the testimony was vital, comply with all their demands about the media and leave them no alternative but to testify or to face a clear charge of contempt? Obviously, Cain and Welker were suggesting that publicity rather than information motivated the Committee's actions. Kefauver and O'Conor were able to amass enough votes to defeat Cain's resolution to reconsider contempt citations, but only a few days later the Committee capitulated on the issue when another witness, Irving Sherman, raised objections to the presence of the media. This time the senators heard their witness without benefit of television, newsreels, or still photographers.[32]

Like most congressional committees, the Kefauver–O'Conor Committee held certain prejudices for or against witnesses. Because of the nature of the matter with which it dealt and because of the past, perhaps current, activities of many of the witnesses, it was acting in a semijudicial capacity but was willing to grant only a limited number of judicial rights. In some cases, as with its enemies in the Miami press and in seeking to use the cloudy immunity laws against certain witnesses, the Committee was essentially punitive. If a witness testified falsely, he faced perjury charges; if he testified truthfully of violating state and some federal laws, he faced prosecution partly based on his own statements; and if he refused to testify on matters not covered by the immunity laws (such

32. *Congressional Record,* March 30, 1951, p. 3040; April 2, 1951, p. 3113; July 30, 1951, pp. 9137–39; August 9, 1951, p. 9703; August 10, 1951, pp. 9765–80, 9872–74, 9788–93, 9795, 9801–2; August 15, 1951, p. 10011; August 16, 1951, p. 10104. Kefauver had so little knowledge of the operation of television that he was not sure whether the voice of a witness would carry over television if the lights and cameras were trained elsewhere. The courts ruled that the general confusion was sufficient to justify Rothkopf's and Kleinman's refusals to talk and indeed dismissed virtually all of the Committee's contempt cases on similar grounds. Ibid., August 10, 1951, pp. 9767–70. United States v. Kleinman et al., 107 F. Supp. 407. New York *Times,* November 4, December 12, 1952; February 13, June 25, 1953. Ronald L. Goldfarb, *The Contempt Power* (New York: Columbia University Press, 1963), p. 248.

as violations of state gambling laws), he faced contempt charges. Due to its momentary popularity, the Committee escaped serious criticism for these tactics, but an undercurrent of opposition sprang up in respected legal circles as well as among the witnesses. As Murray Humphries correctly observed, "Yes, . . . the longer you fellows work, the more we understand what our rights are."[33] If the critic might have wished at times for greater civility on the part of the Committee, he would also have to concede that the type of witnesses and the nature of the questioning created a different—and more sensational—atmosphere than that of most congressional hearings. If the reporters and television technicians occasionally were allowed to take advantage of the witness's plight, it must also be noted that the Committee conceived part of its legislative function to be public enlightenment and that the novelty of television presented the senators with a unique problem for which there were no reasonable precedents. If the situation opened up the possibility for Senator Joseph McCarthy's abuses in the mid-1950s, it also sparked an effort, fully joined by Committee members, to study the role of television, draw up clearer rules for committee procedure, and clarify the unpardonable confusion of the immunity laws.

Understandably, O'Conor, referring to his chairmanship as a "thankless task," laid down his duties with little regret. Wiley and an ailing Tobey joined Homer Capehart and a small group of Republicans in an effort to obtain funds for the Commerce Committee to continue the crime investigation, but the Commerce Committee killed the proposal by a strict party vote of 7 to 6. On September 1, 1951, the Committee turned over its files to the Commerce Committee, as the Senate had directed, and expired almost unnoticed.[34]

In its *Final Report* the Committee had no startling discoveries and very few additional recommendations to make. Recognizing that Kefauver's plan for the creation of a Federal

33. Crime *Hearings,* Pt. 13, p. 59.

34. *Congressional Record,* October 19, 1951, p. 13529; September 14, 1951, p. 11343. Wiley to Adlai Stevenson, October 6, 1951; Stevenson to Wiley, November 13, 1951; George M. Shapiro, Counsel to Thomas E. Dewey, to Wiley, October 26, 1951, Folder 7, Box 9, Series 4, Wiley Papers. Tobey to Edwin C. Johnson, September 13, 1951, Box 105, Tobey Papers. *Congressional Record,* August 22, 1951, p. 5317; October 11, 1951, pp. 12968–69. Moser to O'Conor, September 1, 1951, Box 27, Hunt Papers. New York *Times,* September 27, 1951.

Crime Commission had little chance of passage, the O'Conor Committee tried to secure support for a supposedly less controversial National Crime Coordinating Council. With an initial grant from the federal government, this agency would stimulate the formation of privately financed citizens' crime commissions and would promote the exchange of information among them. At the same time, through the collection and publication of intelligence, the National Crime Coordinating Council would encourage—and sometimes prod—vigor and cooperation among local law enforcement officials. Once launched, the National Crime Coordinating Council and local anticrime commissions would replace periodic reform outbursts with consistent long-term pressure for efficient law enforcement; it would, in short, institutionalize reform and lessen cynicism and frustration, as well as corruption. The Committee again called for the passage of uniform state laws on gambling, vice, and racketeering and for greater state-wide rationalization of the cumbersome local law enforcement structures.[35] While the federal government had such incidental responsibilities as the closing of interstate commerce to gambling syndicates and the tightening of tax laws and policies against racketeers, the larger responsibilities remained with local officials and the public at large.

For a brief period of time, Kefauver's policy of law enforcement harassment caught on in areas throughout the nation. The Justice Department enlarged its racket squad (only to disband it in 1952); the Treasury appointed a special group to explore gangsters' income tax returns; and the Bureau of Naturalization and Immigration renewed efforts to deport certain underworld figures. By 1957 the Treasury Department claimed it had conducted 28,742 racketeering investigations involving over $336 million in taxes and penalties and through the Justice Department had secured the conviction of 1,018 persons in racketeering cases. Although the Committee's wire service bill failed, the shrill public criticism forced Continental to dissolve. While some of the same services were provided by telephone and telegraph, the large horse parlors began a steady decline. Grand juries, special racket squads, and legislative "little Kefauver Committees" sprang up in most states. The American Bar Association encouraged the framing of uniform state laws and drafted a number of model

35. *Final Report*, pp. 6–7, 11–13.

codes with some success. In New York, Governor Dewey appointed a five-man crime commission, which attracted considerable praise for its work on the waterfront; in California, a new study group was authorized; in Michigan, the legislature restored the "one-man grand jury"; in Florida, a number of anti-wire service laws won the approval of both the legislature and Governor Fuller Warren. In Texas, the state's attorney general called a conference of prosecuting attorneys and won legislative approval of bills outlawing slot machines, punchboards, and policy games; the state's House of Representatives, moreover, launched a "little Kefauver Committee" of its own. Kefauver personally encouraged the development of citizens' crime commissions in New York City, Charleston (South Carolina), Boston, Minneapolis, Philadelphia, New Orleans, Dallas, Burbank, Houston, Wilmington, and numerous other cities. One Committee investigator, Ralph Mills, headed a citizens' group in Tampa; James Walsh joined the private citizens' group in New York City; Joseph Nellis aided the Dewey group in its waterfront project; and Investigator John McCormick became Cleveland's director of public safety. Kefauver claimed that the federation of the private citizens' crime commissions in the fall of 1951 substantially accomplished what he had urged in his proposals for a Federal Crime Commission or a National Crime Coordinating Council.

The local crackdowns on gambling, the defeat of tarnished politicians at the polls, and the conviction of such figures as Mickey Cohen on tax charges created substantial excitement for the moment. Kefauver later asserted that the awakening of public opinion by his Committee had been his most significant achievement. As the enthusiasm for voluntarism flagged in the mid-1950s and the visible and dramatic passed from the scene, some critics suggested that Kefauver's "reforms" had served only to intensify long-range frustration and cynicism. So inadequate are crime statistics and definitions, however, no one can document whether organized crime and corruption declined or increased during the 1950s.[36]

36. "The Kefauver Cure for Crime," *U.S. News & World Report,* May 11, 1951, p. 25. New York *Times,* September 7, 1952. *Third Interim Report,* pp. 188–92. Rufus King to Henry Patrick Kiley, July 24, 1954, Crime Box 1, Kefauver Papers. *Final Report,* pp. 19–23. *Congressional Record,* March 28, 1951, pp. A1690–91. Kirwan, *O'Conor,* p. 464. John E. Canaday, President of Burbank Citizens Crime Prevention Commit-

Although Congress refused to pass the various measures recommended by Kefauver in 1951, it did approve a wagering tax bill over the strenuous objections of both Kefauver and O'Conor. The measure, in effect, placed bookmakers, policy operators, and any professional gamblers on a basis similar to gambling devices by requiring a yearly occupational tax and imposing a 10 per cent excise tax on gross operations. Congress hoped to hurt professional gamblers, first, directly through the tax and second, through a registration requirement that would expose those who registered to local harassment. The Committee, with the backing of such public figures as Illinois Governor Adlai Stevenson, thought that a federal tax would be interpreted locally as quasi-legalization and would hence discourage local enforcement of antigambling laws. Precisely such a tax, they argued, had contributed to the confusion and corruption then surrounding the ubiquitous "one-armed bandits." Pushed through Congress in the heated atmosphere Kefauver had helped create, the act had some initial effectiveness, but never returned the revenue its sponsors had promised and certainly did not destroy illegal professional gambling. It did mark, however, the complete collapse of the Kefauver initiative on the crime issue.[37]

---

tee, to Senator Harley Kilgore, May 6, 1955, Crime Box 5; "Constructive Results of the Kefauver Crime Committee" by Stephen A. Langone, Reference Service, Library of Congress, April 5, 1957, Crime Box 1; Jack Younger to Kefauver, September 26, 1951; Kefauver to Younger, October 4, 1951, Crime Box 5, Kefauver Papers. *Congressional Record,* October 18, 1951. Richard Arch Holland, "Legislative Investigations of Organized Criminal Activities in Texas, 1951–1952," (Master's thesis, University of Texas, 1967). Telegram, Sam F. Davis, President Hillsborough County Crime Commission to Kefauver, February 21, 1951; Kefauver to Davis, February 23, 1951, Crime Box 5; Kefauver to Thomas A. Burke, Mayor of Cleveland, Ohio, April 20, 1951, Crime Box 2, Kefauver Papers. "A Big Laugh on the Law," *Life,* October 1, 1951, pp. 19–23. Willard Shelton, "Cast No Stones," *The Nation,* March 31, 1951, pp. 293–94. Robert C. Ruark column, n.d., Buffalo *Courier Express;* Tobey to Kefauver, April 18, 1953; Kefauver to Tobey, April 23, 1953, Crime and Corruption Box 1, Kefauver Papers. Walter Winchell column, Washington *Post,* April 17, 1953. William Lee Miller, *Piety Along the Potomac* (Boston: Houghton Mifflin, 1964), p. 31. Kefauver to Bill Gold, Washington *Post-Times Herald,* February 14, 1957, Crime Box 1, Kefauver Papers. Alexander Heard, *The Costs of Democracy* (Chapel Hill: University of North Carolina Press, 1960), p. 159.

37. New York *Times,* August 17, September 9, 28, 1951. Rufus King, *Gambling and Organized Crime* (Washington: Public Affairs Press, 1969), pp. 88, 92–93. Stevenson to Wiley, November 15, 1951, Folder 7,

The failure of the Kefauver–O'Conor Committee to generate legislation resulted from a number of factors. The decision to continue the investigation, as Kefauver had feared, did in effect diffuse public interest that might have been mobilized to support the Committee's legislative program. The exhaustion, confusion, and mistakes of the senators and staff, the complexity and controversial nature of some of the proposals, the competition for public and official attention by other events, and, to a lesser extent, the jealousy and resentment directed toward the Committee by other legislators, all created impediments to swift enactment of the Committee's program.

One should note, moreover, that the entire thrust of the Committee's recommendations was within the narrow law enforcement perspective it had adopted at the outset. Given the excitement over interstate ethnic conspiracies the Committee had helped foster, it is highly doubtful if Congress and the states would have acted any more favorably on a regulatory approach to gambling. In any event, the Committee rejected the possibility of introducing this alternative and proposed instead a series of complicated acts tightening up the existing law enforcement approach. When Congress rejected these proposals and when state and local groups lost their enthusiasm for voluntarism in the mid-1950s, the very limited legislative and educative accomplishments of the Kefauver Committee became apparent.

Box 9, Series 4, Wiley Papers. "How the U.S. Has Rocked Gamblers," *U.S. News & World Report,* November 16, 1951, pp. 43–45. Lester Velie, "What Are the Gamblers Doing Now," *Saturday Evening Post,* May 3, 1951, pp. 26–27, 112–16. "Legalized Gambling: A Suggestion," *Life,* January 21, 1952, p. 28. Pat Kiley to Kefauver, October 25, 1951, "Miscellaneous Material" Box, Kefauver Papers. In addition to its wire service bill, similar to the Attorney General's proposal of 1950, the Kefauver Committee's principal antigambling recommendations involved federal prohibitions of the theft of race track information and of the use of interstate commerce in connection with any bets or wagers. It also proposed that both legal and illegal casinos be required to keep more complete records of winnings and losses and would have forbidden the deduction of betting losses by illegal gambling operations. In 1968 the Supreme Court struck down the entire Wagering Tax Act. King, *Gambling and Organized Crime,* pp. 88–89. *Final Report,* pp. 88–90, 93.

9

The Committee's Legacy

Mr. Chairman, this committee has created what will
be, I think, now a national issue.
  —Lester C. Hunt, March 1951

If the Kefauver Committee left no legislative monument, it
did create a national candidate and it defined a national problem with which later politicians would deal. The most immediate result of the Committee's work was Kefauver's campaign for the Presidency.

Buoyed by the popular response to the Committee's work,
the efforts of associates and old friends to line up support, and
his rise in the public opinion polls, Kefauver began sounding
out support on a nationwide trip in the fall of 1951. By the end
of the year, Halley had demonstrated the continued public
appeal of the Committee by winning the presidency of the
New York City Council without the support of either the Democratic or Republican parties, and Kefauver stood second only
to Truman in polls as the Democratic choice for the Presidency in 1952. During an interview at the White House, Kefauver indicated that he was considering a race for the Presidency unless Truman ran, but the President replied that he
himself had reached no decision. When Truman continued to
hesitate, Kefauver explained that he meant no offense to the
President, but in view of the primaries he expected to enter,
he had to announce his candidacy.[1]

Kefauver had wide grass-roots support, probably second

1. *Time,* March 24, 1952, pp. 20–24. New York *Times,* June 6, July 29,
September 18, 21, 25, October 20, 30, November 5, 7, December 9, 1951.
Jack Anderson and Fred Blumenthal, *The Kefauver Story* (New York:
The Dial Press, 1956), pp. 166–74.

only to that of a military hero like Eisenhower, and he could obviously best counter the corruption issue the Republicans were developing. Donning a coonskin cap, symbol of his victory over Tennessee bossism, and calling upon his almost limitless physical stamina, Kefauver trudged through sixteen preferential primaries, shaking an endless number of hands in a campaign that was unprecedented at that time for its intensity. His upset victory over a pro-Truman slate in New Hampshire shook the party leaders and embarrassed the President, who shortly thereafter announced his decision not to seek reelection. In Illinois, he drowned a Lucas-backed write-in campaign for Governor Stevenson by over 400,000 votes; in Nebraska, he defeated millionaire Oklahoma Senator Robert Kerr; in California, with the support of James Roosevelt, he defeated the state's attorney general, Edmund G. Brown, by more than 2 to 1. Kefauver lost the District of Columbia to W. Averell Harriman, and Georgia's Senator Richard Russell defeated him in Florida.[2]

In the wake of his primary victories, Kefauver went into the convention with the largest single bloc of delegates, but he did not have the necessary majority, and on the third ballot a group of party leaders that included Harriman, Senator Hubert H. Humphrey of Minnesota, Governor G. Mennen Williams of Michigan, and, later, President Truman prompted a "draft" for the reluctant Governor Stevenson. Lucas, Russell, Speaker Sam Rayburn, and the President vetoed Kefauver's chances for the vice presidential nomination, a prize the Senator would have accepted.[3]

2. *Time*, March 24, 1952, pp. 20–24. Anderson and Blumenthal, *Kefauver Story*, pp. 174–81. William Carleton, "No Mandate for a Bolt," *The Nation*, May 17, 1952, pp. 475–77. Senator Tobey, an Eisenhower Republican, loaned two Kefauver aides his Chevrolet to make preliminary surveys of support in New Hampshire, and he also introduced them to prominent Democrats in the state. Scott Lucas's appearance in New Hampshire and his blast against Kefauver's "televised road-show" did Kefauver's campaign little damage, but at the same time was not a major issue. Tobey to Perry Maynard, February 7, 1952; Tobey to Robert C. Bingham, February 7, 1952, Box 68, Tobey Papers. Joseph Bruce Gorman, *Kefauver: A Political Biography* (New York: Oxford University Press, 1971), pp. 117–30. In Florida, Governor Warren, who was not seeking reelection, continued to charge that Kefauver had made a political deal with Miami politicians while chairman of the Committee, but he avoided a face-to-face debate with Kefauver. New York *Times*, September 16, 1951. Gorman, *Kefauver*, pp. 136–40. Anderson and Blumenthal, *Kefauver Story*, pp. 176–77.

If Kefauver had lost his best chance for the Presidency, he did not give up the fight nor did he lose his knack for developing a dramatic issue. He accused his 1954 primary opponent of having the financial backing of gamblers. Twice, in 1954 and in 1958, he made rumbles that he wished to reconstitute the crime committee. In 1955, he launched a nationwide study of juvenile delinquency that attracted considerable attention, and he initiated hearings that led to cancellation of the controversial Dixon–Yates contract. In 1956 he made a second bid for the presidential nomination, but after upsetting Stevenson in the Minnesota primary, he lost in Florida and California and withdrew from the race. When Stevenson, again the nominee, threw the vice presidential nomination open to the floor, Kefauver edged out Massachusetts Senator John F. Kennedy for the position. After his party's defeat in the second Eisenhower landslide, Kefauver returned to the Senate and the chairmanship of the Senate Subcommittee on Antitrust and Monopoly, from which he launched investigations into price fixing and economic concentration in the steel, automobile, and drug industries. Here Kefauver found a forum for his strong Brandeisian economic views and probably made the most significant contributions of his career. Hearings were in progress when Kefauver, drained by more than a decade of almost constant campaigning and committee exertion died of a heart attack in 1963.[4]

While advancing Kefauver's public career, the Committee also contributed materially to the development of a host of popular and official ideas about organized crime. Essentially, it adopted a conspiratorial, law enforcement perspective rather than a sociological regulatory one. Largely ignoring the economic, legal, and social conditions giving rise to organized crime, the Committee implied that it essentially originated outside of American society and was imposed upon the public by a group of immoral men, bound together by a mysterious ethnic conspiracy.

Through its analysis of the wire service and through its

3. Anderson and Blumenthal, *Kefauver Story*, pp. 195–96. Gorman, *Kefauver*, pp. 154–57.

4. Gorman, *Kefauver*, pp. 207–8, 256–64. Chicago *Sun-Times*, July 1, 1958. Bert M. Keating to Kefauver, December 9, 1954; "Crime and Corruption" Box 2; Kefauver to Larry G. Hastings, February 9, 1955, Crime Box 1, Kefauver Papers. Estes Kefauver, *In a Few Hands: Monopoly Power in America* (Baltimore: Penguin Books, Inc., 1965).

speculations on a Mafia, the Committee unquestionably exaggerated the degree of centralization within the underworld. Since organized crime was a conspiratorial evil rather than a socioeconomic problem, the Committee felt the most effective way to combat it was through the criminal law rather than through regulatory measures. Given this mentality, the senators, without serious study, condemned the legalization and regulation of public gambling as a possible alternative to criminal prohibition. Similarly, it dismissed the findings that the use of marijuana was not necessarily a stepping-stone to heroin addiction; it lumped all "drugs" together under harsher criminal laws and under a thick veil of fear and misunderstanding. In its investigation of gambling, the Committee even dragged out a bit of red herring by suggesting that those who supported legalization might themselves be part of an underworld plot.

Having stressed the nationwide implications of their discoveries and ruled out a regulatory approach to the problems, the Committee then recommended only modest federal remedies and thrust the major responsibilities back to the states, local governments, and private anticrime groups. A brief flurry of activity by these groups followed Kefauver's appeal, but soon public enthusiasm lagged and interagency squabbling resumed while the private groups succumbed to infighting and chronic financial difficulties. In the resulting wreckage of the voluntarism the Committee had suggested, only a few effective entities remained—an occasional state-sponsored investigating commission, a surviving private crime commission, and the Law Enforcement Intelligence Unit, a program first initiated in California in 1956 for the exchange of intelligence among member police departments.[5]

On the federal level, efforts to combat organized crime were more persistent. Senator Tobey, who headed the Commerce Committee in the Republican 83d Congress, began a study of criminal domination of labor on the waterfront, but his death in the summer of 1953 ended the investigation. A total of twenty-four aliens or naturalized citizens mentioned by the

5. *The Challenge of Crime in a Free Society: A Report by the President's Commission on Law Enforcement and Administration of Justice* (New York: Avon Books, 1968), p. 461. Ralph Salerno, *The Crime Confederation* (Garden City, N.Y.: Doubleday & Company, Inc., 1969), pp. 288–94.

Kefauver Committee, including Joe Adonis, were deported, and Costello served over a year behind bars for contempt of the Committee. The Treasury Department achieved some modicum of success with its special rackets squad, and Justice launched a weakly organized Crime and Racketeering Section in 1954. Under the prompting of Attorney General Robert F. Kennedy, Congress in 1961–1962 passed four new antigambling bills that outlawed the use of telephone and telegraph facilities by persons engaged in a betting business, forbade the transportation of gambling paraphernalia through interstate commerce, prohibited the use of interstate commerce generally and travel in particular to organized criminal activities, and finally strengthened the Johnson Slot Machine Act of 1950. Enforcement responsibilities were assigned to the Justice Department, from which Kennedy mobilized a concerted attack on organized crime.[6]

Beginning in 1957 Senator John L. McClellan, first as head of the Special Committee on Improper Activities in the Labor and Management Field and later as chairman of the Permanent Subcommittee on Government Operations, explored labor racketeering, gambling, and traffic in narcotics. Following a meeting of nationally known racketeers at Apalachin, New York, in 1957 (which in fact was a gathering of men who came, in the main, from Detroit, Cleveland, New Jersey, Pennsylvania, and New York), McClellan again focused attention on the Mafia. With the assistance of his former chief counsel, Attorney General Kennedy, McClellan held televised hearings in 1963 before which Joseph Valachi, a self-admitted member of "La Cosa Nostra," appeared.[7]

6. Memorandum, Downey Rice to Tobey, January 26, 1953, Box 106, Tobey Papers. "Vacant Seat," *Newsweek,* August 3, 1953. "Federal Effort Against Organized Crime: Report of Agency Operation," *House Report No. 1574,* 90th Cong., 2d sess. (1968), pp. 31, 13, 14. "Humbling 'The King,'" *Newsweek,* April 19, 1954, p. 30. Rufus King, *Gambling and Organized Crime* (Washington: Public Affairs Press, 1969), pp. 95–97.

7. "A Searching Look at Big Crime," *Life,* February 13, 1959, p. 26. John L. McClellan, *Crime Without Punishment* (New York: Duell, Sloan and Pearce, 1962), pp. 13, 201. Peter Maas, *The Valachi Papers* (New York: G. P. Putnam's Sons, 1968), p. 46. After the Apalachin meeting had been broken up, Attorney General William P. Rogers established a "Special Group on Organized Crime" to gather intelligence and prosecute those arrested. Twenty of the men were later

Valachi's testimony had two important results. First, following the sensational accounts of the Apalachin conference, it stimulated fresh public interest in a Mafia-like conspiracy interpretation of organized crime. It explained the assassination of Albert Anastasia and the attempted assassination of Frank Costello in 1957 in terms of the rise to authority in the organization of Valachi's own *bête noire*, Vito Genovese. It strengthened a theory, emerging from police work, that organized crime was dominated by a hierarchy of twenty-four "families" linked by a "commission" at the top. Second, Valachi's references to "La Cosa Nostra" gave the FBI, which had refused to acknowledge existence of "the Mafia," a means of joining the Kennedy anticrime fight without undue loss of face. The broad conspiratorial view of organized crime found further endorsement in President Johnson's Commission on Law Enforcement and the Administration of Justice. Even in 1970, when Attorney General John N. Mitchell, in response to pressure from the Italo-American community (including Joseph Colombo's controversial Italian-American Civil Rights League) ordered the Justice Department to discontinue use of the words *Mafia* and *Cosa Nostra,* the concept of organized crime as conspiracy continued to dominate thinking in government circles and in press reporting.[8]

No one can accurately gauge the extent of organized crime or the effectiveness of the steps taken to combat it. Estimates of the volume of illegal gambling usually vary between $20 billion and near $50 billion—figures as impressive for their range as for their size. Even if one could approximate the dollar volume and profits of illegal gambling, narcotics, loan sharking, prostitution, and the other goods and services generally classed as organized crime, it would still be impossible to measure its social damage or to evaluate the public's loss of

convicted of conspiracy, but the convictions were reversed. The Special Group's functions were absorbed by the Organized Crime and Racketeering Section. Salerno, *Crime Confederation,* pp. 300–301. "Federal Effort Against Organized Crime," *House Report No. 1574,* 90th Cong., 2d sess., p. 13.

8. Maas, *Valachi Papers,* pp. 239–44. Donald R. Cressey, *Theft of the Nation: The Structure and Operations of Organized Crime in America* (New York: Harper & Row, Publishers, 1969), pp. 20–24. *The Challenge of Crime in a Free Society,* pp. 437–86. Milwaukee *Journal,* July 24, 1970. Nicholas Pileggi, "The City Politic: Why They Had to Shoot Colombo," *New York,* July 12, 1971, pp. 8–9. "The Mafia: Back to the Bad Old Days?" *Time,* July 12, 1971, pp. 14–21.

faith in a political system frequently rendered impotent by corrupting powers. If former Attorney General Ramsey Clark was correct in arguing that the extent of organized crime is vastly exaggerated, even he acknowledged that it remains an active and threatening factor in the nation's life.[9]

By disseminating press and crime commission interpretations of organized crime, the Kefauver Committee set the limits for action against it for a generation.[10] The widespread publicity and authority granted the Committee's conclusions on national crime syndicates and the Mafia have been elaborated upon as crime "families" and "commissions" of La Cosa Nostra but have not essentially been altered. President Johnson's commission's definition of organized crime as a "society" that operates through "intricate conspiracies" to flaunt public control and "amass huge profits" shows the tenacity of the conspiratorial perspective.[11] In fact, of course, organized crime springs from inconsistencies between moralistic laws and less moral economic and human appetites. Efforts to modify its influences have been complicated by the deeply embedded tradition of decentralized law enforcement, which has facilitated corruption and contributed to the defeat of spasmodic popular protest and reform waves.

The Kefauver Committee's debatable judgments on the structure of organized crime could be overlooked if the senators had seriously considered broad policy alternatives for fighting the problem. In effect the Committee brushed aside consideration of legalization and regulation as possible alternatives to the law enforcement approach. If it is unfair to criticize the Committee for an investigation it did not make, it is hardly unjust to point out that they did not make it and

9. Salerno, *Crime Confederation,* pp. 227–28. King, *Gambling and Organized Crime,* p. 33. Ramsey Clark, *Crime in America: Observations on Its Nature, Causes, Prevention, and Control* (New York: Simon & Schuster, Inc., 1970), pp. 73–84.

10. In the 1970s the reconsideration of laws on marijuana and drug addiction and the experiments with legalized gambling schemes in a number of Northeastern states certainly suggests a departure from the Kefauver Committee's conclusions. Less clear is the future of the Mafia stereotype. The combination of growing resentment by certain Italian-American groups at the image, the deaths and imprisonment of a number of Italian crime figures, and the increasing attention paid to Black and Puerto Rican gangsters may foreshadow a significant shift in the older stereotype.

11. *Challenge of Crime in a Free Society,* p. 437.

that the scope of their authoritative judgment should have been lessened by that failure. The real tragedy, of course, is that the public thought such a study had been made, and popular opinion being set, later investigations enjoyed less flexibility for reeducating the public.

Perhaps, in the final analysis, no congressional committee, surrounded by political considerations, dependent upon press sources, and limited in time, could have done better. Probably some other mechanism for exploring the problem would have been preferable. Like most congressional committees, the Kefauver Committee's perspective was already determined before its actual work began, and most of its investigation was little more than a dramatization of its adopted point of view. The fact that it was a supremely effective and magnificent show should not obscure its fundamental failure.

Bibliographical Essay

Manuscript and Film Sources

When the Kefauver–O'Conor Committee expired, its authority and voluminous files passed to the Senate Commerce Committee. Various federal agencies, such as the FBI, went through these files to extract and remove certain materials, and reporters allegedly pilfered some of the documents. The inadequate protection and storage of these files by the Senate Commerce Committee aroused the criticism of former personnel of the Kefauver Committee, and eventually the ninety linear feet of material was physically transferred to the National Archives for safekeeping. The Commerce Committee at the same time retained control over access to the Kefauver Committee's files and apparently began opening them only upon the request of Kefauver or certain official agencies.

Members of the Commerce Committee's staff refused my initial requests for access to the Kefauver files, with the explanation that the unindexed material contained records of scurrilous and unproven charges and held little material of historical value. My offers to submit all notes to Commerce Committee agents for censorship—a practice satisfactorily followed by the State Department in similar circumstances—proved unavailing. An attempt to enlist the aid of a member of the Commerce Committee, Senator Howard H. Baker, Jr., and Kefauver's friend and colleague, Senator Albert Gore, brought a more sympathetic hearing but no change of policy.

To a large extent the papers of four Kefauver Committee members compensated for the unavailable Committee files. The Kefauver Papers at the University of Tennessee in Knoxville contain extensive documentation on the Chairman's painful courtship of the press and constitute the single most fruitful collection on the Committee. Because the Senator temperamentally avoided expressing his deeper feelings or motivations even to close associates and family, the Kefauver Papers provide only fleeting insights into the inner man. Senator Tobey's Papers, at Dartmouth College in Hanover, New Hampshire, yield most on the public reaction to the televised hearings in New York, and they strongly suggest that the Committee's gadfly acted as much from calculation as from impulse. The Wiley Papers at the State Historical Society Archives in Madison, Wisconsin, are less voluminous on the Crime Committee than those of Kefauver or Tobey, but they clearly demonstrate that Wiley and his staff were conscious of the political implications of the crime study from an early date. Senator Hunt's Papers at the University of Wyoming in Laramie contain a few documents on the Committee not found elsewhere. What remained of the O'Conor Papers were stored in a cellar and later destroyed by a flood.

Supplementing the Committee members' papers are those of the Chicago Crime Commission; of William H. Standley, head of the California Crime Commission, at the University of Southern California in Los Angeles; and of Robert P. Patterson, chairman of the American Bar Association Commission on Organized Crime, in the Library of Congress. In the Harry S. Truman Library, the Presidential Papers, the papers of Presidential Assistant George M. Elsey, and those of Attorney General J. Howard McGrath sketch the picture of an administration as it gradually lost control of the "crime issue." The papers of Victor R. Messall, also in the Truman Library, contain a few documents on the influence-peddling charge leveled at the President's former campaign manager. Of superficial value only are the papers of Mayor DeLesseps S. Morrison in the Public Library in New Orleans and in the Howard-Tilton Memorial Library, Tulane University; those of Senator Joseph O'Mahoney at the University of Wyoming; those of Senators Tom Connally and Theodore Green in the Library of Congress; those of Senator Styles Bridges at Dartmouth College; those of Senator Homer Capehart at the Indiana State Library in Indianapolis; those of Senator James Kem in the Western Historical Manuscripts Collection, University of Missouri at Columbia. Inquiries about the papers of Senators Patrick McCarran, Thomas Hennings, Jr., and Herbert Lehman, Vice President Alben Barkley, Director Harry Anslinger of the Narcotics Bureau, and Governor Forrest Smith of Missouri reveal no material of significance on the Kefauver Committee. The Collections of Sidney Shalett, ghost writer of Kefauver's *Crime in America,* at the University of Oregon turned out to be largely newspaper clippings as was the private collection of Committee Counsel Joseph Nellis in Washington, D.C. Materials on the late Rudolph Halley and William O'Dwyer in the Columbia Oral History Project are unfortunately closed, as are the papers of Governor Thomas E. Dewey and Senators Scott W. Lucas and Forrest C. Donnell. Neither the late Edwin Johnson's Papers nor those of Senators Ernest McFarland and Homer Ferguson, or Governor Fuller Warren have been placed in depositories. Efforts to obtain access to pertinent material in the Department of the Treasury, the Justice Department, the Federal Communications Commission, and the Senate Commerce and Judiciary committees were unproductive.

Movietone News compiled an hour-long film from segments of the New York hearings and showed this film at theaters across the country in the early 1950s. The film is presently available at the Twentieth Century Fox Film Center in New York. The Library of Congress, Motion Picture Division, holds a number of "Meet the Press" interviews with Kefauver, Halley, and Tobey about the Committee in early 1951 as well as a CBS special, "Crime and the Committee," made in 1958.

Government Documents and Studies

The four Kefauver Committee reports, particularly the much-cited *Third Interim Report,* are indispensable for determining what information impressed the Committee and how it argued its case. Even more important are the nineteen volumes of printed hearings, running to approximately twelve thousand pages of testimony plus several hundred pages of appendices and supportive evidence. The published hearings clearly reveal that the Committee approached organized crime with preconceived judgments and occasionally slanted the evidence in its reports. A few volumes of unpublished stenographic minutes available in the Kefauver Papers reveal little that is not in the printed hearings.

The often overlooked McFarland Report, "Transmission of Gambling Information," *Senate Report No. 1752,* 81st Congress, 2d session (Washington, 1950), and the hearings and reports of the Senate Select Committee on Improper Activities in the Labor and Management Field and the Senate Permanent Subcommittee on Investigations, both later headed by Senator John L. McClellan, help round out the record of the Senate's work on organized crime. The Subcommittee on Investigations, particularly in its highly publicized Valachi hearings in 1963, expanded the Kefauver Committee's views on the Mafia. The Senate's interpretation was accepted by

President Johnson's Commission on Law Enforcement and the Administration of Justice both in *The Challenge of Crime in a Free Society* (New York: Avon Books, 1968) and *Task Force Report: Organized Crime* (Washington, 1967). The House Committee on Government Operations has surveyed the federal antiorganized-crime campaign in "Federal Efforts Against Organized Crime: Report on Agency Operations," *House Report No. 1574,* 90th Congress, 2d session (Washington, 1968).

Personal Interviews

All the Committee members and a distressingly large number of the staff, including Rudolph Halley, are now dead. Approximately fifteen persons who were associated in one fashion or another with the Committee granted interviews, but little material that is not available elsewhere developed during these sessions. Committee counsels Downey Rice, Rufus King, George S. Robinson, and Joseph Nellis provided interesting insights into the personal interactions of both the senators and the staff, but their reminiscences were limited by a strong personal devotion to Kefauver and the fuzziness on details to be expected after the passage of two decades. Edward Cooper, counsel to the McFarland Subcommittee, provided a counterbalance to those who were inclined to condemn Kefauver's senatorial critics. Virgil W. Peterson, former operating director of the Chicago Crime Commission and now a lecturer in criminology at Northwestern University, reminisced about his association with the Committee and about his analysis of organized crime. Judge Morris Ploscowe, Charles Siragusa, Julius Cahn, Edward Jarrett of the Senate Commerce Committee staff, and Charles G. Neese and Richard Wallace of the Kefauver staff were all cordial but either recalled less or were deliberately circumspect. Herbert R. O'Conor, Jr., provided introductions to three of his father's Committee aides, but again the passage of time had dulled memories and little not already known developed from the interviews. Former Senators Homer Capehart and John Bricker provided an insight into Republican skepticism about Kefauver and the Committee.

Newspapers and Periodical Literature

The popular press devoted substantial attention and comment to the formation and work of the Committee. Several major newspapers assigned full-time reporters to travel with the Committee and report on its activities. Because of its superb index, the New York *Times* provided the most usable running account of daily Committee news, but except for the hearings in New York, it did not deal to any significant extent in the excitement and rumors engulfing the investigation. Kefauver maintained close contact with the publisher and editor of the Washington *Post* as well as with Drew Pearson, whose syndicated column appeared in the *Post*. Both the *Post* and the Washington *Evening Star* adopted a pro-Kefauver perspective in reporting the behind-the-scenes maneuvering and hearings in the capital. The *Christian Science Monitor* also had surprisingly good national coverage.

Two Miami newspapers, the *Daily News* and the *Herald,* gave Kefauver the most enthusiastic support of all the press, reporting with great relish both the hearings and off-the-record comments and observations. The St. Louis *Post-Dispatch*, Kansas City *Star,* New Orleans *Item,* Detroit *Free Press*, and the Cleveland *Plain Dealer* catalogued and generally praised the Committee's local appearances but followed hearings elsewhere with less interest. The McCormick-owned Chicago *Tribune* remained skeptical of the Committee until the defeat of Democrats Scott Lucas and Daniel Gilbert in the November election. The tabloid New York *Mirror* cooled toward Kefauver as its columnist-critic Lee Mortimer drifted into opposition. An excellent clipping service compiled several large scrapbooks on the Committee for Senator Kefauver, and less complete scrapbooks were maintained by the offices of Senators Tobey, Wiley, and Hunt and Mayor Morrison and the Chicago Crime Commission.

The major news magazines, such as *Newsweek, U.S. News and World Report,* and *Time,* delighted in the Committee's sensational exposures but never cultivated the close partnership with Kefauver the big-city newspapers enjoyed. Even while sponsoring the New York hearings, *Time* attempted to maintain a certain snickering distance from the "crime circus." *Editor & Publisher* and *Printers' Ink* provided the best perspective on the novel use of television and also reviewed the anticrime campaigns of local dailies. From 1947 to 1953 Herbert Asbury and Lester Velie wrote valuable series of feature articles for *Collier's* on Costello, Halley, District Attorney Hogan, Ambassador O'Dwyer, Arthur H. Samish, and other persons who were caught up in the furor. (Samish and feature-writer Bob Thomas later produced *The Secret Boss of*

California: The Life and High Times of Art Samish [New York: Crown Publishers, Inc., 1971], an expansion of the Velie article.) *American Mercury* in 1951–1952 published a series of bitter articles on the Committee by Lee Mortimer.

Secondary Accounts on Organized Crime

The secondary literature on organized crime remains unbelievably distorted. Criminologists have generally concentrated on such topics as juvenile delinquency for which statistics are readily available or on theories of aberrant psychology. The more popular textbooks generally have one chapter on organized crime, which is based on the standard government studies, including those by the Wickersham Commission, President Hoover's Council on Social Trends, the Kefauver and McClellan committees, and more recently the President's Commission on Law Enforcement and the Administration of Justice. As pointed out in the text, while portions of these studies are quite valuable, they suffer from a too narrow concept of organized crime and from a decided antiregulatory bias.

The recently renewed interest in organized crime has spawned several books that reflect this perspective. Rufus King, former Kefauver Committee legislative counsel and consultant on President Johnson's Commission, has expressed his views in *Gambling and Organized Crime* (Washington: Public Affairs Press, 1969). Criminologist Donald R. Cressey, who helped draft the President's Commission's chapter on organized crime, has in effect updated Joseph Valachi's testimony with appropriate sociological jargon in *Theft of the Nation: The Structure and Operations of Organized Crime in America* (New York: Harper & Row, Publishers, 1969). A third member of the task force on organized crime of the Johnson Commission, New York City policeman Ralph Salerno, has written *The Crime Confederation* (New York: Doubleday & Company, Inc., 1969), the best summary to date of the predominant law enforcement perspective on the problem.

Journalistic exposés, generally of an inferior quality, constitute the bulk of the secondary literature. One of the better such efforts is Lloyd Wendt and Herman Kogan, *Bosses in Lusty Chicago: The Story of Bathhouse John and Hinky Dink* (Bloomington: Indiana University Press, 1967), a study of political machine leaders with extensive underworld ties. In the 1920s and 1930s Herbert Asbury wrote a series of informal histories of the underworlds of New York, New Orleans, Chicago, and San Francisco. Probably the best is *The Gangs of New York* (New York: Alfred A. Knopf, Inc., 1928), an entertaining volume with some value as social history. Asbury dates the end of the "gangs" and the beginning of "mobs" with the development of large business organizations in the late nineteenth century. In these earlier works, in contrast to his postwar articles on Costello, Asbury saw no nationwide organization of criminal syndicates.

Most commentators date the rise of modern organized crime from the Prohibition experiment, yet there is no good account of this development. Andrew Sinclair, *Prohibition: The Era of Excess* (Boston: Little, Brown and Company, 1962), is a social history of the period with a reasonably good chapter on the underworld, but Sinclair's analysis falls far short of the need. Fred D. Pasley's *Al Capone: The Biography of a Self-Made Man* (New York: Garden City Publishing Co., 1930) places the Chicago underworld leader in the same league as the older robber barons, a theme that was updated by British journalist Kenneth Allsop in *Bootleggers and Their Era* (Garden City, N.Y.: Doubleday & Company, Inc., 1961) and reporter John Kobler in his recent *Capone: The Life and World of Al Capone* (New York: G. P. Putnam's Sons, 1971). John McPhaul underscores the role of Capone's predecessor in *Johnny Torrio: First of the Gang Lords* (New Rochelle, N.Y.: Arlington House, Inc., 1971). Virgil W. Peterson, in his *Barbarians in Our Midst* (Boston: Little, Brown and Company, 1952), presents his own law enforcement perspective on the so-called "Capone syndicate," and John H. Lyle's *The Dry and Lawless Years* (Englewood Cliffs, N.J.: Prentice-Hall, Inc., 1960) is a second general account of the Chicago scene. Leo Katcher's *The Big Bankroll: The Life and Times of Arnold Rothstein* (New York: Harper and Brothers, 1958) superficially assesses the pioneering organizational impact of the notorious New York gambler. Paul Sann sketches the failure of one underworld figure to accommodate himself to the emerging business structure in *Kill the Dutchman! The Story of Dutch Schultz* (New Rochelle, N.Y.: Arlington House, Inc., 1971). *The Dillinger Days* (New York: Random House, Inc., 1963) by John Toland is a lurid account of the dramatic bank robbery and kidnapping chases on which the FBI based its reputation for fearless crime fighting at the end of Prohibition.

The "Murder, Inc." cases, with their implications of nation-

wide organization, would probably have produced a number
of books had not World War II intervened to absorb the nation's attention and energies. This theme was not developed
until the newspaper articles and the Lait and Mortimer volumes of the Kefauver period. The bulk of the literature produced since the Kefauver hearings has been based on the Kefauver and McClellan hearings and is highly sensational. The
only major criticism of the Kefauver Committee, other than
the later Lait and Mortimer books, was Burton B. Turkus and
Sid Feder, *Murder, Inc.: The Story of "The Syndicate"* (London: Victor Golancz, Ltd., 1953). Turkus, an O'Dwyer assistant
in the District Attorney's office, related the details of the famous prosecutions and took the Committee to task for confusing the Mafia and Black Hand. Feder, a journalist, collaborated with Joachim Joesten in *The Luciano Story* (New
York: David McKay Co., Inc., 1954), a pro-Dewey account of
the controversial commutation of Luciano's sentence, but
Joesten then privately printed *Dewey, Luciano, and I* (Great
Barrington, Mass., 1955), in which he sided with the Kefauver
Committee and accused Dewey of releasing Luciano to prevent the underworld leader from showing that the Governor
had framed him. Although its criticisms of the Kefauver Committee betray a certain peevishness, the Turkus book remains
the accepted account of the "Murder, Inc." cases; the contradictory Joesten accounts have no redeeming merits.

Ed Reid, who won a Pulitzer prize for his exposures of the
Gross bookmaking ring in the Brooklyn *Eagle,* capitalized on
the Kefauver Committee's publicity for his *Mafia* (New York:
Random House, Inc., 1952), a wildly exaggerated story of how
a small conspiracy controls virtually all of organized crime.
Reid joined the Las Vegas *Sun* and collaborated with Ovid
Demaris on the successful *The Green Felt Jungle* (New York:
Trident Press, 1963), an exposé of outside control of the gam-
bling city. Reid brought his Mafia theories up to date but did
not improve on them in *The Grim Reapers: The Anatomy of
Organized Crime in America* (Chicago: Henry Regnery Com-
pany, 1969). Demaris developed a more narrow theme in
showing how the underworld still makes Chicago a *Captive
City* (New York: Pocket Books, 1970).

The Mafia theory that the Kefauver Committee renewed has
unquestionably attracted the widest attention. George Redston, a right-wing ex-bookmaker, is coauthor of *The Conspiracy of Death* (Indianapolis: The Bobbs-Merrill Co., Inc.,

1965), which focuses on the California world of Mickey Cohen, "Bugsy" Siegel, and Virginia Hill. More recent accounts of the late gangster moll are Dean Jennings, *We Only Kill Each Other: The Life and Bad Times of Bugsy Siegel* (Greenwich, Conn.: Fawcett Publications, Inc., 1968), and Ed Reid, *The Mistress and the Mafia: The Virginia Hill Story* (New York: Bantam Books, Inc., 1972). The police chief of Santa Ana, California, Edward J. Allen, produced *Merchants of Menace—The Mafia: A Study of Organized Crime* (Springfield, Ill.: Charles C. Thomas, Publisher, 1962) and Raymond V. Martin wrote *Revolt in the Mafia* (New York: Duell, Sloan and Pearce, 1963), the story of the Gallo-Profaci gang war of the early 1960s in New York. The classic Narcotics Bureau position is stated in Frederic Sondern, Jr., *Brotherhood of Evil: The Mafia* (New York: Farrar, Straus and Cudahy, 1959), an account that seized upon the Apalachin meeting of 1957. Peter Maas's best-selling *The Valachi Papers* (New York: G. P. Putnam's Sons, 1968)— later made into a motion picture—revisits the famous McClellan Committee witness and renames the dread conspiracy *La Cosa Nostra.* Fred J. Cook, a newspaper reporter, drew heavily upon state and congressional investigations for his *A Two Dollar Bet Means Murder* (New York: The Dial Press, 1961), *The Secret Rulers* (New York: Duell, Sloan and Pearce, 1966), a Valachi-based review of Joe Adonis and the New Jersey underworld of the late 1940s and 1950s, and the more sweeping *Mafia!* (Greenwich, Conn.: Fawcett Publications, Inc., 1973). Nicholas Gage's *The Mafia Is Not an Equal Opportunity Employer* (New York: Dell Publishing Co., Inc., 1972) is a short, readable summary of the conventional journalistic wisdom on organized crime. Gage, a reporter for the New York *Times,* recently edited *Mafia, U.S.A.* (Chicago: Playboy Press, 1972), a selection from writers associated with the conspiratorial perspective.

A dissenting perspective on the Mafia–Cosa Nostra theme has been put forth by newsman Hank Messick in *The Silent Syndicate* (New York: The Macmillan Company, 1967), *Syndicate Abroad* (Toronto: The Macmillan Co. of Canada, 1969), *Lansky* (New York: G. P. Putnam's Sons, 1971), and several other volumes. Messick emphasizes the Jewish element in organized crime and claims that the Rothkopf–Kleinman gambling syndicate in Cleveland and Meyer Lansky from New York expanded into Nevada, Florida, and the Caribbean while the politicians and the press were pursuing an overblown Italian conspiracy. Journalist Wallace Turner also focuses on the Cleveland gambling syndicate in his case study of *Gamblers' Money: The New Force in American Life* (Boston: Houghton Mifflin Company, 1965).

Messick's most recent work is *John Edgar Hoover* (New York: David McKay Co., Inc., 1972), which argues that Hoover avoided a fight against organized crime because he shared with it a powerful right-wing constituency. The best part of *John Edgar Hoover* is Messick's almost hilarious attack on the Valachi testimony and the FBI's role in building up La Cosa Nostra. Fred J. Cook's *The F.B.I. Nobody Knows* (New York: The Macmillan Company, 1964), because it attacks Hoover on civil liberties as well as organized crime, is still of some value. Jay Robert Nash's *Citizen Hoover* (Chicago: Nelson-Hall, 1972), too intent in denying the FBI any glory, is distinctly inferior to both the Messick and Cook books. Victor S. Navasky also predicates much of his criticism of Hoover in *Kennedy Justice* (New York: Atheneum Publishers, 1971) on the Director's reluctance to accept the old Mafia interpretation of organized crime and to join the fight with vigor. A more balanced, less emotional analysis of the FBI's approach to organized crime is one of the most pressing needs of scholars in the field, but may well have to wait until the academic world rethinks the problem of organized crime and more reliable information becomes available on the Bureau's decision making.

Periodic law enforcement breakthroughs have fueled the expanding literature on organized crime. The Reles case, the Apalachin convention, the Valachi testimony have each been cited as new and conclusive proof of the old conspiracy view. One recent instance was the release by the U.S. Attorney in 1969 of 2,300 pages of transcript based on the FBI's electronic bugging of the office of Simone Rizzo "Sam the Plumber" DeCavalcante in Kenilworth, New Jersey. The recorded conversations show that mention of "the Commission," of "Cosa Nostra," and of underworld courts do occur in underworld conversations. Reporters Joseph Volz and Peter J. Bridge edited a 200-page condensation of the DeCavalcante tapes in *The Mafia Talks* (Greenwich, Conn.: Fawcett Publications, Inc., 1969). Aside from the mechanical pitfalls of deciphering the tapes (such as the Kefauver Committee experienced with the Frank Costello–George Morton Levy telephone conversations), one should bear in mind that the DeCavalcante recordings refer to the New York–New Jersey underworld circles and do not establish the existence of a tightly knit national organization. Nor, judging from the contents of the tapes, does "the Commission" appear to be of particularly ancient vintage. The intriguing possibility that the underworld itself is influenced by press speculation and the dramatic testimony of such witnesses as Valachi has never been explored. Interestingly, the greater number of references to "the Commission" in *The Mafia Talks* occurs during the "Bonanno War," after Valachi's testimony, and DeCavalcante appears to be explaining the functions and powers of "the Commission" to a confused friend in post-Valachi terms. The very latest exposé by a person supposedly "inside" the structure of organized crime is *My Life in the Mafia* (Garden City, N.Y.: Doubleday & Company, Inc., 1973) by Vincent Teresa and journalist Thomas C. Renner. Teresa claimed to be a ranking member of a New England crime family who was betrayed by his syndicate friends, once he had been apprehended. Most of the sensationalism in Teresa's book appears to be the handiwork of Renner, and the combined effort is less than convincing.

Popular acceptance of the law enforcement conspiracy perspective about organized crime has been immeasurably advanced by a series of best sellers in the late 1960s and early 1970s. That part of Gay Talese's *Honor Thy Father* (New York: World Publishing Company, 1971) based on Talese's personal contacts in the troubled Bonanno family provides interesting insights into what Talese believes to be a declining Italian underworld. Unfortunately, Talese supplements his personal observations with the official studies discussed above and reduces the merits of a potentially major contribution. Mario Puzo's sensational novel, *The Godfather* (New York: G. P. Putnam's Sons, 1969), and the successful motion picture based on it clearly reinforce the traditional view. The careful student would do well to read the sequel, *The Godfather Papers and Other Confessions* (New York: G. P. Putnam's Sons, 1972), in which Puzo admits his heavy reliance on the traditional government sources and the newspapers. Charles Durbin's *Vendetta: A Novel of the Mafia* (New York: Coward, McCann & Geoghegan, Inc., 1970) and a spate of other "Mafia novels" portray the same kind of world but in a decidedly less readable manner. Jimmy Breslin's *The Gang that Couldn't Shoot Straight* (New York: The Viking Press, Inc., 1969) spoofs the legendary mechanical efficiency of the underworld but does little to reeducate the public. Beginning in August of 1973,

Playboy has published a series of articles by journalist Richard Hammer, which promises to strengthen the older Mafia stereotype.

The Mafia is an issue in Italian and Sicilian politics as well as in the United States. Unfortunately, no systematic study of the Old World background of American figures, past and present, has been made, and the value of studies on the Italian and Sicilian underworld is hence limited. E. J. Hobsbawn's pioneering *Primitive Rebels: Studies in Archaic Forms of Social Movement in the 19th and 20th Centuries* (New York: W. W. Norton & Company, Inc., 1965) has an excellent chapter on the Sicilian Mafia but makes no serious effort to show its relationship to the American underworld. Luigi Barzini's *The Italians* (New York: Atheneum Publishers, 1964) suggests that talk of international conspiracies is vastly overblown and that American-style greed has helped to destroy the social benefits of the old Sicilian mafia. Neither Norman Lewis's *The Honored Society: A Searching Look at the Mafia* (New York: G. P. Putnam's Sons, 1964) nor Michele Pantaleone's *The Mafia and Politics* (New York: Coward, McCann & Geoghegan, Inc., 1966) adds any understanding to the American scene.

Slowly there is emerging what one commentator calls a revisionist school of "Mafiaology,"[1] which is inclined either to deny the existence of a Mafia-like structure, to minimize its impact, or to stress broader socioeconomic injustices as the root cause of organized crime. The literature is scattered through several periodicals and enjoys nothing like the circulation of the more popular law enforcement-conspiracy school. Two outstanding examples include the insightful "Mafia" article by Gaetano Mosca in the *Encyclopedia of Social Sciences* and Daniel Bell's indispensable article "Crime as an American Way of Life" in his *The End of Ideology: On the Exhaustion of Political Ideas in the Fifties* (New York: The Free Press, 1962). *The Annals of the American Academy of Political and Social Science* devoted its September, 1941, issue to consideration of crime and included a number of significant articles such as Morris Ploscowe's "Crime in a Competitive Society." The *Annals* published special issues in May of 1950, May of 1963, and November of 1967 on gambling and organized crime, but the general tone has not been revisionist.

1. Tom Buckley, "The Mafia Tries a New Tune," *Harper's* (August 1971), 46–56.

John Landesco's excellent study, "Organized Crime in Chicago," buried in the *Illinois Crime Survey* of 1929, was resurrected in 1968 as a separate volume by the University of Chicago Press. Gus Tyler has edited a superb volume, *Organized Crime in America: A Book of Readings* (Ann Arbor: University of Michigan Press, 1962), which samples the literature from all points of view and includes the Mosca, Bell, and Ploscowe articles. Tyler's own introduction to "The Mafia" chapter is a valuable contribution in itself.

The Public Interest periodically publishes revisionist articles on organized crime. Thomas C. Schelling's "Economics and Criminal Enterprise," a plea for regulatory rather than prohibitive legislation, appeared in the spring of 1967. Schelling's article has been lost in the index of the *Task Force Report: Organized Crime* of the President's Commission on Law Enforcement and the Administration of Justice. Gordon Hawkins's article, "God and the Mafia" (Winter 1969), is a scathing indictment of the verbal inconsistencies of the Kefauver and McClellan committees. Hawkins concludes that the persistence of the Mafia conspiracy view reveals more about the public than about organized crime.

Joseph L. Albini's *The American Mafia: Genesis of a Legend* (New York: Appleton-Century-Crofts, 1971) is a solid book-length attack on the old conspiracy myths. The most promising effort thus far has been Francis A. J. Ianni's superb anthropological field study, *A Family Business: Kinship and Social Control in Organized Crime* (New York: Russell Sage Foundation, 1972). Through his close observations and discussions with a crime "family" in New York, Ianni concludes that the dominant characteristic of organized crime operations among Italians is kinship rather than business efficiency—the commonly accepted model previously offered by sociologist Donald Cressey. While acknowledging that there are kinship ties between Italian criminal families in cities throughout the country, he finds no evidence of a national commission that manages or controls operations. Nor does he attempt to move beyond his findings to assess how much of organized crime in the United States is controlled by Italians as opposed to other ethnic groups. Though Ianni's study leaves many questions unanswered, he has carefully demonstrated how the expertise of social scientists can be useful in clarifying a historical question too long clouded by verbal overkill.

An example of revisionist overstatement can be found in the

Italian nationalist Giovanni Schiavo's *The Truth About the Mafia and Organized Crime in America* (El Paso: Vigo Press, 1962). Schiavo in effect tries through a strident tone and verbal acrobatics to define away the problem. While former Attorney General Ramsey Clark accepts the existence of a Cosa Nostra in his *Crime in America: Observations on its Nature, Causes, Prevention and Control* (New York: Simon & Schuster, Inc., 1970), he belongs in the revisionist group insofar as he denies that it controls all of organized crime or that organized crime itself is as extensive as others claim.

The real tragedy of the Mafiaology debate has been that it led the public to ask the wrong questions, to concentrate upon the dramatic rather than upon the more substantive legal, social, and economic problems that gave rise to organized crime or upon the broad policy alternatives to combat it. Two historians have begun to make significant contributions that may help reorient the public. Humbert S. Nelli, in his "Italians and Crime in Chicago: The Formative Years, 1890–1920" in *The American Journal of Sociology* (January 1969) and *The Italians in Chicago, 1880–1930* (New York: Oxford University Press, 1970) has laid the groundwork for a broader study on the relationship of crime and ethnic mobility. Mark H. Haller, working toward a book on crime and the criminal justice system in Chicago, has already published such insightful articles as "Organized Crime in Urban Society: Chicago in the Twentieth Century" in the *Journal of Social History* (Winter 1971–1972) and "Urban Crime and Criminal Justice: The Chicago Case" in the *Journal of American History* (December 1970).

Secondary Accounts on the Kefauver Committee

Aside from the occasional mention of the Kefauver Committee in the literature on organized crime, little attention has been directed toward the crime study itself. Kefauver's *Crime in America* (Garden City, N.Y.: Doubleday & Company, Inc., 1951), drafted with the literary aid of a free-lance writer, Sidney Shalett, sums up the Chairman's conclusions on the various field hearings but touches gingerly on the political context of the investigation. Joseph Bruce Gorman's *Kefauver: A Political Biography* (New York: Oxford University Press, 1971), which will probably become the standard biography, certainly overrates the Senator from Tennessee. Hewing closely to his political orientation, Gorman completely ignores the interpretive problems of organized crime in two chapters on the Crime Committee. While entirely too laudatory of Kefauver, Harvey Swados in his *Standing Up for the People: The Life and Work of Estes Kefauver* (New York: E. P. Dutton & Co., Inc., 1972) properly places the Senator in the antimonopoly tradition. Still of some limited value is an earlier campaign biography, Jack Anderson and Fred Blumenthal, *The Kefauver Story* (New York: The Dial Press, 1956). Harry W. Kirwan's biography, *O'Conor: The Inevitable Success* (Westminster, Md.: Newman Press, 1962) contains a chapter on the Crime Committee, but does not penetrate beneath the surface. Ralph Jerome Woody pays only passing attention to the Kefauver Committee in his "The United States Senate Career of Lester C. Hunt," a Master's thesis completed at the University of Wyoming in 1964. Senator Tobey wrote his own homiletic impressions of the investigation in *The Return to Morality* (Garden City, N.Y.: Doubleday & Company, Inc., 1952), an account of little value.

One can find only passing references to the Kefauver Committee in the existing literature on the Senate during the Truman Administration. The best general studies of the Senate during the period are Donald Matthews, *U.S. Senators and Their World* (Chapel Hill: University of North Carolina Press, 1960), and David B. Truman, *The Congressional Party: A Case Study* (New York: John Wiley & Sons, Inc., 1959), but these add nothing specifically on the Kefauver Committee. William S. White, *Citadel: The Story of the U.S. Senate,* reflects the hostile attitude of the Senate "establishment," a view one can also detect in White's works on Senator Robert A. Taft, *The Taft Story* (New York: Harper and Brothers, 1954), and *The Professional: Lyndon B. Johnson* (Boston: Houghton Mifflin Company, 1964). Senator Johnson's hostility to Kefauver is better explained in Rowland Evans and Robert Novak, *Lyndon B. Johnson: The Exercise of Power* (New York: The New American Library, Inc., 1966). One of Kefauver's friends in the Senate, Paul H. Douglas, defends the Crime Committee and has some comments on the Chicago political situation in *In the Fullness of Time: The Memoirs of Paul H. Douglas* (New York: Harcourt Brace Jovanovich, Inc., 1971). Neither Allan Nevins, *Herbert H. Lehman and His Era* (New York: Charles Scribner's Sons, 1963), Winthrop Griffith, *Humphrey: A Candid Biography* (New York: William Morrow & Co., Inc., 1965), Donald J. Kemper, *A Decade of Fear: Senator Hennings and Civil Liberties* (Columbia: University of Missouri Press, 1965), nor

Marvin E. Stromer, *The Making of a Political Leader: Kenneth S. Wherry and the United States Senate* (Lincoln: University of Nebraska Press, 1969) add anything on the Kefauver Committee or on the Senate's reaction. Frank Madison, *A View from the Floor: The Journal of a U.S. Page Boy* (Englewood Cliffs, N.J.: Prentice-Hall, Inc., 1967), catches the essence of the Senate leadership's aversion to Kefauver the maverick, and Robert S. Allen and William F. Shannon present a series of illuminating vignettes in *The Truman Merry-Go-Round* (New York: Vanguard Press, Inc., 1950). Robert Griffith in *The Politics of Fear: Joseph R. McCarthy and the Senate* (Lexington: University of Kentucky Press, 1970) analyzes the development of the Communist issue in the Senate in the late 1940s and early 1950s, a controversy with several parallels in the crime problem. Douglass Cater has a few insightful comments on the symbiotic relationship between legislators and the press corps in *The Fourth Branch of Government* (Boston: Houghton Mifflin Company, 1959).

Virtually no studies of the Administration have touched on the Crime Committee. Neither the President in the second volume of his *Memoirs:* Vol. II, *Years of Trial and Hope, 1946–1952* (Garden City, N.Y.: Doubleday & Company, Inc., 1956), Alfred Steinberg in *The Man from Missouri: Life and Times of Harry S. Truman* (New York: G. P. Putnam's Sons, 1962), nor Cabell Phillips, *The Truman Presidency: The History of a Triumphant Succession* (New York: The Macmillan Company, 1966), make more than passing references to the investigation. Jules Abels summarizes the 1952 Republican "corruption" issue in *The Truman Scandals* (Chicago: Henry Regnery Company, 1956). One can hope that the research presently in progress, including Richard Kirkendall's biography of Truman and the studies of Attorney General J. Howard McGrath and the 1952 campaign, will deal more fully with the "crime issue." A solid biography of Scott Lucas, touching on both his career in the Senate and his post-Senate lobbying activities, might be insightful, as would an examination of Senator Patrick McCarran's Washington career.

One Committee counsel, Joseph L. Nellis, quickly surveyed the complex "Legal Aspects of the Kefauver Investigation," in the *Journal of Criminal Law, Criminology and Police Science* (July–August 1951). "The Kefauver Investigation in Perspective" in *Dickinson Law Review* (March 1951) by Harold Newcomb Morse sketches previous antiracketeering efforts, and

Rufus G. King in "The Control of Organized Crime in America," *Stanford Law Review* (December 1951) discusses the Committee's failures to obtain remedial legislation. King gives vent to his criticism of the Committee's conclusions on the Mafia in *The Drug Hang-Up: America's Fifty Year Folly* (New York: W. W. Norton & Company, Inc., 1972). Both Alan Barth in *Government by Investigation* (New York: The Viking Press, Inc., 1955) and Telford Taylor in *Grand Inquest: The Story of Congressional Investigations* (New York: Simon & Schuster, Inc., 1955) touch upon the troublesome issue of television and civil liberties before legislative committees. Ellsworth Scott Bryce completed a germane Master's thesis, "The New York Hearings of the Kefauver Crime Committee: A Rhetorical Analysis," for the Department of Speech and Theatre at Indiana University in 1963.

The best studies of comparable congressional committees are John E. Wiltz, *In Search of Peace: The Senate Munitions Inquiry, 1934–1936* (Baton Rouge: Louisiana State University Press, 1963), and Jerold S. Auerbach, *Labor and Liberty: The La Follette Committee and the New Deal* (Indianapolis: The Bobbs-Merrill Co., Inc., 1966). Walter Goodman's study of the House Un-American Activities Committee, because of the extended life of *The Committee* (Baltimore: Penguin Books, Inc., 1969), is necessarily less detailed. Ironically, the Truman Committee has not yet attracted thorough study. Both John L. McClellan in *Crime Without Punishment* (New York: Duell, Sloan and Pearce, 1962) and Chief Counsel Robert F. Kennedy in *The Enemy Within* (New York: Harper & Row, Publishers, 1960) have written on the Labor–Management hearings of the late 1950s but with predictable first-person bias.

Index